YUGOSLAVS in LOUISIANA

YUGOSLAVS
in
LOUISIANA

Published on the occasion of the
United Slavonian Benevolent Association
Centennial 1874–1974

by
MILOS M. VUJNOVICH

A
FIREBIRD
PRESS
BOOK
Gretna 2000

Manufactured in the United States of America
Published by Pelican Publishing Company, Inc.
1000 Burmaster Street, Gretna, Louisiana 70053

FOR
Vera

Contents

List of Tables

Preface

THE YUGOSLAV IMMIGRANTS and their descendants have been living in Louisiana for the past 140 years, yet when the demographers, sociologists, and historians write about the people of Louisiana, the Yugoslavs are not even mentioned. This is not surprising when we realize that practically nothing has been published about them; nor is any information about them readily available in the state's libraries. With the publication of this study we hope to fill this void. The Yugoslavs came to Louisiana seeking freedom and fortune, and in doing so they contributed their share in building this great state. It is therefore fitting and proper that their story should be recorded and published. It is also most appropriate that the book should be published to commemorate the one hundredth anniversary of the founding of the second oldest Yugoslav organization in the Western Hemisphere: the United Slavonian Benevolent Association.

I hope that the reader will find the statistical information useful (Tables and Appendixes). I feel that this information is essential for the complete story of the Yugoslav immigration to Louisiana. It is intended to serve as a source of information to genealogists, and to writers interested in the origin and composition of the people of Louisiana. Appendix II, with the names and birthplaces of the Yugoslav immigrants, should assist those Louisianians of the Yugoslav background who wish to know from which Dalmatian town their ancestors came, so that, when they travel abroad, they can visit these places and locate their long lost "cousins." During the past few years I have answered many such inquiries by telephone or letter, and with the publication of this information I hope to be relieved of this task.

I first became interested in the Yugoslavs in Louisiana in 1949 when a publicist, Vlaho S. Vlahovic, of New York asked me to write a paper on Yugoslav immigration to Louisiana for a book about the Yugoslav contribution to America, *Builders of America*, which he was then writing. Researching for this paper aroused my interest in the subject so that during the intervening years, as the information came to my attention, I simply filed it for future reference. When at one of the Slavonian Association's meetings during the late 1960s it was suggested that a book should be written about "our people" in Louisiana I took the challenge, gathered additional material, and wrote this book.

My primary sources have been the records of the United Slavonian Benevolent Association, Civil War records, United States Census records, and, of course, personal communication with the older immigrants who narrated their experiences, sometimes spontaneously and sometimes as a response to my inquiries. The New Orleans newspapers dating back to the Civil War period have been most helpful, especially the reports of the October, 1893, hurricane.

In writing this book I contacted many individuals for information contained herein; others I asked to read the manuscript and offer suggestions. All these persons have been most generous with their time and advice, and it is with heartfelt appreciation that I acknowledge their assistance. I especially wish to thank the following: Marko Cibilich, Adam Eterovich, Frank Glavina, John P. Gentilich, Frank Kopanica, Mary Perlman, Dr. George Prpic, George Seferovich, and Dr. Richard Vidacovich, and Otokar Lahman and Stipe Vujnovic of Yugoslavia.

New Orleans
August, 1973

YUGOSLAVS in LOUISIANA

HIMNA SLOBODI
(HYMN TO LIBERTY)

O lijepa, o draga, o slatka slobodo
(Oh beautiful, oh dear, oh sweet liberty)

Dare, u kome sva blaga višnji nam Bog je do
(Gift, by which the eternal God made us wealthy)

Uzroće istini od naše sve slave
(True source of all our glory)

Uresu jedini od ove Dubrave
(The only adornment of this our land)

Sva srebra, sva zlata, svi ljudski životi
(All the silver, all the gold, and all human lives)

Ne mogu biti plata tvoj čistoj ljepoti!
(Cannot compensate for your pure beauty!).

From pastoral play *Dubravka*, by Croatian
poet from Dubrovnik, Ivan F. Gundulić (1588–1638).

1

Introduction

THIS BOOK DEALS with the Yugoslavs in Louisiana, with their arrival here, their transition from immigrants to Americans, their part in the state's oyster industry, their organization of a benevolent association, and with their everyday life in Louisiana. However, before we get into the main theme of the study, the following few pages, which describe the old country background, will be helpful for better understanding of their story.

The Yugoslavs (literally *South Slavs*[1]) were united in a common state: Yugoslavia (originally called the Kingdom of the Serbs, Croats, and Slovenes) in 1918. Therefore this is a relatively young country, but the peoples living there have a long, glorious, and a somewhat troubled history.

The original home of the Slavs was in the area north and east of the Carpathian Mountains in present-day Poland and Ukraine; roughly between the Oder and Dnieper rivers. The exact boundaries of the Slavic settlements are unknown, for the records about early Slavs are scanty. During the migration of nations they too became restless and during the sixth and the seventh centuries migrated in several directions including south to the Balkan Peninsula. From then on the Slavs are usually grouped in three distinct groups: the Eastern Slavs (Russians, Ukranians, and Bjelorussians); the Western Slavs (Poles, Czechs, and Slovaks); and the Southern Slavs (Serbs, Croats, Slovenes, and Bulgarians[2]).

[1] The two terms *Yugoslav* and *South Slav* are used interchangeably throughout this book.

[2] Strictly speaking the Bulgarians, too, belong to the South Slavic group. However, since the creation of Yugoslavia, the term *South Slavs*, as a rule, applies to the Slavs of the present-day Yugoslavia.

After their arrival in the Balkans the Slavs subdued and assimilated the natives (Macedonians, Greeks, Illyrians, and Romans) and eventually Slavicized the region presently occupied by Yugoslavia and Bulgaria.

The Serbs settled in the eastern and southeastern part of present-day Yugoslavia; the Slovenes in the northwestern part and the Croats in the middle, including most of the eastern shore of the Adriatic Sea.

THE SERBS

When they first arrived in the Balkans the Serbs were organized in *zhupanije* (duchies) and ruled by tribal chieftains called *zhupani*.

Between their coming to the Balkans and the middle of the twelfth century they recognized the suzerainty of the Byzantine Empire and consequently came under the religious and cultural influence of Constantinople. Their conversion to Christianity took place during the eighth and the ninth centuries, but it was completed by two Greek missionaries, brothers Cyril and Methodius, who became the apostles to the Slavs and translated the Bible into the ancient Slavonic language. The alphabet used by the Serbs, Russians, and Bulgarians, which the brothers and their followers constructed on the Greek model, is called the Cyrillic alphabet after Cyril. The Serbs adopted the Eastern Orthodox rite whereas the Croats and the Slovenes adopted the Catholic.

Throughout this period the Serbs were in constant strife with the Greeks, Bulgars, and the Byzantines. In 1159 the grand *zhupan* (overlord) of Rashka, Stefan Nemanja, succeeded in uniting most of Serbia under his rule. He established the Nemanjic dynasty which ruled Serbia for the next two hundred years.

During the reign of the Nemanjics, Serbia's territory expanded southward to include the Vardar Valley and northward toward the Danube and Save rivers. The greatest expansion—although short-lived—took place during the reign of Stefan Dusan who ruled from 1331 to 1346 as king, and from 1346 to 1355 as czar of the Serbians. A powerful and an aggressive ruler, constantly warring for the expansion and consolidation of his empire, he dreamed of replacing the decaying Byzantine Empire with the Serbian Empire, but his death in 1355 cut short his ambitions. During his reign he gave Serbia its greatest hour, establishing internal order and promoting commerce and general well-being.

Dusan was succeeded by his son Uros, who did not measure up to his father's greatness; in fact he was called Uros the Weak. Dusan's empire soon fell apart so that it was unable to stop the oncoming expansion of the Ottoman Turks from the East.

The battle on the Maritsa River in 1371 was the beginning of the Turkish conquest of Serbia, and the defeat of the outnumbered Serbian and Croatian armies on *Kosovo Polje* (field of black birds) in 1389 sealed the fate of Serbia for the next four hundred years. Tens of thousands of soldiers died in the battle, and both the Serbian Prince Lazar and the Turkish Sultan Murad lost their lives that fateful day. Serbia now became completely subjugated by the Turks whose pashas ruled it from Belgrade. For centuries after this battle the Serbian troubadors and peasant poets composed and sang songs about the heroic deeds of their warriors, resulting in the Cult of Kosovo. They sang about Milos Obilic, who killed Murad, and about Kraljevic Marko and other heroes.

It was the memory of their dead heroes, glorified and given supernatural powers through this epic poetry, and the Serbian Orthodox Church that kept the Serbian national consciousness and tradition alive during these four centuries.

However, the Turks were never able to conquer the mountainous areas northeast of the Bay of Kotor. Originally known as the province of *Zeta*, it later acquired the name of *Crna Gora* (Montenegro) due to its forbidding mountains. Montenegro eventually became an independent state ruled by prince-bishops. In 1910 it was declared a kingdom, and in 1918 it became a part of Yugoslavia.

In 1804 a rebellion for independence broke out in Serbia under the leadership of George Petrovic, called *Kara* (Black) *George* by the Turks. Petrovic founded the Karageorgevic dynasty. The rebellion was successful but short-lived. In 1813 the Turks reoccupied the autonomous territory and temporarily crushed the independence movement.

In 1815 a new leader, Milos Obrenovic, led another revolt against the Turks and with Russian help won limited independence for Serbia. Milos in turn established the Obrenovic dynasty. These two families alternated in ruling Serbia; which ruled when depended on the abilities of the rulers, their popularity among the Serbian people, and on the will of the Parliament. The Obrenovic dynasty died out with the assassination of Alexander Obrenovic and his queen Draga Masin in 1903. Peter Karageorgevic, the grandson of the original George, was installed on the throne. As King Peter I he gave Serbia an enlightened and a democratic rule. He successfully led Serbia through the Balkan wars and abdicated in June, 1914, in favor of his son Alexander. Serbia was attacked by Austria in 1914, and, after initial successes, the remnants of the Serbian army were forced to retreat to Albania. Enforced by the new enlistments, including volunteers from America, this Serbian army participated on the Salonika front and helped defeat the Austrians. In 1918 Serbia became a part of the newly formed Kingdom of the Serbs, Croats, and Slovenes.

THE SLOVENES

The Slovenes, who even today do not number two million, are the least numerous of the South Slavs. They arrived in their present home in the northwestern corner of Yugoslavia during the second half of the sixth century. They subdued the natives but were never successful in creating their own independent state, as were the Croats and the Serbs. At first they were under the influence and partial domination of the Avars and later under the Franks. During Charlemagne's reign (768–814) they were converted to the Christian (Catholic) Church. In 843 when Charlemagne's empire was divided Slovenians came under the rule of dukes of Bavaria.

During the thirteenth century they were a part of the Slav empire of Ottokar of Bohemia. However, soon after, in 1278, they came under the rule of the Austrian Habsburgs where they remained until 1918. The foreign rule therefore lasted over twelve hundred years, and that the Slovenes survived as a nation is somewhat of a miracle. The credit for survival of the Slovene nation goes to the Slovene peasants who for centuries tilled the land, fed the nobility—foreign and domestic—and preserved their language and culture from foreign oppression and obliteration.

During the short period of Napoleon's rule (1809–1813), when Slovenia was included with the other South Slavs in one administrative unit, law and order were introduced, and road building, postal service, and other forms of progress were initiated. However, the most important contribution to the Slovenian national renaissance by the French rule was the introduction and encouragement of the Slovene language in schools and in public life.

After the fall of Napoleon, Austria once more took over Slovenia and restored German as the dominant language. The Austrians, however, were unsuccessful in Germanizing the Slovenes, for the seeds of national awakening took root, and henceforth the Slovene language was espoused by the emerging intellectual class, and the Slovene literature flowered.

THE CROATS

The Croats,* who settled in the Balkans during the second half of the sixth century, and the first half of the seventh, were the first among the South Slavs to organize their own state. They easily overpowered and assimilated most of the people found there. However, some of the Roman population which resisted Croat assimilation found refuge in the fortified cities along the Dalmatian coast. For a number of years the Croats were dominated by the Avars who then ruled that part of Europe. In 796 the Franks under Charlemagne destroyed the Avar state, and although in Croatia the Franks were assisted by the Croat forces under Duke Vojnomir, they now extended their control over the Croats who were forced to recognize Frankish suzerainty for another eighty-odd years. During this time the Croats embraced Christianity and were permitted by Rome the use of their own language in the liturgy which caused considerable friction with the higher Catholic clergy of the Dalmatian cities, who favored Latin.

In 880, under the able leadership of Duke Branimir, Croatia became an independent state and in 925 a kingdom under King Tomislav. Tomislav expanded the territory of the new kingdom to include the coastal cities and the islands, improved the civil administration, and established a strong army and navy so that Croatia became a leading state in southeastern Europe. The next two hundred years marked the glorious period of the Croatian history. This was their Camelot.

The kingdom had its ups and downs, reaching the zenith of its power under Peter Kresimir IV (1058–1073).

The last Croat king of note, Zvonimir, was crowned in the basilica of St. Peter's in Solin near Split in 1076, with the blessings of Pope Gregory VII. However, when Zvonimir sought the unified support of the Croat nobles to assist Pope Urban II against the Seljuk Turks, the nobles opposed military expeditions outside their borders. At an assembly on the Knin Field an armed disagreement ensued and in the melee the king fell mortally wounded.

* Since most of the South Slav immigrants to Louisiana were/are of Croatian nationality the history of the Croats is given a more detailed treatment.

After his death some of the Croat magnates invited the Hungarian king, Ladislaus—brother of Zvonimir's widow—to occupy the vacant Croatian throne. The dissenting nobles elected a fellow nobleman, Peter Svacic, who ruled but a short time. Later (in 1102) King Koloman of Hungary negotiated a treaty with the Croatian nobles, the so-called *pacta conventa* where he agreed to honor the Croatian sovereignty and asserted that Croatia and Hungary were two separate kingdoms under one king. He also agreed to respect the laws passed by the Croatian *Sabor* (Parliament) and to a separate coronation which took place at Biograd-by-the-Sea. This association with Hungary lasted eight long centuries.

For the next three or four hundred years the internal rule of Croatia was left to the Croats. The Hungarian feudal nobles ruled the Hungarians, and the Croat feudal nobles ruled the Croats. This feudal development in Hungary and Croatia—similar to that of the West—facilitated the union between the two kingdoms for the nobles easily agreed to the status quo as long as they ruled their respective estates unmolested.

However, the eastern Croats living in Bosnia did not like this arrangement with the Hungarians, and they rebelled several times. Under *Ban* (Governor) Kulin (1180–1204) Bosnia became a separate state and in 1377 was declared a kingdom by its ruler, Stjepan Tvrtko. Tvrtko expanded the territory of his kingdom at the expense of the neighboring states and thereby changed the ethnography of Bosnia. Soon after his death, however, the Bosnian nobility's jealousy of each other caused the disintegration of the kingdom so that it offered only a token resistance to the Turks who conquered it in 1463. The Turks held Bosnia until 1878 when it was occupied by the forces of the Austro-Hungarian Empire.

In 1409 the Venetian Republic gained the control of most of Dalmatia and held it until 1797 when Dalmatia became a part of the Austrian Empire where it remained until 1918.

Meanwhile, the Turkish menace continued westward. After the fall of Bosnia, the invincible Turkish forces turned on Hungary and Croatia. In 1493, at the battle of Krbava plain, the Croats were defeated, and the flower of Croatian nobility lost their lives. Hungary was defeated in 1526 at the battle of Mohacz. The Croato-Hungarian king fell in the battle, and since he had no heirs the throne became vacant. The Croatian Parliament then elected Ferdinand Habsburg of Austria as king, and the following year the Hungarians followed suit. Thus began the association with the Austrians which lasted until 1918, during which time the Croats had to contend with the Austrians and the Hungarians.

However, the greatest historical tragedy to befall the Croatian people was the Turkish onslaught against which they struggled for two long centuries. They lost a battle at Krbava but did not surrender; they fought on and on, relinquishing their defense outposts (fortified cities) only when further resistance became useless against overwhelming odds. They made the Turks pay dearly for each city that they were forced to surrender. The Croatian territory kept shrinking but they never laid down their arms. They retreated from one city only to take a stand in the next one. In 1593 the Turks were finally checked at Sisak. This prolonged, tenacious resistance, which decimated the Croatian population, scorched the land, and destroyed Croatian cities, checked the Turkish menace, and removed the threat to the western civilization, but it almost destroyed Croatia as a nation. The popes praised the heroic Croats, sent them a few ducats now and then, preached for Christian crusades against the "infidels," and bestowed upon the Croats the epithet of *Antemurale Christianitatis* (Ramparts of Christianity). To protect their interests the Austrians, in 1578, established a military frontier along the then Turkish border; a sort of a defense corridor garrisoned by military forces and connected with fortified outposts, but it was primarily the Croatian blood that was spilled in its defense.

During the seventeenth century the Turkish supremacy in this part of Europe began to decline, and by the beginning of the eighteenth century most of Croatia proper was free from the Turkish rule. However, the Croatians did not regain their pre-Turkish territory or self-rule. With the approval of the Habsburgs from Vienna, they were forced by the Hungarians into a subordinate role. They insisted on their rights, whenever they could, using every legal means available to them in defending their national identity, language, and culture.

A strong impetus to the renaissance of nationalism was given by the short (1809–1813) French occupation. Napoleon united the South Slavs ceded to him by Austria in his Illyrian Provinces. The French administration encouraged the establishment of schools, literary pursuits and other cultural endeavors. After the French left, the association with Austria and Hungary was reestablished, but the desire and struggle for self-government continued. The disagreements with the Hungarians continued until 1848 when they culminated in an armed conflict when *Ban* (Governor) Josip Jelacic marched into Hungary at the head of the Croatian Army of 50,000 troops, not only to help quell the Hungarian revolt against the Habsburgs but much more to protect the Croatian interests against the encroachment of the Hungarian nationalistic leaders who were unwilling to grant the Croats the same liberties they demanded from the Austrians.

In 1867 the Austrians reorganized the governmental structure. A compromise *Ausgleich* was reached with Hungary, creating a dual monarchy of Austria and Hungary. The following year the Hungarians and the Croats reached an agreement giving Croatia autonomy in domestic matters. The Dalmatian Croats, however, still remained directly under Austria with its own Diet at Zadar.

This arrangement only whetted the people's appetite for complete freedom, and the next fifty years saw the rise of agitation for complete self-determination. Certain elements favored the unification of all Slavs in the monarchy on equal footing with the Hungarians and the Austrians, others sought an establishment of an independent ethnic Croatia, while still a third group favored the creation of a South Slavic state in union with Serbia. By the eve of the First World War the last group emerged as the strongest and led Croatia into the union with Serbia and Slovenia.

In the meantime, the cultural renaissance continued alongside the political agitations. Cultural, literary, and learned societies rose across the land. An Academy of Arts and Sciences was established at Zagreb in 1867, and a national Croatian University was founded, also at Zagreb, in 1874. Historical research, pioneered by Franjo Racki, was encouraged. The Academy, the literary-scientific society *Matica Hrvatska* (established 1847), and other publishing houses published the scientific, literary, religious, and cultural works and distributed them among the people. The Croatian literature, whose roots go back to the humanist Marko Marulic (1450–1524) of Split, playwright Marin Drzic (1509–1567), and poet Ivan Gundulic (1588–1638) of Dubrovnik, flowered into full bloom, producing hundreds of new works.

While most of the Croats had to continually—through the long centuries—fight the invaders to defend their liberties, there was one Croatian area, an oasis of peace and prosperity, that escaped foreign oppression until the Napoleonic era. That was the small maritime

Republic of Dubrovnik. Since the mariners of this area played a leading role in initiating the South Slavic immigration to America and Louisiana, the history of the republic is pertinent to the main theme of this book.

REPUBLIC OF DUBROVNIK

The city of Dubrovnik, located in southern Dalmatia, was founded on the rocky promontory at the end of the seventh century by the Greek and Roman refugees from the nearby ancient city of Epidarus as they escaped the Avar and the Slav onslaught.

Here they built a fortified city, called *Ragusa* in Latin. It was separated from the mainland by a shallow lagoon which was the dividing line between the Roman Ragusa and a Slav (Croat) settlement. Soon the two settlements, Croat and Roman, became one, and a new city was born. Later the Croats called it Dubrovnik, after *dubrava* (woodland), and the two cultures merged to produce a city republic which lasted a thousand years. Subsequently, the lagoon was filled and became the city's main street.

The republic's geographic location, providing an easy access to the hinterland on one hand and an access to all the seas through its ports on the other, facilitated its development into an important trading center. For a time the infant republic was under the protection of the Byzantine Empire and later under the influence of Venice. It traded both on land and on the sea. Its land caravans traded throughout the Balkans all the way to Constantinople, and its ships sailed throughout the Mediterranean carrying goods available in one area and needed in the other.

Eventually (1358) Dubrovnik and its immediate vicinity became a completely independent state making its own laws and coining its own money. Its government was headed by a *knez* (rector), a sort of a modern chairman of the board who served for only a month at a time, and could be reelected only after an interval of two years. An interesting characteristic of his tenure of office was that during the month in office he had to take permanent residence in the rector's palace and could leave it only on official business of the republic, accompanied by members of his council. The city fathers feared any emerging strong ruling personality who could become a dictator. So to prevent this, the tenure was limited to three, then two, and finally to one short month. This seems to have worked, for during its long history of one thousand years, a dictator never took over the government.

Dubrovnik's greatest period was from the beginning of the fifteenth to the middle of the seventeenth century. During this time its area increased so that it extended along the Adriatic seaboard, from the Bay of Kotor in the southeast through Konavli to the mouth of Neretva River in the northwest, including the islands of Kolocep, Lopud, Sipan, Lastovo, Mljet, and the Peljesac Peninsula. For a short time (1413–1417) its territory included the islands of Korcula, Hvar, and Brac.

During the sixteenth century Dubrovnik dominated and controlled most of the trade between the Balkan states and western Europe. This dominance lasted well into the seventeenth century. According to Luetic: "During this time the Republic of Dubrovnik had its great mercantile fleet, and in the world's trade and shipping it occupied one of the most prominent positions. Proportionally to the size of the republic it seems that Dubrovnik in that century was one of the greatest maritime centers in the world."

The Ragusan (as the republic was known as Ragusa throughout the world) ships sailed most of the known seas under the republic's standard of its patron, St. Blaise, and an accompanying flag bearing a single word *Libertas* on it. They traded with faraway countries including England, and its ships gave the English language the word *argosy*, originally meaning a rich, laden ship from Ragusa (Dubrovnik).

This worldwide trade produced substantial wealth for the republic. The ruling merchant class built beautiful palaces, churches, government buildings, and the great fortified wall around the city, all supervised by domestic and imported architects. The republic enacted progressive laws governing sanitation and building codes for the city. It established benevolent societies to care for the orphans, widows, and the destitute. In 1317 it established a pharmacy (still operating) to dispense medicine to its citizens; in 1347, a home for the aged; in 1512, a foundling house, and in 1517, a day nursery. As early as the first decade of the fifteenth century, it forbade its ships to trade in, and transport, slaves. Architecture, art, literature, and the sciences were encouraged and subsidized, and they reached a point where Dubrovnik rivaled the greatest cities of Europe. Physicist Roger Boscovich, whose theories rivaled that of Newton and who for a time lived in London where he held membership in the Royal Society, was proud that he was from Dubrovnik. Writers and poets such as the above mentioned Gundulic and Drzic, and Jakov Bona, Sisko Mencetic, Andro Cubranovic, and many others wrote in Croatian and produced excellent works, many of which are popular to this day. The city well earned the sobriquet, The Croatian Athens.

The people insisted on integrity and honesty in all their government officials. Honor, service, and fairness were the bywords of all its dealings as early as the thirteenth century. The business ethics of the republic were so well established and respected that Cromwell adapted them for England.

The ships of Dubrovnik participated in many foreign naval engagements; they played a part in the annihilation of the Turkish fleet in the Battle of Lepanto (October 7, 1571), and out of the 130 ships of the invincible Spanish Armada, 33 belonged to Dubrovnik. Many did not return from the English waters. These ships were built in the Dubrovnik shipyards and manned and commanded by sturdy Dalmatians.

The shift in trade from the Mediterranean to the Atlantic and the great earthquake of 1667, when most of the city was leveled and over four thousand killed, contributed substantially to the republic's decline. The earthquake survivors rebuilt the city, which still stands, and carried continued trade on a reduced scale. By the beginning of the eighteenth century its fleet had recovered, and its ships once more plied the world's trade routes.

The French occupied the city in 1806, and two years later (January 31, 1808) Napoleon decreed the end of the one-thousand-year-old republic. However, the marine tradition and navigational skills could not be abolished with a decree, and mariners from Dubrovnik and vicinity continued to sail the seven seas. It is thus that they become a part of our story when they started leaving the ships to settle in the New World.

YUGOSLAVIA

Throughout the long history of the South Slavs there were sporadic limited attempts to unite the Croats, the Serbs, and the Slovenes into one state. As early as the seventeenth century a Croatian Jesuit, Juraj Krizanic, who preached ecumenism, advocated Slav unity. At the beginning of the nineteenth century, as the nationalistic feelings were awakened partly by Napoleon's unification of the Croats and other South Slavs in the Austrian Empire and partly by the successful insurrections of Serbs against the Turks, the Yugoslav movement gained wide support. During the nineteenth century the movement was further enhanced by Ljudevit Gaj's and Vuk Karadzic's work in unifying and standardizing the literary language of the Croats and the Serbs and by Yugoslav-minded Bishop Juraj Strosmajer's encouragement and generous patronage of arts, sciences, education, and literature. However, it was not until World War One that definite steps were taken for the unification. After the initial successes against the Austrians the Serbian army and the government were forced into exile. In the meantime many political leaders from Croatia and Slovenia under the leadership of Ante Trumbic went abroad to seek help and understanding from the Allies in establishing a South Slavic state. Toward this end they established a Yugoslav Committee with headquarters in London. Discussions and negotiations between this committee and the Serbian government regarding the formation of a unified state were carried on intermittently during the war years. In July, 1917, an agreement was reached on the island of Corfu, the so-called *Krfska Deklaracija* (Declaration of Corfu) between the Serbian government and the Yugoslav Committee. The main provision of the agreement was the establishment of an independent democratic "Kingdom of the Serbs, Croats, and Slovenes under the Karageorgevic dynasty."

Toward the end of the war, as Austro-Hungary disintegrated, the plan received backing from the victorious Allies, and steps were taken by the South Slavs to finally bring unification to a reality. On October 29, 1918, the Croatian Parliament declared its association with the Austro-Hungarian Empire at an end and transferred its authority to the National Council of the Serbs, Croats, and Slovenes, which on December 1, 1918, joined with the Kingdom of Serbia in declaring the establishment of the new state. Thus Yugoslavia was born.

But all was not well with the new state. The Serbs looked at it as the enlargement of Serbia; the Croats and Slovenes hoped for a decentralized democratic arrangement; consequently friction developed from the beginning. In 1921 a constitution was adopted, with a majority of Croats abstaining, creating a strong central government. The governing apparatus, including the army, was primarily in Serbian hands, which created resentment among the non-Serbian population. These disagreements and quarrels culminated in violence in the Yugoslav Parliament when during a debate, the Croatian leader Stjepan Radic was mortally wounded. A crisis ensued, and in January, 1929, King Alexander dissolved the Parliament, suppressed the constitution, and assumed dictatorial powers. In October, 1929, he officially changed the name of the country to Yugoslavia and ruled by decrees until his assassination in Marseilles in October, 1934.

After Alexander's death the royal powers were exercised by a regency, notably by its principal member, Prince Paul, Alexander's cousin. Negotiations were carried on with the Croatian leaders, and in 1939 an agreement *sporazum* was reached, creating an autonomous Croatian region, *Hrvatska Banovina*. This improved relations and conditions within the country, but the arrangement was short-lived as the war clouds approached and Europe was engulfed in the Second World War.

At the beginning of the war Yugoslavia tried to remain neutral, but continued German political pressure forced the government to join the Tripartite Pact. However, before the ink was dry a coup, led by a group of army officers, overthrew the government, forced Prince Paul to leave the country, installed the youthful son of the late King Alexander as King Peter II, and proclaimed Yugoslavia neutral. As soon as Hitler learned of the coup he ordered the destruction of Yugoslavia. German forces attacked the country without a formal declaration of war. The youthful king and his ministers fled the country, most of the generals surrendered, and in a few days it was all over; Yugoslavia was conquered, or so the Germans thought.

Resistance to the occupying German and Italian forces started almost immediately, and it was hardened by the occupational forces' inhumane treatment of the population. At first there were two organized resistance movements; one, the *Chetniks*, led by a prewar army colonel Draza Mihajlovic, mainly Serbian in character; and the other, the Partisans, led by a communist, Josip Broz, called Tito, whose forces from the very beginning were led by the monolithic, efficiently organized, and disciplined Communist Party. While the Partisans fought the enemy at every occasion, suffered heavy casualties, liberated pockets of territory inside Yugoslavia, and gained a following among the people, the *Chetniks* lingered and only occasionally engaged the enemy. They eventually collaborated with the Italians and Germans against the Partisans. After the Italian surrender, Tito's forces disarmed several Italian divisions and armed their own men.

Their ranks grew daily so that the Germans were forced to keep over twenty-six divisions in Yugoslavia to contain the Partisans.

During the war several political meetings were held on the liberated territory where important decisions were made for the conduct of war and the future of Yugoslavia. At the political meeting in Jajce in November, 1943, Tito was declared a marshal, and King Peter was forbidden to return to Yugoslavia.

Towards the end of the war the Partisans held large areas of the Yugoslav territory and with help from the Soviet troops liberated the country from the Germans. They took control of the government and by November, 1945, abolished the monarchy and declared Yugoslavia a republic. They divided the country into six "people's republics" (Serbia, Croatia, Bosnia and Herzegovina, Slovenia, Montenegro, and Macedonia), and two autonomous regions within Serbia (Vojvodina and Kosovo), established a strong central government, and adopted a constitution patterned after the 1936 Soviet constitution, which was later revised to provide for more local autonomy. Immediately after the war Yugoslavia cooperated closely with Russia, but when Stalin tried to impose his will on the Yugoslav Communists, Tito resisted and broke away from the Soviets. The country then received substantial financial and military aid from the West, primarily the United States. Since then, however, Yugoslavia has mended her fences with the Soviets and has in the meantime become an exponent of the nonalignment policy professing a "national" special brand of communism.

Present-day Yugoslavia occupies an area of 98,760 square miles (approximately equal to the combined areas of Louisiana and Mississippi) with a population of a little over 20 million. The Serbs number about 8.5 million (including 500,000 Montenegrins); Croats 6 million; Slovenes 2 million; and Macedonians 1.2 million. There are also about 1.3 million Albanians; 0.5 million Hungarians, and a scattering of other minorities. The three main religions are the Greek Orthodox, Roman Catholic, and Moslem. Serbs and the Macedonians use the Cyrillic alphabet while the Croats and the Slovenes use the Latin. Both alphabets enjoy official status, and one edition of a periodical, book, or a newspaper may be printed in both alphabets.

Yugoslavia's predominant agricultural character is being changed by planned, government-controlled industrialization. The metal, petrochemical, and textile industries are well developed. Yugoslavia produces more copper, bismuth, antimony, and lead than any other country in Europe. Immediately after the last war the emphasis was on heavy industry which since has shifted to the production of consumer goods (automobiles, television sets, radios, tractors, etc.). The shipbuilding industry, with large yards at Rijeka, Pula, Split, and Kraljevica, is also well developed, producing ships, large and small, for domestic shipping companies as well as for export to other nations. (During 1972, for instance, it delivered a 225,000-ton ship to Norway, and for 1973 the shipyards have contracted for three 265,000-ton giants for Sweden). Yugoslavia enjoys substantial trade with the West and since the thaw with the Soviets, moderate trade with the east European nations.

The climate in the northern part of Yugoslavia is continental; along the Dalmatian coast it is Mediterranean. In winter the average temperature along the coast is fifty degrees Fahrenheit, and in the north (Vojvodina) it is a much cooler twenty-seven degrees, and the summer temperature is eighty and seventy-two degrees respectively. Yugoslavia as a whole has many tourist attractions but the Adriatic coast with its mild climate, well-developed coastline including many islands, attracts visitors from all over the world. The coast of the mainland and of the islands is dotted with historically rich, quaint villages and towns. With natural attractions such as hundreds of sandy and sun-swept beaches washed by crystal-clear sea water, it rivals, and in some respects surpasses, other European tourist centers. Lately, modern hotels have been constructed, roads built, and transportation and service improved to properly accommodate the tourists. Consequently, since the mid-1960s Yugoslavia has become part of a normal tourist itinerary. Americans, too, have begun to visit Yugoslavia in ever growing numbers. During the 1972 tourist season over 200,000 Americans visited Yugoslavia and more are expected during 1973. Among these are many immigrants who visit their native land for a nostalgic look and the Americans of Yugoslav ancestry from all the states, including Louisiana.

YUGOSLAVS IN AMERICA

The Dalmatian Croats have been renowned sailors and navigators for centuries, and, as already mentioned, Dubrovnik Republic was free to fully develop its merchant fleet. As expert seamen and captains the mariners of Dubrovnik and vicinity were sought after by many foreign naval powers. Once the trade center switched from the Mediterranean to the Atlantic, Spain and Portugal needed mariners who could sail and command their ships. The mariners from Dubrovnik participated in most of the New World discovery expeditions during the fifteenth and the sixteenth centuries. Many reached high positions in the Spanish service. Vicko Buna (born in 1559), for instance, served as an envoy to Philip II and Philip III in many foreign lands. While in Mexico, Buna was made a viceroy of that country and performed admirably.

Around 1520 two brothers, citizens of Dubrovnik, Mato and Dominik Konkedevic, left for America where, during the next thirty years, they accumulated wealth worth 12,000 ducats and returned to Europe in their own ship. Basilije Basiljevic left Seville for Peru in 1537 with 1000 ducats worth of merchandise for trading. In 1606 Dubrovnik historian Jakov Lukarevic wrote that men of Dubrovnik often traveled to America. After 1750 merchant ships from Dubrovnik sailed to the New World (Brazil, Havana, Cap Haitien, Santo Domingo, Philadelphia, and New York) regularly, and many sailors settled there for good. For instance, in 1788 there were several immigrants from Dubrovnik in Cap Haitien on the island of Hispaniola and one of them, Rado Sisevic, ran a store where his countrymen gathered. When in 1783 Dubrovnik's consul in Paris, Frano Savi, paid his government's respects to the American peace commissioners, Benjamin Franklin, John Jay, and John Adams, they informed him that the ships of Dubrovnik would be welcome to trade with the ports of the newly formed United States.

Most of the first immigrants came to better their economic conditions, but there were others who came to give of themselves. These were the Catholic missionaries, from Croatia and Slovenia. They came to spread the Scriptures and civilization. A nobleman, Baron Ivan Ratkaj, born in Veliki Tabor, Croatia in 1647, who became a Jesuit in 1675, came to Mexico in 1680 to work among the Indians. For the next three years—until his death in 1683—he worked among the Taramuhari Indians as a missionary baptizing and instructing hundreds of Indians. His records of his travels in New Mexico and other regions were invaluable to the settlers who came after him. Another Jesuit, Father Ferdinand Konscak (Consag), who was born in Varazdin in 1703, came to Mexico in 1730 as an Indian missionary. Two years later he was transferred to California. San Ignacio Mission in the San Vicente Ferrer Valley was the base from which he traveled far and wide baptizing the Indians and exploring the territory. He made a detailed map of Lower California and proved that Lower California is a peninsula rather than an island. The most popular of his many writings, *Historia de las Misiones de la California* and *Diario de California*, describe the experiences of his interesting life. He died in 1759. The Consag Rocks in the Gulf of California are named in his honor. Frederic Baraga, a Slovenian, was another outstanding missionary who became a bishop in Michigan. He served the Indians of Upper Michigan from 1830 until his death in 1868. His grammar and dictionary of the Ojibwa language are used to this day. Baraga County in Michigan was named in his honor. There were many other missionaries too numerous to mention here. However, it should be noted that during the nineteenth century, money was collected in Croatia for Indian missions in America. During the 1830–1840 decade Croatians contributed and sent to America 57,400 florins (over $10,000).

These early South Slav contacts with America were on an individual and an isolated basis. After 1830 they began to come in greater numbers. The ships from the Dalmatian ports sailed regularly to America and many sailors, as noted elsewhere in this book, simply left their vessels and settled in New York, San Francisco, Philadelphia, Mobile, and New Orleans. This type of immigration continued until the 1870s when the mass immigration from southeastern Europe began. From then on until the First World War hundreds of thousands of South Slavs left their homes to settle in the "promised land."

The official statistics of the total number of Yugoslav immigrants are not available, for no accurate records were kept by nationalities until after the 1920s. However, over a million (about 650,000 Croats; 200,000 Slovenes; and 150,000 Serbs) settled in America. About 180,-000 settled in Pennsylvania; 110,000 in Ohio; 100,000 in Illinois; 50,000 in New York; 40,000 in Michigan; 30,000 in Minnesota; 28,000 in California, and from 15,000 to 20,000 in each of the following states: Indiana, New Jersey, Colorado, Montana, Kansas, Missouri, West Virginia, and Washington. A smaller number settled in other states so that today they are found in all fifty states of the union.

They found employment in the coal mines, steel mills, as longshoremen in New York and other ports, and in the stockyards of Chicago, or took whatever jobs they could find. Many opened restaurants, saloons, grocery stores, and boardinghouses. In California they became farmers, producing some of the best figs and grapes in that state.

Dalmatian Croats settling along the Pacific and the Gulf of Mexico became expert fishermen, some of them acquiring large fleets of boats and canning plants. The South Slav contribution to America has been substantial. Nikola Tesla, the inventor of the alternating current transmission, who was granted hundreds of patents in the electrical field, and Michael Pupin who perfected the long-distance telephone communications, are among the many who contributed in the field of science. Captain Anthony Lucas (Lucich), who was born in Split in 1855, pioneered the Texas oil industry. It was Lucas who on January 10, 1901, brought in the first oil well at Spindletop near Beaumont which gushed oil at a rate of 75,000 to 100,000 barrels a day until it was capped. Unfortunately, Lucas did not develop the Spindletop but sold his interest for $400,000. Frank J. Lausche, governor of Ohio and later a U.S. senator; John A. Blatnik, congressman from Minnesota; the late Nick Begich, congressman from Alaska; and Mike Stepovich, first native governor of Alaska, did well in the political field.

The above are only a few of the Yugoslav immigrants and their descendants who achieved prominence in America. It is beyond the scope of this introduction to list many others, but there are thousands who became successful, and many who became famous, in their chosen fields. We find them in all occupations: in medicine, education, science, engineering, clergy, research, sports, literature, politics, military, entertainment, the arts, farming, and industry.

The first generation served as a bridge between the old and the new, but the subsequent generations, born and schooled in this country, entered the mainstream of American life as fully participating members, distinguished from the *Mayflower* and Jamestown descendants only by the surnames they proudly bear.

2

Immigration to Louisiana

THE FIRST SOUTH SLAVS* to come to Louisiana were the Dalmatian sailors and officers who served on the sailing vessels that traded with the American ports including New Orleans. There were a few individuals from north and central Dalmatia, but most of them came from the area of the old Dubrovnik Republic and from the Bay of Kotor. They began settling in New Orleans during the middle 1830s.

The South Slavic immigration to America is usually considered to belong to the so-called "new immigration" which started during the 1870s, for it was not until that time that the southeastern Europeans began immigrating to the United States in substantial numbers. Yet decades before, there were sizable settlements of South Slavs in New Orleans, San Francisco, and New York. That they were able to travel to these places, and especially Louisiana, half a century before the immigration fever overtook southeastern Europe is due to the centuries-old maritime tradition of Dalmatia, particularly the Peljesac-Dubrovnik-Bay of Kotor region.

The Dubrovnik Republic was a maritime republic whose very life and prosperity depended on its ships and the skill of its sailors and captains. These mariners, second to none, for centuries successfully competed for the maritime trade with Venice and other seafaring nations. In 1800 the cities of the Bay of Kotor (Perast, Dobrota, Hercegnovi, and Kotor) possessed around three hundred ships, large and small, which were manned by three thousand to four thousand men.

* The pioneer South Slav immigrants who settled in New York, San Francisco, and New Orleans called themselves *Slavonians* (translated from *Slovinci*) . The term was popular in Dalmatia during the first half of the nineteenth century, but it is no longer used there. However, in Louisiana and Mississippi the name—perpetuated by their *Slavonian* associations—still persists, especially among the old-timers.

The Republic of Dubrovnik had at this time hundreds of small boats and two hundred eighty large ships which navigated throughout the world. Therefore, at the beginning of the nineteenth century this region had a centuries-old tradition, skill, and means of navigating and trading with the faraway places including the American continents. The profits from this maritime trading created a snug prosperity and a high standard of living which Napoleon's armies were soon to destroy.

When the French troops occupied Dubrovnik in 1806, the Dubrovnik Senate, recognizing the gravity of the situation, and not wanting the ships to become the property of the French, sent the following message to all its consuls who were located in all the leading ports: "Order all national (Dubrovnik's) ships to discharge their crews, leaving only the necessary guards aboard; let the ships remain where they are and await our further instructions. The owners are free to sell their ships if they wish."

A few captains, who were also owners, did sell their ships and discharge the crews, each man to go his own way. Several ships, with crews, entered the services of other nations. However, the rest of the vessels which were not captured or destroyed during the Continental Blockade remained loyal to the traditions of the republic and eventually reported home to make the best of an undesirable situation. When, at the Congress of Vienna in 1815, the new and permanent (until 1914) European boundaries were decided, the area of the Dubrovnik Republic became Austrian territory and the people found themselves as Austrian subjects. The sailors and the officers sailed their ships, however grudgingly, under the Austrian flag. Needless to say the fleet was decimated, and it did not recover until many years later, never reaching its pre-Napoleonic strength. A similar fate befell the Bay of Kotor merchant fleet.

After the dust cleared and the Austrian occupation became permanent, the living conditions of Dubrovnik and the Bay of Kotor area declined rapidly. This was primarily due to the drastic reduction of their lucrative maritime trade. The Austrian authorities did nothing to improve the situation. The nobility of Dubrovnik, the ruling class of yesteryear, abandoned its responsibility of leadership and decided on the passive resistance of nonfraternization with the "foreign occupiers," carrying its domestic passivity somewhat to the extreme by refusing to have any progeny. For many years afterwards, the people of

Dubrovnik hoped for some miracle, for the restoration of the Old Republic, for the prosperous times "when the duke ruled," "*kad je knjaz vlado.*" A lethargy overtook the people—a generation—who never quite recovered from the shock of losing their independence.

By the 1830s, however, the merchant fleet of this region had recovered somewhat, and by this time the other Dalmatian port cities began to build large oceangoing vessels which sailed all over the globe. It is axiomatic that for any movement of people to take place over a great distance with any permanency, three elements must be present: the push from the place where they are, the pull to where they are going, and the means of getting there.

The declining economic conditions of Dubrovnik and vicinity, during the 1830s and 1840s, and the dissatisfaction with the oppressive Austrian authorities provided the push. The rapidly growing prosperity of the American port cities to which many of them had sailed, such as Baltimore, Philadelphia, New York, Mobile, and especially the bustling river port of New Orleans, where the climate and culture were similar to their own, created the desire to settle there. This provided the pull. Sailing ships provided the means.

They, as millions of others before and after, came to this promised land seeking freedom and fortune. Some did amass fortunes, but all found freedom. The typical early South Slav immigrant made several trips to American ports before he made the final decision to remain in the United States. Consequently, when he decided to jump ship he knew where he was going; probably to contacts made on previous trips. Many left their vessels and settled in New Orleans. Others settled in New York and later in San Francisco and to a lesser degree in Baltimore and Mobile. This was on an individual basis or in small groups so that the vessels were able to return to Dalmatia for replacements.*

By 1840 some of the South Slavs in New Orleans were already

---

* It is appropriate to note here that the captains of the Dalmatian ships were required to report the names of all deserters from their ships to the deserters' home ports. The archives of these ports should, therefore, yield valuable data on the early South Slav immigration to New Orleans and other American ports. However, this type of research is beyond my reach at this time. For example, the *JADRANSKI ZBORNIK*, Adriatic Anthology, Rijeka, 1969, notes that the archives of the port of Bakar contain an entry that a sailor, Mate Jelencich, from Kostrene Sv. Barbara, deserted from the Brigantine *Piccollo Gioachino* (Captain Frane Badesich) in New Orleans in 1839.

established residents making their living by running their own businesses. Among those were: D. Ajmerich, grocery; Frank Ajmerich, coffee house; M. Giuranovich, coffee house; N. Ivanovich, restaurant; and Theodore Stanich, fruit stand. By mid-1840s their number increased to include among others, the following, who according to the New Orleans city directories, owned and operated various businesses ranging from coffee houses to billiard parlors: Andrew Bajanovich, Anthony Cognevich (who came to Louisiana from Konavle in 1835), John Dancevich, Marco Givanovich, N. Marich, George Mascovich, Nikola Matulich, Luke Orlich, L. Pablovich, Henry Pavelich, J. Petrovich, John Petrovich, Marko Petrovich, Marko Radovich, Tripo Raichevich, and P. Vidich.

Most of the early settlers, however, found employment on the New Orleans riverfront and on the New Orleans-based vessels; others became oystermen; John, Steven, and Anthony Vidacovich, and Marko Givanovich became planters.

John Vidacovich came to Louisiana around 1839 from Hercegnovi, Bay of Kotor, when he was about twenty-five years of age. He settled on the west bank of the Mississippi River in Plaquemines Parish and at first made his living fishing oysters and later as a planter. In 1844 he married Charlotte Brenny, a native of suburbs of Paris, France. Of this union the following children were born: Jerome in 1845; George, 1846; Annette, 1849; Robert, 1851; Nicholas, 1853; Desirée, 1856; and Paul François in 1859. Today his many descendants live in New Orleans and in Plaquemines Parish. The late Dimitry Vidacovich, who was killed in action in France during World War I, was the sixth child of Nicholas Vidacovich. Anthony P. Vidacovich, prominent in New Orleans Knights of Columbus circles and the oldest of five sons of Paul François, is still living in New Orleans. His youngest brother, the late Pinky (Irvine John) Vidacovich was a popular New Orleans entertainer for many years. Pinky's son—a great-grandson of the original John—Dr. Richard P. Vidacovich is a practicing ophthalmologist in New Orleans.

John Vidacovich became a prominent planter in Plaquemines Parish. The census of 1850 lists him as having one slave and the census of 1860 lists six. He died in 1886.

Marko Givanovich was born in Dubrovnik in 1823 and came to Louisiana in 1842. For a while he lived in New Orleans and apparently amassed a fortune, for in 1863 he purchased Home Place Plan-

Plaquemines Parish planter John Vidacovich (1815–1886) came to Louisiana from Hercegnovi in 1839.

Luke Jurisich, a native of Duba, Dalmatia, began cultivating oysters in Bayou Cook, Louisiana, around 1860.

The 1892 South Slav tug-of-war team; sitting, left to right: Matthew Perisich, Matthew Drazeta, Samuel M. Fucich (captain), Gregory Kacich-Miosich, and Anthony Protich; standing: George Slavich and John Radovich (sixth and seventh from left, respectively) ; others unidentified.

tation, located on the Cane River a few miles north of Alexandria, Louisiana, from his uncle, Nicola Gracia, for $325,000. The purchase included the plantation with land on both sides of the river, all the slaves, the plantation house with all the furnishings, other buildings on the plantation, and all the livestock.

The mansion house was built with care by his uncle Nicola Gracia, an educated Spaniard. It was one of the best examples of the early Louisiana-type plantation homes. It soon became known as the Marco House.

Givanovich was a bachelor who lived the life of a country gentleman. He made frequent trips to New Orleans and stayed at the best hotels and ate at the best French Quarter restaurants. On one such visit on February 16, 1896, he died while dining with his friends. He left all his property and possessions to a nephew in Dalmatia who, upon his death, left them to his seven children, and they later sold the entire estate. The new owner demolished the plantation house.

The Louisiana plantation houses and the communities which grew around them were usually named after the family name of the owners but Givanovich was probably too difficult to pronounce for his French and English-speaking neighbors and the workers, so he simply called it Marco, after his first name. Today there is a thriving community on the Cane River called Marco in memory of this nineteenth-century Louisiana planter from Dalmatia.

Since most of the South Slav immigrants before 1860 came from the same geographical area that stretched for a distance of about sixty miles along the Dalmatian coast from the mouth of Neretva River through the Bay of Kotor, many were known to each other and some were related. Also, many were in daily contact with each other on their jobs along the riverfront. So it is not surprising that they lived in the same sort of area in New Orleans. This area radiated around the French Market stretching from Bienville Street to Esplanade Avenue along Chartres and Decatur streets including the streets at right angles to Chartres and Decatur. They felt at ease on the waterfront of New Orleans which was similar to the other ports that they visited. These early immigrants were not illiterate peasants, but were "men of the world" who navigated the seven seas. The officers spoke two or three languages, including English, which they learned in the nautical academies of Dubrovnik, Kotor, Perast, and other coastal cities of Dalmatia. New Orleans with its Latin culture and a European flavor

The bark *Elena*, captained by A. Miloslavich. One of the many vessels which sailed between Dalmatia and New Orleans from 1830 to 1870.

Photo courtesy Dubrovnik Marine Museum

Port of New Orleans in 1852.

Photo courtesy Leonard V. Huber Collection

presented no obstacles to adjustments—social or occupational. Its prosperity and ability to absorb additional newcomers is effectively re-
flected in its increase of population from 17,000 in 1810 to 46,000 in
1830, to 102,000 in 1840 and 168,000 in 1860. Of the city's 168,000
population in 1860, over 63,000 were foreign born. Therefore, they
felt at ease among other European groups: the French, the Germans,
the Irish, the Spanish, the Portuguese, and the Italians whose language they probably spoke.

Based on the early New Orleans city directories, on the United
States Census of New Orleans and Plaquemines Parish for 1850 and
on the recollections of the early settlers, we conclude that by 1850
there were over two hundred South Slav immigrants in Louisiana.
Since only a handful came as bonafide passengers on regular passenger
vessels, most of them must have come over by simply getting off their
ships and remaining in New Orleans. No complicated documents
were required in those days. Many of them, according to Emily G.
Balch, in *Our Slavic Fellow Citizens*, went unrecorded. The first immigration laws by the federal authorities regarding the Caucasians
were not enacted until 1875. They simply stepped ashore with their
meager belongings and did not return to their ships. The list of those
who arrived on the regular passenger boats (before 1850), the names
of the early businessmen (listed on a previous page), and the ninety
or so names from the 1850 United States Census of New Orleans are
submitted here as documentary evidence that by 1850 the South Slav
immigrants were well established in Louisiana.

From over two hundred in 1850 their number, by 1860, grew to
about five or six hundred, an increase of over four hundred persons
for the decade. Coincidentally the years from 1850 to the Civil War
were the boom years for the city and port of New Orleans and for the
Dalmatian merchant shipping. Those were the last years when the
sailing vessels reigned supreme. Also, the pre–Civil War years saw
the greatest increase of the foreign-born population in New Orleans.
The South Slavs settling in New Orleans merely followed a popular
trend of other Europeans for whom New Orleans was a place to come
to make a fresh start. The New Orleans foreign-born population by
1860 reached 41 percent, declining to 25 percent in 1870, to 19 percent in 1880, to 14 percent in 1890, and to a mere 3 percent in 1940.
(The state of Louisiana foreign-born population in 1940 was a little

TABLE I

SOUTH SLAV IMMIGRANTS WHO ARRIVED AT NEW ORLEANS
ON REGULAR PASSENGER VESSELS FROM 1821 TO 1870.
Source: Passenger Lists of Ships Entering Port of New Orleans
from 1813 to 1870.

NAME	VESSEL	LAST PORT DOCKED BEFORE COMING TO NEW ORLEANS	DATE OF ARRIVAL
Matthew Pandich	Brig *Beldvin*	Cape Hayta	December 1, 1821
M. Reindich	Brig *Balvidere*	Baltimore	December 22, 1821
Mrs. M. Gurlich	Ship *Nestor*	La Havre	1825
A. Lorich	Ship *Corinne*	Bordeaux	December 1, 1825
Joseph Gavenich	Brig *Conveyance*	Vera Cruz	December 1, 1827
Hortense Galmich	Bark *Virginia*	La Havre	November, 1837
Felicite Galmich	Brig *Virginia*	La Havre	November, 1837
Mark N. Radovich[1]	Brig *Titi*	Havana	March 6, 1848
John Savich	Ship *Cato*	Liverpool	December 17, 1853
M. Irmich	Steamship *Cahawba*	Havana	February, 1857
D. Y. Masich	Brig *Black Warrior*	Havana	October, 1858
Simon Radovich	Brig *Hope*	Matamoras	April 1, 1864
M. N. Radovich	Brig *Hope*	Matamoras	April 1, 1864
Giacomo Covachevich	Brig *Hope*	Matamoras	August 25, 1864
Anthony Cognevich[2]	Schooner *Gleaner*	Matamoras	December 9, 1864
Estefano Vidovich	Schooner *Neptune*	Matamoras	August 26, 1865
Luka Jonovich	Schooner *Neptune*	Matamoras	August 26, 1865
Ante Milanovich	Schooner *Alonzo*	Havana	October 17, 1865
Luka Jurisich[3]	Steamship *Bolivian*	Liverpool	December 2, 1865
Ante Tomasovich	Steamship *Bolivian*	Liverpool	December 2, 1865

[1] Mark N. Radovich was the captain of Brig *Titi* in 1840 and later of Brig *Union*. He sailed these ships between the Caribbean ports and New Orleans. Apparently, after October 30, 1851, his last recorded trip, he settled in New Orleans. Around 1867 he was the captain of river steamer *Aloe*.

[2] Anthony Cognevich's trip from Matamoras was probably a business trip, because he had arrived in New Orleans many years before. During the Civil War he organized and led the Cognevich Company which served in the Louisiana Militia.

[3] Luke Jurisich and Ante Tomasovich, natives of Duba on Peljesac, also arrived much earlier, probably on one of the merchant vessels of Peljesac. They fished oysters in Bayou Cook, Louisiana, for many years and immediately after Appomattox returned to Duba for a visit with their families. They came back to New Orleans on December 2, 1865.

TABLE I (Continued)

NAME	VESSEL	LAST PORT DOCKED BEFORE COMING TO NEW ORLEANS	DATE OF ARRIVAL
Vlaho Petrovich	Schooner *Ada*	Vera Cruz	April 3, 1866
George Barbich	Schooner *Angelina*	Matamoras	August 6, 1866
M. Stiglich	Schooner *Angelina*	Matamoras	August 6, 1866
M. Marinkovich	Bark *Rio Grande*	Genoa	May 23, 1866
G. Carlovich	Steamship *Darian*	Havana	August 9, 1867
James Radich	Brig *Hope*	Havana	August 4, 1868
Maria Barbalich	Steamship *Saxonia*	Hamburg	October 24, 1868
Luke Radesich	Ship *Trade Wind*	Honduras	August 9, 1869

over 1 percent.) New Orleans reached and passed the melting-pot phase decades before the rest of the nation.

The South Slavs, however, did not restrict themselves to New Orleans. Many settled in nearby Plaquemines Parish, especially in its lower part near the mouth of the Mississippi River. Others used New Orleans as the embarkation point or a place for a short stay and moved on to St. Louis, Missouri, or to California. After gold was discovered in California many ex-sailors signed on the California-bound vessels either as passengers or as crew and became gold prospectors once they reached California. Some sailed around the Horn while others disembarked at the Isthmus of Panama, crossed over by horse or foot, and boarded the next available vessel for California. Many of the early San Francisco Yugoslavs came through New Orleans. John V. Tadich, a prominent San Francisco restaurateur wrote in his reminiscences about the nineteenth-century San Francisco Yugoslavs: "Repeatedly I would hear my uncle (Nikola Buja) discuss New Orleans with his old-time friends. . . . I asked several of our people why New Orleans was always the topic of conversation among many of our men, and was informed that the majority of our earliest pioneers in San Francisco came from New Orleans."

Once the very first immigrants achieved some economic stability in New Orleans, many naturally wrote back home about it and perhaps exaggerated a little about their successes. These letters whetted the appetites of their younger brothers, cousins, and other relatives, many of whom soon joined them in New Orleans. These "second-wave" immigrants were more fishermen than career sailors, and upon arriving in New Orleans, instead of remaining on the city's riverfront

TABLE II

SOME OF THE SOUTH SLAV IMMIGRANTS LIVING IN NEW ORLEANS
DURING 1850. EXCERPTS FROM THE UNITED STATES POPULATION
CENSUS FOR NEW ORLEANS, LOUISIANA, FOR 1850.
Source: Slavonic American Historical and Genealogical Society,
edited by Adam S. Eterovich.

NAME	AGE	OCCUPATION
Nicholas Ankini	30	Seaman
Peter Ankini	45	Seaman
Anthony Ban	28	Fruit dealer
Andrew Bojanovich	40	Fisherman
Madalina Bojanovich	38	Housewife
Nicholas Borich	34	Sailor
John S. Boza	35	Coffeehouse owner
Leon Cartovich	37	Sailor
Ignacio Colorich	35	Fruit dealer
John Dancenovich	50	Boardinghouse operator
Julia Danilovich	20	Housewife
L. Danilovich	35	Fruit dealer
Steven Danilovich	1	Child
L. Dantzic	35	Fruit dealer
Alborlini Davidovich	30	Fruit dealer
J. Davidovich	35	Sailor
Mario Davidovich	30	Fisherman
Luke Doncovich	25	Fruit dealer
M. Doncovich	28	Fruit dealer
Vincent Donovich	50	Cook
Jacob Frankibusich	21	Laborer
A. Garani	35	Fruit dealer
Luke Gobovich	45	Marketman
P. Godinavich	35	Fruit dealer
F. Gravolina	30	Fruit dealer
Joseph Gravolina	2	Infant
Louiza Gravolina	25	Housewife
Lawrence Gregovich	19	Fruit dealer
Blaise Jacovich	43	Fruit dealer
John Jacovich	23	Fruit dealer
Peter Lomovich	24	Laborer
Nicholas Jovinon	25	Fruit dealer
Michael Larini	23	Fruit dealer
John Luchich	44	Clerk
T. Lucovich	35	Sailor
Matthew Marlovich	42	Fruit dealer

TABLE II (Continued)

NAME	AGE	OCCUPATION
Andrew Marovich	34	Sailor
Anthony Marovich	30	Fruit dealer
Marko Marovich	40	Fruit dealer
John Matovich	28	Fruit dealer
Maria Matovich	28	Housewife
Michael Matovich	37	Fruit dealer
F. Medin	28	Waiter
Jacob Medovich	31	Seaman
Stephen Melich	48	
I. Meranovich	24	Fruit dealer
Louis Miriovich	51	Clerk
Gregory Naneza	40	Barkeeper
Stephen Nicolich	29	Sailor
Catherine Orlich	42	Housewife
Luke Orlich	42	Grocer
Nicholas Palovich	22	Fruit dealer
Ann Pavelich	23	Housewife
Henry Pavelich	44	Coffeehouse owner
Gregorio Pavlovich	35	Sailor
Jacob Perovich	36	Fruit dealer
Louis Perovich	33	Fruit dealer
Joseph Perovich	30	Seaman
Mario Petrovich	25	Grocer
Paul Petrovich	35	Fruit dealer
Philip Puscovich	45	Fruit dealer
Tripo Reicevich	38	Fruit dealer
Joseph Rimitich	36	Fruit dealer
Anthony Robira	20	Fruit dealer
Franusia Rostevich	22	Housewife
Manuel Rostevich	27	Oyster shop owner
Peter Rostevich	1	Infant
Mark Sargovich	30	Fruit dealer
Vincent Sartovich	34	Fisherman
Theodore Stanich	55	Fruit dealer
Gaspar Steglich	24	Fruit dealer
Luke Stica	27	Ice-cream dealer
John Teric	30	Seaman
I. Tuma	35	Fruit dealer
Anthony Varan	34	Clerk
Anthony Yorina	35	Fruit dealer
Nicholas Zambelich	25	Fruit dealer
Amadeo Zorlovich	25	Fruit dealer

or signing on one of the New Orleans-based vessels, they moved down to the fish, shrimp, and oyster waters of Plaquemines Parish. Raised on the shores of the Adriatic, expertly trained in the art of fishing and small craft handling, they had no difficulty in adapting to the Louisiana bays and bayous and to the Gulf waters in general. They soon became expert fishermen, shrimpers, and oystermen. A few became farmers and planters, but oystering proved to be most dependable and profitable, and it soon became their chief occupation. Their story is told in another chapter of this book.

Among those who settled in Plaquemines Parish before the Civil War were the following: Anthony Ban, Peter Barich, Frank Benushi, Ilia Catovich, Nicholas Cartovich, Joseph Churlich, Anthony Cibilich, Joseph Cibilich, Nikola Cibilich, Stephen Cognevich, John Cornavich, P. Escovencovich, Anthony Franovich, Andrew Juraditich, Andrew Jurich, Joseph Jurisich, Luke Jurisich, George Lusich, Frank Matovich, Stephen Matulich, Peter Merlich, Matthew Murina, Bosko Musselivich, F. Novasina, Anthony Ozmanovich, Luke Pastrovich, Anthony Payitich, Frank Pergovich, John Petrovich, Marko Petrovich, Peter Petrovich, Nicholas Suich, Nicholas Tanovich, Anthony Tomasovich, John Vukovich, and Peter Yankovich.

By 1870 their number increased considerably as is evidenced by the 1870 United States Census (Table III). Of course there were many more South Slavs living in this area at that time than were listed by the census. Not all who were on camps and boats could be reached to be counted.

HOW MANY CAME?

It is difficult to estimate accurately the number of the South Slav immigrants that came to Louisiana during the last 140 years. At the beginning they did not come through the regular passenger routes, and therefore were not recorded anywhere. Nor can their exact number be determined from the United States census records of foreign-born, because many—since their homeland was a part of Austro-Hungary—declared Austria as their country of birth and consequently were listed as Austrians. Therefore their number can only be estimated from the local sources, i.e., the American Civil War service records, the Slavonian Association, and from the old-timers. Also by meticulously reading the actual census lists of Orleans and Plaquemines parishes for 1860, 1870, and 1880 (1890 census records were accidentally destroyed

TABLE III

SOUTH SLAVS IN PLAQUEMINES PARISH, LOUISIANA, IN 1870.
Source: National Archives Microfilm Publications Population
Schedules of the Ninth Census of the United States, 1870.

NAME	AGE	OCCUPATION	PLACE OF BIRTH
Luka Babin	62	Farmer	Austria*
Anthony Ban	47	Farmer	Dalmatia
Genevieve Ban	34	Housekeeper	Louisiana
Marie Ban	15		Louisiana
Frank Ban	13		Louisiana
Julia Ban	10		Louisiana
Mathilde Ban	8		Louisiana
John Ban	2		Louisiana
Nikola Bendich	30	Seaman	Dalmatia
Uranie Bendich	17	Housekeeper	Louisiana
Peter Bendich	26	Fisherman	Dalmatia
Anthony Brocadovich	30	Farmer	Dalmatia
Joseph Camovich	46	Fisherman	Dalmatia
George Canka	48	Carpenter	Dalmatia
Jeannette Canka	37	Housekeeper	France
Joseph Cascarich	45	Fisherman	Dalmatia
George Catach	18	Fisherman	Dalmatia
Simon Catach	21	Fisherman	Dalmatia
George Catanovich	62	Fisherman	Dalmatia
George Catanovich	27	Fisherman	Dalmatia
A. Ceheovich	52	Fisherman	Dalmatia
Ignacio Cognovich	26	Fisherman	Dalmatia
Michael Conrac	23	Seaman	Dalmatia
P. Conivicich	40	Fisherman	Dalmatia
Elias Cussevich	51	Fisherman	Dalmatia
Louis Dascovich	28	Fisherman	Dalmatia
L. Dracotonovich	21	Fisherman	Dalmatia
Vincent Dulsich	48	Fisherman	Dalmatia
Luka Escobedo	35	Seaman	Dalmatia
Armantine Escobedo	19	Housekeeper	Louisiana
Nikola Franovich	18	Fisherman	Dalmatia
M. Frenkovich	28	Seaman	Dalmatia
Spiro Gobelich	26	Fisherman	Dalmatia

* In 1870 Dalmatia was a crown province of the Austro-Hungarian Empire.
Hence when they emigrated they were the subjects of the Austrian Empire. A few
listed Austria as the country of birth while most of the others listed Dalmatia; apparently detesting the Austrian rule over their homeland.

TABLE III (Continued)

Name	Age	Occupation	Place of Birth
George Grandolich	49	Fisherman	Dalmatia
Anthony Granich	42	Fisherman	Dalmatia
Ivan Granich	32	Fisherman	Austria
N. Gusmanovich	46	Fisherman	Dalmatia
Andrea Iaduc	33	Seaman	Dalmatia
Rachel Iaduc	23	Housekeeper	Prussia
Annette Iaduc	4		Louisiana
Michael Iancovich	35	Fisherman	Dalmatia
Peter Iancovich	26	Fisherman	Dalmatia
Anthony Iasprich	40	Fisherman	Dalmatia
Hyacinthe Illisich	28	Fisherman	Dalmatia
John Istanovich	41	Fisherman	Dalmatia
Luka Itirinich	49	Fisherman	Dalmatia
Joseph Jasprizza	25	Farmer	Dalmatia
Ivan Jucurovich	37	Fisherman	Dalmatia
Paul Jurivich	30	Fisherman	Dalmatia
Adam Lapovich	27	Fisherman	Dalmatia
Luka Lidotich	24	Fisherman	Dalmatia
Peter Littovich	21	Fisherman	Dalmatia
Leo Lusich	40	Fisherman	Dalmatia
Bosko Maloscich	46	Fisherman	Dalmatia
John Maloscich	11		Louisiana
Ivan Margodich	30	Fisherman	Dalmatia
Joseph Mascovich	40	Fisherman	Dalmatia
Joseph Masich	24	Fisherman	Dalmatia
R. Matonich		Fisherman	Dalmatia
H. Mattanich	28	Fisherman	Dalmatia
Nikola Matulich	57	Farmer	Dalmatia
Sarah Matulich	42	Housekeeper	Louisiana
Henry Matulich	15		Louisiana
Jerome Matulich	13		Louisiana
Mary Matulich	11		Louisiana
George Matulich	10		Louisiana
Margueritte Matulich	8		Louisiana
Thomas Meladin	30	Fisherman	Dalmatia
Josephine Meladin	18	Housekeeper	Louisiana
George Mestrovich	33	Seaman	Dalmatia
Adam Millanovich	32	Fisherman	Dalmatia
Bogdan Millanovich	30	Fisherman	Dalmatia
C. Millanovich	58	Fisherman	Dalmatia
Joseph Millovich	24	Fisherman	Austria
Thomas Millovich	60	Fisherman	Dalmatia

T A B L E I I I (Continued)

NAME	AGE	OCCUPATION	PLACE OF BIRTH
George Missiaborich	30	Seaman	Dalmatia
Mikola Mladineo	30	Fisherman	Dalmatia
Dominick Monaspina	51	Fisherman	Dalmatia
P. Mumanovich	32	Fisherman	Dalmatia
Anthony Munich	31	Fisherman	Dalmatia
Matthew Murina	35	Fisherman	Dalmatia
M. Pabolovich	26	Fisherman	Dalmatia
N. Parivaporich	30	Fisherman	Dalmatia
Marko Patovich	28	Fisherman	Dalmatia
Vincent Pederich	40	Fisherman	Dalmatia
Peter Pedrocorach	45	Fisherman	Dalmatia
Ilia Pendo	42	Fisherman	Dalmatia
Tony Perag	49	Boatman	Dalmatia
Peter Perovich	41	Fisherman	Dalmatia
Anthony Petanovich	25	Fisherman	Dalmatia
Perani Petrovich	30	Fisherman	Dalmatia
Peter Picolich	42	Fisherman	Dalmatia
Peter Pilotich	37	Fisherman	Austria
Luka Portovich		Fisherman	Dalmatia
Lazar Radovich	30	Fisherman	Dalmatia
Vlaho Rana	28	Fisherman	Dalmatia
Bosko Rastianovich	30	Fisherman	Dalmatia
R. Rastovich	35	Fisherman	Dalmatia
Nikola Ruffalich	47	Fisherman	Dalmatia
Vincent Sansovich	22	Fisherman	Dalmatia
Thomas Sapatovich	28	Fisherman	Dalmatia
Stefan Sturlitza	39	Farmer	Dalmatia
Françoise Sturlitza	23	Housekeeper	Louisiana
Jacques Sturlitza	5		Louisiana
Antoine Sturlitza	3		Louisiana
Peter Taliantich	30	Fisherman	Dalmatia
Gaspar Tertorich	30	Fisherman	Dalmatia
Marko Todorich	40	Fisherman	Dalmatia
V. Tomasich	24	Fisherman	Dalmatia
Ilia Tosich	39	Fisherman	Dalmatia
Irene Tosich	37	Housekeeper	Louisiana
Genevieve Tosich	18		Louisiana
Helene Tosich	17		Louisiana
Sava Tripcovich	34	Seaman	Dalmatia
Suzanne Tripcovich	19	Housekeeper	Louisiana
Annette Tripcovich	4		Louisiana
John Ubirichich	40	Fisherman	Dalmatia

TABLE III (Continued)

Name	Age	Occupation	Place of Birth
Kristo Ubirichich	56	Fisherman	Dalmatia
John Uchinovich	34	Seaman	Dalmatia
Rose Uchinovich	22	Housekeeper	Louisiana
Antonio Uchinovich	6		Louisiana
Angeline Uchinovich	3		Louisiana
George Uchinovich	1		Louisiana
Andrea Undich	40	Farmer	Dalmatia
Odile Undich	36	Housekeeper	Louisiana
Joseph Undich	12		Louisiana
Marie Undich	11		Louisiana
Frank Undich	4		Louisiana
Jacques Undich	1		Louisiana
Stefan Urich	26	Fisherman	Dalmatia
Frank Uridich	38	Farmer	Dalmatia
Elodie Uridich	24	Housekeeper	Louisiana
Josephine Uridich	7		Louisiana
Marie Uridich	4		Louisiana
Hyacinthe Uridich	2		Louisiana
John Vidacovich	54	Farmer	Dalmatia
Charlotte Vidacovich	48	Housekeeper	France
George Vidacovich	21	Steamboat pilot	Louisiana
Nicholas Vidacovich	12	Student	Louisiana
Paul Vidacovich	9		Louisiana
Desiré Vidacovich	7		Louisiana
Lazar Viscovich	54	Fisherman	Dalmatia
Anthony Volich	40	Fisherman	Dalmatia
Peter Yancovich	39	Carpenter	Dalmatia
Joseph Zibilich	57	Farmer	Dalmatia
Louise Zibilich	35	Housekeeper	Louisiana
Angeline Zibilich	9		Louisiana
Josephine Zibilich	6		Louisiana
George Zibilich	4		Louisiana
Paul Zibilich	2		Louisiana

by fire and the lists for 1900 and later cannot yet be released to the public, under existing law) and counting the South Slavic names additional statistics are obtained. But at best these numbers are only indicative, because a few did change the spelling of their names, and some who were scattered throughout the Louisiana marshes on boats and in camps were never recorded.

From the meager beginnings of the middle 1830s their number climbed steadily so that on the eve of the Civil War there were between 500 and 600 South Slavs in Louisiana: over 400 in New Orleans and over 100 in Plaquemines Parish. The number 400 for New Orleans is obtained from the Civil War service records. The Cognevich Company numbered 110 men, Slavonian Rifles I, 118, and assuming that the Slavonian Rifles II numbered about 100 men, a total of 328 is obtained. Counting the women, the aged, and those men who did not join, it can conservatively be estimated that by 1860 there were over 400 South Slav immigrants in New Orleans.

After Appomattox their number in New Orleans declined because of unemployment and the general economic decline which set in during Reconstruction. Many left the city. Some returned to Dalmatia, some moved to Plaquemines Parish to fish oysters, a few moved to St. Louis, Missouri, while others migrated to California where many had relatives and acquaintances.

From the late 1860s to the early 1890s their number in Plaquemines Parish increased steadily so that on the eve of the 1893 storm there were over four hundred South Slavs living in the Louisiana delta. After the 1893 hurricane there was a rapid decline in the Plaquemines Parish population, partly because of the storm deaths and partly because of the survivors who migrated to New Orleans or returned to the old country.

From 1895 to the eve of World War I their number, both in Plaquemines and Orleans parishes, grew steadily, reaching its highest mark of over a thousand Dalmatian-born around 1914, when the legal emigration from Dalmatia was radically curtailed because of the war. After the armistice in 1918 and the creation of Yugoslavia, many returned, with their savings, to live the rest of their lives on native soil. From then on the number of native-born fluctuated around six hundred, the newcomers replacing those who died and those who returned to Yugoslavia. Of course, the total number who have come to Louisiana since the 1830s is several times that—somewhere around five thousand. However, many of them stayed here only a few years and returned home, and many others, far too many, never married, and died without leaving any descendants.

Starting with the 1920 United States census, the Louisiana South Slavs are classified as Yugoslavs, but the figures reported are somewhat low when compared to the estimates from other sources. In the 1920 census 312 Louisianians reported Yugoslavia as the country of birth; 397 in 1930; 445 in 1940; 427 in 1950; 358 in 1960; and 411 in 1970.

In addition to the above-mentioned six hundred Yugoslav-born Louisianians, there are the descendants of first-generation immigrants. Counting the second and the subsequent generations there are between five thousand and six thousand Louisianians of Yugoslav ancestry living in the Pelican State.

CAUSES FOR EMIGRATION

As was previously stated, the early South Slav immigrants left their native land because of declining economic and political conditions in Dubrovnik and vicinity after the fall of the Dubrovnik Republic. From those early years to the present the principal cause for emigrating has always been deficient economic conditions. However, there were also secondary causes such as the desire to be united with the relatives already here, to escape oppression of the Habsburgs and compulsory military service in the Austrian armed forces, and for some to satisfy their adventurous spirit.

The reasons that many sailors deserted their ships while in foreign, especially American, ports were many and varied. In perusing the Croatian maritime literature dealing with this subject, I found the following to be mentioned most often: better pay on ships of other nations; maltreatment by the captains; wars breaking out at home or rumors of wars; news of contagious diseases (especially yellow fever) in the next scheduled port of call; disease aboard ship; termination of sign-on agreements; unseaworthy conditions of the ships; discovery of gold in California and later in Alaska; and better monetary rewards and working conditions on shore.

For instance, in 1854 three sailors, one each from Makarska, Kostrena, and Boka Kotorska deserted from Brigatine *Fidente* after the outbreak of yellow fever aboard the ship in the port of New Orleans. A few days later Juraj Sikic died from yellow fever onboard, and they abandoned all plans of returning to the *Fidente*. In 1878 a first mate on the *Fanny P.* deserted because the captain demoted him to second mate and hired a new first mate. Many who had no intentions of deserting their ships at first were persuaded to do so by their countrymen and acquaintances who had "done well" in the New World. This was especially true at the port of New Orleans where the vessels made regular runs and the crew could visit their sailing mates on shore, who had deserted on previous voyages.

During the second half of the nineteenth century, sailing merchant vessels were replaced by larger and costlier steam vessels. Small companies and individual owners in Dalmatia lacked the necessary capital to build steamships, and consequently sailors and merchant marine officers found themselves without jobs. The prosperous towns of Kotor, Dobrota, Dubrovnik, Perast, Hercegnovi, Korcula, Orebic, and other coastal towns whose prosperity rested on the commerce and wealth generated by the sailing vessels declined rapidly. Many sailors and unemployed youth left home and settled in America, some in Louisiana.

Another factor that contributed to the emigration from Croatia and other parts of the present-day Yugoslavia was the destruction of the vineyards by the grape insect *phylloxera* during the last half of the nineteenth and the beginning of the twentieth century. True, to prevent complete destruction of the vineyards the *phylloxera*-immune American rootstocks were transplanted and the domestic vines grafted to it. This restored the vineyards somewhat, but wine production never reached its pre-*phylloxera* days. The younger male members of the impoverished families left for the United States. Many settled in California where they helped develop a thriving wine industry. Others came to Louisiana.

Creation of the new South Slavic state (Yugoslavia) in 1918 did not improve economic conditions, and immigration to Louisiana (America) continued on a smaller scale for the new immigration laws enacted by Congress during the early 1920s made it difficult for large masses to enter the United States.

Most of the immigrants had been generous about sending part of their earnings to the families back home. This, the letters describing the favorable conditions in America, and the impression of prosperity created by the returning or visiting immigrants also encouraged restless youths to emigrate.

The visiting immigrant was always welcomed by his native villagers. I remember many such visits by *Amerikantsi* from Louisiana to our village during the 1930s. The youngsters were impressed by his dress: by his starched white shirt, loud new tie, blue serge suit, shinning leather shoes, and a gold pocket watch on the end of a gold chain across his vest. As he recounted his adventures in America in the native Croatian, an English word would be thrown in now and then, which should have made the narrative unintelligible to us—for we knew no English—but it only created an aura of mystery in our imaginative, adventure-seeking minds. The visitor, especially if he were an eligible bachelor, would be wined and dined from house to house, and more especially where there were marriageable young ladies. Many selected their brides and returned to America with them, to the envy of the most of the villagers.

The "pull" to Louisiana has always been the promise of good wages and eventual success in one's own business. Before leaving his homeland, the new immigrant usually arranged for employment with a relative or a friend who was already in Louisiana. This arrangement was done by correspondence or in person, when the "sponsor" visited his homeland. He usually owned an oyster-producing enterprise in the Louisiana bayous or a business establishment in New Orleans. He also paid for the passage, which was subsequently deducted from the newcomer's wages.

Each of these factors added to the desire to emigrate, and the result was a steady stream of immigrants who hoped to improve their economic status whether by temporarily emigrating and returning with a few thousand dollars or by settling in America for good.

PLACES OF ORIGIN

Most of the Yugoslavs coming to Louisiana emigrated from southern Dalmatia; specifically from an area extending from, and including, the Bay of Kotor through the town of Podgora and embracing the nearby islands of Korcula, Hvar, and Brac; a distance of about one hundred miles along the Adriatic coast. Sixty or so persons came to Louisiana from Molat Island and its immediate vicinity. The rest come from towns and villages scattered along the whole length of Dalmatia.

The Dalmatian birthplaces of the Louisiana Yugoslavs are typical Mediterranean communities. Most of the ports are crescent- or u-shaped, with a quay extending into the sea on the exposed side to enlarge their areas and to give additional protection to the harbors. The houses, two-to-three-story stone structures, built to last for centuries, hug the shoreline. They are simply constructed, square- or rectangle-shaped. The fronts of the houses are decorated with stone carvings and some of them have elaborate stone porches protruding above the main entrance. The ground floor or *konoba* is used for storing the family supply of wine, olive oil, tools, small boats, nets, and other fishing and farming gear. The other two levels are used for sleeping and living quarters. These homes are simply furnished, for the Dalmatians are an outdoor people who enjoy the freedom of nature.

The church, the school building, the town hall, and the other public buildings are located in the center of town bordering on a public square. The town hall usually has a tall square-shaped tower—competing with the church campanile—with a large clock which can be seen from almost all points within the town. Some of these town halls and churches date back centuries while others are of recent vintage (late nineteenth or the early twentieth century). A few were completely demolished by bombs during World War II and some have been rebuilt.

The chief occupations in these coastal communities are: fishing, small stock raising on a limited scale, small-scale farming including olive oil and wine producing, navigating the seas as merchant mariners, and since the 1950s, tourism.

Living along the seashore they naturally turned to the sea for additional food and profit. They fish by traps, hooks, spears, and nets. However, sardine fishing on warm moonless nights is the primary and the most interesting and adventurous fishing activity.

A small boat equipped with a powerful light lures the schools of sardines from the open sea to a favorable position near the shore. The fish follow the boat as it moves inland slowly and silently, with muffled oars. When near the shore the sardines are encircled with a large net and scooped into a boat which delivers the catch to a nearby factory for canning.

Through the centuries the Dalmatians built their houses close together for protection against invaders by land and from pirates by sea. The result is a coast dotted with close-knit villages and towns surrounded by plots of farmland, vineyards, olive groves, and pastures owned by its inhabitants who commute back and forth between their homes and the land they work, a distance of several miles each way, either by foot, horse, or boat. One family may own land at several different locations because of the parceling of inheritances through the centuries and acquisition of land by marriages.

The southernmost part of the area from which the Louisiana Yugoslavs originated is the Bay of Kotor (Boka Kotorska), where the Adriatic penetrates the mainland for several miles and forms a sinuous bay—or rather bays, for there are four distinct bays (Hercegnovi Bay, Tivat Bay, Kotor Bay, and the Risan Bay), each separated from the other by a narrow strait. Bordered on all sides by high mountains it looks more like a Norwegian fjord than a Dalmatian seacoast bay.

The towns and villages, dating back to the Illyrian, Greek, and the Roman times, are located along the bayshore. The principal city is Kotor, which gave the bay its name. Some of the other towns are: Hercegnovi, Perast, Dobrota, Risan, Lepetane, Lastva, Tivat, and Morinj.

These towns produced first-rate sailors for centuries. Peter the Great of Russia sent his naval cadets to the bay's maritime academies. During the sixteenth and seventeenth centuries the merchant marine fleet of the Bay of Kotor was at its prime. Kotor, Perast, Dobrota, and other towns were the home ports of hundreds of merchant sailing vessels. The prosperity of these towns was greatly reduced with the decimation of the fleet during the Napoleonic wars. Later, when the steamships came into use and the owners, either from lack of capital or from slavery to tradition, stubbornly refused to adapt to steam, the larger sailing vessels all but disappeared from this area. During this era of decline many sailors and officers emigrated to other lands, some to Louisiana.

The sailors and the officers of the sailing merchant marine of the bay, which traded with the port of New Orleans, settled in Louisiana between 1830 and 1890. The Louisiana families with the following names trace their origin to this region: Abramovich, Amanovich, Benovich, Berberovich, Bjelich, Dolanich, Ercegovich, Franovich, Gojkovich, Ivovich, Krsanac, Pavlovich (Pablovich), Radovich, Ramadanovich, Ribica, Rusovich, Seferovich, Surdich, Trazivuk, Tripkovich, Trojanovich, Vasiljevich, Vidacovich, Vucinovich, Vuinovich, Vuskovich, and Yuncevich.

Moving northward along the Adriatic coast from the Bay of Kotor we come upon a fertile valley called: Konavli, named after the canals which were dug there during the middle ages to drain the area. Konavli is a narrow valley only a mile or so wide and about fifteen miles long, with a number of friendly and picturesque villages. On

The Louisiana Yugoslavs came from . . .

Bay of Kotor . . .

. . . Dubrovnik

Photo by author

Ston . . .

. . . Trpanj

. . . Duba

Photo courtesy Ante Cibilich

Korcula . . .

. . . Sucuraj

Photo by author

Igrane . . .

. . . Podgora . . .

. . . and Molat

the north it is bounded by a mountain chain Sjeznice and on the south by the hills of Donja Gora which separate it from the sea. This is the most populous area of Dalmatia.

Since 1420 Konavli has constituted a part of the Dubrovnik Republic and for centuries has produced the foodstuff for the republic and furnished some of the sailors for its ships. After the fall of the republic it became a part of Austro-Hungary and in 1918 was incorporated with the rest of the South Slavic lands into the new state of Yugoslavia.

Some of the villages of Konavli are: Durinici, Mikulici, Gruda, Popovici, Cilipi, and Mocici. The area is famous far and wide for its quaint national costumes and beautiful girls.

The young men of Konavli emigrated to America in large numbers. Many went to California where they became successful farmers. Jack London describes them in his *Valley of the Moon* in which he calls their settlement Little Dalmatia; others came to Louisiana.

The following Louisiana families trace their origin to the region of Konavli: Ban, Cognevich, Draskovich, Gjuratovich, Kandich, Levata, Mijoch, Mustahinich, Popovich, Puh, Rasica, Skalamija, Spremich, Sukno, Vidak, and Zupancich.

Next on our list as we move northward is the historic city of Dubrovnik and its immediate vicinity. The city's history is recorded elsewhere in this study, but it should be noted here that today it is one of the principal tourist attractions of southern Europe.

Dubrovnik is well preserved, and, by legislation, its historic buildings are protected from destruction and alteration. The streets, shops, buildings, and fortifications of the inner-walled city still remain as they were during the seventeenth century when they were constructed.

There are, however, several public buildings dating back to the thirteenth and the fourteenth centuries. As an example there is a Franciscan church with a monastery built in 1315. The monastery contains a most valuable library with ancient manuscripts and the oldest pharmacy in the world, dispensing medicine since 1317. There are numerous other pre–seventeenth-century buildings standing as mute reminders of a thousand years of independence and commercial prosperity of this small maritime republic.

After the disastrous earthquake and subsequent fire of 1667 the city was almost completely rebuilt. The nobles and the wealthy merchants built large three- and four-story palaces of stone and marble according to citywide planning and based on the plans of the best architects of the day. These buildings and the few that survived the earthquake and fire comprise the Dubrovnik that the tourists see today.

Subsequent to the fall of the republic during the Napoleonic wars, many of its sailors and officers emigrated to foreign lands. Between 1830 and 1880 hundreds abandoned their ships and settled in San Francisco, New York, and in New Orleans.

The following Louisiana families proudly point to Dubrovnik as the birthplace of their ancestors: Antoncich, Antulovich, Apoloneo, Baccich, Bautovich, Berbera, Bozanja, Drcelja, Gusina, Kutzum, Muhoberac, Picoli, Prislich, Salatich, Skobelj, Slabowski, Soljacich, and Strbinich.

About twenty-five miles northwest from Dubrovnik lies the Peljesac Peninsula which has contributed a number of its youth to Louisiana. The peninsula projects itself into the Adriatic and is connected to the mainland by a narrow strip of land about a mile wide. It has all the characteristics of a Dalmatian island. It is about forty-four miles long and from one to four and a half miles wide. Its highest point, the three thousand two hundred-foot Mount of Sveti Ilija (St. Ellias), offers a panoramic view of the surrounding islands, the mainland seacoast, and of the azure Adriatic all the way to the Italian coast. It is dotted with towns and villages from which came many an immigrant to Louisiana to seek his fortune. Its largest town is Ston and the other towns and villages which have contributed to the Louisiana population are: Cesvinica, Hodilje, Duba near Ston, Brijesta, Janjina, Sreser, Kuna, Vrucica, Duba near Trpanj, Trpanj, Orebic, and Viganj.

The history of the peninsula goes back to prehistoric times. It includes the Illyrians, the Greeks, and the Romans. The Roman ruins can still be seen in Ston and Janjina. As the Croats arrived on the Adriatic, during the migration of nations, they intermingled with, and eventually (as elsewhere in present-day Croatia) conquered the people they found there.

From 1326 to 1808 Peljesac was a part of the Dubrovnik Republic whose political and economic fate it shared for five centuries.

Ston and vicinity are well known for salt production from the sea on its shallow well-developed enclosures. Salt was one of the chief exports of the Dubrovnik Republic to the Balkan interior, and Ston soon became an important factor in the economy of this small maritime republic. In fact the peninsula was once called *Stonski Rat* (Cape of Ston).

In the vicinity of the Mali Ston (Little Ston) which is located on the northern shore of the peninsula about a mile from Ston proper there is a large area of shallow water where the cultivation of oysters is highly developed; this fact perhaps explains why some of the best Louisiana oystermen come from the Peljesac Peninsula.

The town of Trpanj, located on the northern side of the peninsula, has, due to its accessible location and mild climate, developed into an important tourist center. There are several sun-swept beaches nearby, which, during the summer months, accommodate tourists from far and near.

On the southern side of the peninsula, across from Korcula, nests a small seaside town of Orebic. Due to its location it has served, through the centuries, as an important governing and maritime center for the Dubrovnik Republic. At first it was called *Trstenica* and during the sixteenth century adopted its present name after the Orebic family from Bakar which settled there and in 1568 built a castle for protection against the Turks and the pirates. Traditionally, through the centuries, Orebic has been a hometown of many captains who commanded local as well as the oceangoing ships. Many a family has produced generations of seagoing captains who after retirement built imposing villas, many of which still remain as a lasting testimony of its past maritime glory.

However, of the many towns and villages of Dalmatia that have contributed youth to Louisiana, the village of Duba near Trpanj has contributed the most. Every family in Duba has at least one member in Louisiana, some two or more, and some entire families have been transplanted. It has been estimated that if the youth of Duba did not emigrate, its present population would be at least three-fold.

The peninsula has produced excellent sailors and hundreds of well-trained and valiant captains who served on the ships of the Dubrovnik Republic as well as on the ships owned by fellow Peljescanis. These sailing ships were in contact with the American ports, including New Orleans, from the 1820s to the end of the nineteenth century. From the beginning, many sailors and officers chose to remain in New Orleans and settled in Louisiana. When, due to the inability to compete with the steam-operated vessels, their sailing merchant fleet declined, the number of immigrants from the peninsula increased rapidly. The Peljesac Peninsula has contributed some of the earliest and some of the most recent immigrants to Louisiana; they still continue to come. The following names trace their origin to Peljesac: Bajurin, Ficovich, Gerica, Hajtilovich, Kresich, Pendo, and Tovarac from Ston; Ficovich, Kopanica, Rozich, and Zile from Cesvinica; Antunica, Delo, Garbini, and Marinovich from Hodilje; Balovich, Korac, and Vulich from Duba near Ston; Dimak, Popich, and Prcevich from Brijesta; Jurisich, Nozica, and Pekich from Janjina; Masich and Turcich from Sreser; Bjelancich, Jurovich, Mestrovich, Palihnich, and Vidos from Kuna; Barach, Belin, Butirich, Frankovich, Glavina, Keko, Markovich, Markotich, Miljak, Mucalo, Nesanovich, Porobil, Suljaga, Vezich, and Zaninovich from Trpanj; Dragicevich, Lepetich, Pausina, Seput, Stipeljkovich, Stuk, and Tesvich from Vrucica; Bilich, Cibilich, Jurisich, Mihocevich, Murina, Petrovich, Slavich, Tomasovich, Zegura, and Zibilich from Duba near Trpanj; Koludrovich, Marinovich, and Ruvo from Orebic; Lupis and Mazuran from Viganj, and Kristichevich from Podobuce.

The island of Korcula is separated from the Peljesac Peninsula by a narrow channel only about 1½ miles wide. It is one of the few Dalmatian islands from which some of its residents emigrated to Louisiana. Twenty-four miles long, four to five miles wide, a little over one hundred square miles in area, it supports about twenty thousand people who make their living by farming, fishing, boat building, tourism, and stone quarrying. The island is rich in history having first been settled by the Greeks who maintained extensive vineyards there. One of the best Dalmatian grapes *Grk* (the Greek) is still grown on Korcula.

When the Greeks first settled there the island was covered with thick black forest which cast dark shadows, so they called it the Black (*Korkyra Melaina*; Latin *Corcyra Nigra*). This was later Croaticized to Korcula. Up to 1420 it was ruled by various peoples; Greeks, Illyrians, Romans, Franks, Croats, and Hungarians. In that year it came under Venetian rule and remained so until 1797. Most of the architecture on the island, especially in its main city Korcula, dates from this period. The following names now found in Louisiana originated in Korcula: Anzulovich, Carevich, Druskovich, Farac, Persich, Radovanovich, Separovich, and Stella.

The other island in this area from which a number of residents emigrated to Louisiana is the island of Hvar. Hvar lies parallel to Korcula and is separated from it by a 9-mile-wide channel. It is one of the most beautiful and, historically, is the most interesting of the Dalmatian islands. In addition to this, its climate is so pleasant that it has been named "the Adriatic Madeira." It is 42 miles long, from 2 to 6½ miles wide and with 116 square miles in area it has a population of about twelve thousand persons. Its history is similar to the other Dalmatian islands. It was first settled by the Greeks from the island of Paros who called it Pharos, hence Hvar.

With the exception of Sansovich, Mladineo, and Kovachevich families from Stari Grad, all other Louisianians from this island came from a small town of Sucuraj (Suchuray) located on the eastern tip of the island only three miles from the mainland on its northern side and six miles from the Peljesac Peninsula on the southern. Sucuraj is a contraction of Sveti Juraj (St. George), the name of its patron saint. At first it was called *campus s. Georgi in Plame* and later (sixteenth century) *vicus s. Georgi* (village of Sveti Juraj) which was eventually simplified to Sucuraj. In antiquity it was inhabited by the Illyrians and later by the Romans. With the coming of the Slavs to the Balkans, Sucuraj was originally settled by the Croats from the Neretva region. Later, beginning in 1606, its population was augmented by the Croats from the nearby mainland who, led by the Franciscans from Zaostrog Monastery, came to Sucuraj and other island towns to escape the Turkish persecution.

Its population gravitates more to the sea and fishing than to the land and farming. It is well known for its sardine-catching localities and today has a sardine canning factory that cans most of the sardines caught in this area of the Adriatic. However, the people still find time to produce enough wine, figs, and olive oil for its own consumption and some for export. Lately, with the influx of tourists to Dalmatia during the summer months, it too derives a substantial part of its income from tourism, when its population is doubled and trebled by the travelers who swarm here to enjoy its sunshine and its commodious beaches.

During the late part of the nineteenth century its residents, upon learning from the returning immigrants of Peljesac of the successful and profitable oyster cultivation in Louisiana, started immigrating to the Pelican State. The following names are from Sucuraj: Barisich,

Franicevich, Jelicich, Kumarich, Kuluz, Petricevich, Piacun, Rosandich, Slavich, Vojkovich, Vujnovich, and Vuljan.

Across from Sucuraj there is a thirty-seven-mile-long region along the mainland called Makarsko primorje (Makarska Littoral) containing several towns, along the shore of the Adriatic. It is named after Makarska, the largest town in the area. Other towns are: Gradac, Zaostrog, Drvenik, Zivogosce, Igrane, Podgora, and Baska Voda. The chief occupations of this region are fishing, tourism and the producing of olive oil and wine. Tourism is well developed and the littoral is lined with several large, newly constructed hotels near the beaches which abound in this area. Podgora, Igrane, and Zivogosce are well represented in Louisiana by their emigrants.

Podgora is situated about six miles southwest from Makarska, and has a population of about 1600. Old Podgora is located somewhat above the seacoast while New Podgora hugs the shoreline. Old Podgora is chiefly a farming community with vineyards and olive groves terraced on the side of Biokovo Mountain which here rises steeply. The Adriatic highway passes through here so that Podgora is accessible from all points along the seacoast, and during the summer months it is a popular tourist resort.

The town is rich in history. It was a part of Croatia until 1483 when it was conquered by the Turks, who stayed there until 1640 when Podgora voluntarily came under the Venetian protection. During the National (Croatian) Renaissance one of its sons, Miho Pavlinovic (1831–1887), played an active role in the Dalmatian, the Croatian, and the Vienna parliaments in awakening the Dalmatians to their Croatian heritage.

During the Second World War it achieved fame as the birthplace of the new Yugoslav Navy. It was from Podgora that the almost barehanded Dalmatian fishermen, with their small wooden motorized fishing boats, started attacking and capturing the Italian supply vessels with their precious cargo of desperately needed food and war matériel. On November 10, 1942, the first Yugoslav naval units were formed in Podgora. (The prewar Yugoslav Navy ceased to exist once the Adriatic was occupied by the Italians.) This event is celebrated as the birth of the present Yugoslav Navy. An imposing monument in Podgora, erected on the twentieth anniversary, commemorates their heroic actions.

Igrane is another seacoast town which has sent many of its citizens to Louisiana. It is located about eleven miles from Makarska on a small peninsula. It was first inhabited during the Roman times. Above the town there is a fortress Zale built during the seventeenth century as a deterrent against the Turkish invasion, and there is a baroque church built in 1752. Nearby is a small church of St. Michael from the eleventh century. The town boasts an imposing campanile, a gift from one of its returning Louisiana immigrants.

During the last two decades of the nineteenth century the residents of Makarska Littoral started emigrating to Louisiana. Many became skilled oystermen, and some of the later emigrants (1905–1920) from this region settled in Buras, Triumph, and vicinity, where they helped develop the Louisiana orange industry and produced some of the finest Louisiana oranges and orange wine. The names of those coming from the Makarska Littoral are: Rudez from Gradac; Jurisich (Frank) from Brist; Antunovich, Franicevich, Jurakovich, and Marinovich from Zivogosce; Anticich, Bakalich, Cvitanovich, Lovich, Lulich, Morovich, Parun, Pobrica, and Taliancich from Igrane; Alach and Urlich from Drasnice; Devcich, Milicich, Pivach, Sumich, Vela, Vodanovich, and Vrsaljko from Podgora; and Zanki from Makarska.

Ten miles from the seacoast, directly northeast from the coastal town of Zaostrog, lies the town of Vrgorac (literally on top of a mountain). Its population is around fifteen hundred people. It is an important highway junction and a center of the table-grape growing industry. It was a part of Croatia until it fell to the Turks in the second half of the fifteenth century. From 1690 to 1797 it was ruled by the Venetians. In 1815 Vrgorac was transferred (with the rest of Dalmatia) to the Austro-Hungarian rule, under whose jurisdiction it remained until 1918 when it became a part of Yugoslavia.

Although Vrgorac is not a coastal town many of its young men, during the second half of the nineteenth century, sailed the seas for a living. When their ships docked in American ports many jumped ship and remained there. Those who settled in Louisiana usually followed the oyster-fishing occupation, and many became successful oystermen. The following Louisiana families trace their origin to Vrgorac: Barbir (Barbier), Mialjevich, Salinovich, and Vujevich.

The last region on our list of the birthplaces of the Louisiana South Slavs is the island of Molat located in northern Dalmatia twelve miles from the mainland and nineteen miles west of the city of Zadar.

One of the smaller Dalmatian islands, it occupies about eleven square miles in area and has a population of eight hundred. In shape it resembles a giant boomerang. Its coast is irregular and curved, having many small bays and inlets, giving it a total length of thirty miles of shoreline. The three population centers are Molat, Brgulje, and Zapuntale.

The island was first settled by the Romans who named it Melatus after the Latin word *Mel* for honey which abounded there. This was Croaticized to Molat when the Croats settled there sometime in the tenth century. Until 1420, when it came into Venetian possession, it was a part of the Croatian state. Venetians ruled it until Napoleon's time. In 1815 it was transferred to Austria which ruled it until 1918, when it became a part of Yugoslavia.

The main arable land is found in the Molat and Zapuntale fields where the vineyards and olive groves abound. The people are excellent fishermen. Sardines are caught here in large quantities as early as April. They are also skilled seamen, navigating the seven seas on merchant marine vessels. Lately, the island, with the rest of the Zadar Archipelago, has become a popular tourist locaton, and during the summer months the residents derive some of their income from tourism.

In 1895 John Gentilich emigrated from Molat to New Orleans, and in response to his invitational letters many soon followed. The following families trace their origin from this island: Baranich, Baricev, Batinich, Dujmov, Gentilich, Lovretich, Mandich, Marcev, Matulich, Mavar, and Spanich.

THE JOURNEY

Until the Civil War the means of traveling to Louisiana were, as a rule, sailing vessels on which future immigrants sailed either as full-time sailors or with the intention of leaving their ships as soon as they arrived in New Orleans, where most of them—once the colony was established—had friends and relatives. The route may have been direct and may have taken only a few weeks, or it may have been circuitous with stops in many ports and taken as long as two or three years. In any event it was no pleasure cruise.

From 1865 to the middle 1880s some came as sailors on merchant ships while others traveled as passengers on commercial passenger vessels. By the late 1880s, however, the steamship companies were transporting hundreds of thousands (later millions) of immigrants an-

nually from southeastern Europe* From then on the South Slav immigrants to Louisiana traveled as legal passengers with proper papers
and a right to return. The bachelors already in Louisiana sent passage
money and an invitation to their childhood sweethearts to join them,
and the husbands did the same to their wives and children, and many
men hastened to New York to meet them. From the 1880s to World
War I they boarded ocean steamers at Trieste and for twenty-five to
fifty dollars per person traveled to New York in less than a month's
time in relative comfort compared to the conditions of decades before
on the sailing vessels. From New York to New Orleans they traveled
by train which gave them an opportunity to see some of America before arrival in New Orleans or the Louisiana bayous. From 1919 to
the early 1950s—with the World War II interruption—most of them
gathered at Split (in central Dalmatia) and thence by train to Zagreb
and from there by the Orient Express to Paris. After an overnight stay
in Paris they proceeded to Le Havre where they boarded one of the
floating palaces—which plied the Atlantic during this time—to New
York and from there by train to New Orleans. The trip took two or
three weeks.

The youngsters, whose age ranged from eleven to seventeen, and
who immigrated to Louisiana at the invitation of relatives or friends
or who joined their fathers once they were old enough to help with
the oyster fishing usually traveled with relatives or neighbors who
were returning to Louisiana after a summer-long visit with their families. The older guides were looked upon by the immigrating youths
as "Americans," and this gave them confidence and helped them enter
a new and a strange world.

Since the early 1950s the airplane has become the chief mode of
transportation, and the time of travel has been reduced to a matter of
hours. However, the initial step of the journey, as a rule, still begins
(since the 1880s) with a coastal steamer from the native village to Split
or (since the 1950s) to Dubrovnik, where the travelers board an
airplane.

To those immigrating to America the parting from dear ones and
childhood scenes is of a permanent nature. Thus, on the eve of their

---

* Most of the large steamship lines had agents in Trieste, Rijeka, and other
port cities who encouraged and persuaded the emigrants, and those who, at first,
had no intention of leaving, to travel on their lines with promises—more fictional
than real—of lucrative jobs with high pay awaiting them in America.

departure, those leaving make the rounds of the village—where everyone knows everyone else—to take leave of their friends, relatives, and schoolmates and to visit the village priest to receive his blessing for a safe and happy journey and an unasked-for admonition not to lose the religion of one's forefathers in faraway America. The partings are usually sad and sometimes tearful, with wishes for bon voyage and riches in America and with messages for the relatives already in Louisiana.

The coastal steamers pick up the passengers in the morning hours for arrival at Split or Dubrovnik during the afternoon of the same day. Whenever there are people leaving for America all of their relatives and most of their friends come to the quay for a final farewell. While waiting for a steamer they may sing parting songs such as: *"Dide Baba izadjite vanka,* (Grandfather, Grandmother come outside,) / *Da vidite našega rastanka.* (To see our parting.)" and *"Zbogom more, zbogom polje,* (Farewell to the sea, farewell to the fields,) / *I Sućurju milo mjesto moje.* (And to Sucuraj* my dear birthplace.)"

The travelers' parents and immediate relatives accompany them to cities, where at the airports or the railroad stations the final touching farewell takes place. However, with jet transportation the partings are less tearful and less emotional. Since they are only hours away from each other, the separation does not seem so permanent.

Upon arrival in Louisiana the first order of business is writing descriptive letters to those left behind, describing fabulous New York, wonderful New Orleans, and the riches of America. The letters of most of the newly arrived immigrants are full of longing for their homes, friends, and birthplaces and of plans for an early return. But as the years pass, the memories dim, the carefree childhood days are forgotten, and the process of Americanization takes root. Plans to return permanently are abandoned and substituted with plans for a temporary visit sometimes in the future.

* Here a name of the town from which they are leaving is substituted.

3

Life in Louisiana

"I could speak of many ways in which those who came to these
shores have enriched America, but let me point out one
way in particular: They believed in hard work. They didn't
come here for a handout. They came here for an
opportunity, and they built America."

*President Richard M. Nixon in his speech at the
dedication of the Museum of Immigration in
New York Harbor, September 26, 1972.*

THE MAIN REQUISITE for success of immigrants in America, be they
from Yugoslavia or from any other country, was, and still is the ability
to adapt to the American way of life. Invariably this means not only
learning the English language and modifying their social behavior
but also working at occupations heretofore unknown to them. The
Dalmatians are specially adept at this. For centuries they adjusted to
the changing conditions in their homeland and, as seafarers, acquired
a degree of cosmopolitanism and an ability to learn foreign languages.
This helped them greatly in adjusting to the ways of America. They
possessed the four characteristics necessary to succeed in the New
World: the pressing need to earn a living, a strong constitution (the
weak and the sick stayed at home), a driving will to work, and an
ability to adapt to the conditions required of a particular occupation.
When they came here they grabbed at the first available opportunities
or, if none existed, created their own. The heretofore ships' officers,
sailors, fishermen, and peasants became restaurant owners and operators, oyster growers, coffee shop owners, bartenders, teamsters, farmers, butchers, clerks, boardinghouse operators, or whatever was available and profitable.

As mentioned elsewhere in this study, they came in search of "freedom and fortune," and when they arrived in Louisiana they knew that the means of achieving economic security were hard work and thriftiness, and they were willing and able to do the first and practice the second. Of course, only a few acquired fortunes but all were able to earn a decent living.

They believed in saving at least a part of their earnings. They believed, and still do, in owning property. Not a great lot but enough so that they could be a part of America; that a small part, no matter how small, belonged to them and they in turn belonged to it. In Dalmatia they or their families owned the ancestral homes where they lived and a few acres of soil that they tilled. When they left this and came to a foreign land they in effect became homeless, and drifters without roots, so by acquiring at least some property, a home, a small farm, or a campsite and a place to tie their boats, they acquired roots in, and identification with, their adopted country. This gave them stability and permanence.

The South Slav immigrants of 1830s, 1840s, and 1850s had no trouble finding work in the bustling cosmopolitan port city of New Orleans. They found employment along the riverfront as stevedores, cargo packers, teamsters, and as ordinary laborers; some obtained jobs on the Louisiana river vessels as sailors, mates, and a few as captains. Proof of their ability to adjust and prosper in an alien world became evident when they did not find jobs working for others but decided to try on their own. The merchandizing instincts of their forefathers of the Republic of Dubrovnik were deeply ingrained in their blood. The men opened business establishments, some of humble beginnings, but they were their own.

By the middle 1850s there were scores of businesses in New Orleans owned and operated by the South Slav immigrants: M. Guiranovich, Henry Pavelich, P. Vidich, Samuel Jovovich, G. Scenevich, and Peter Masich founded and operated coffee houses. Tripo Raicevich, L. Pablovich, George Mascovich, Vincent Radulovich, John Radovich, Vincent Radovich, George Petrovich, J. Petrovich, D. Petrovich, Anthony Cognevich, Andrew Bajanovich, Lazar Dancevich, Anthony Ban, Matthew Vukovich, Andrew Carnich, and P. Dragicevich opened and operated fruit stands. Frank Masich, G. Masich, and C. Jovanovich established a wholesale fruit importing and distributing firm primarily to supply their countrymen with domestic and imported fruits.

N. Marich, Marko Petrovich, Andrew Garcich, and Jakov Comich opened grocery stores and became grocers.

John Bassich, Peter Ochiglevich, and Lazar Dancevich opened oyster shops (called oyster saloons in those days). John Petrovich opened a shoe store; Luke Orlich a billiard parlor, M. Giuranovich a variety store; Nicholas Racich a jewelry store—selling, repairing, and manufacturing; John Ochiglevich a sail, tarpaulins, and a flag "manufactory"; E. Sigalovich a cigar-making and distributing establishment; John Dancevich set up a boardinghouse where most of the bachelors and those with families in the old country resided.

However, the chief occupation that they followed was and still is oyster fishing. This type of work required no special skills other than the ability to handle a boat and the implements associated with fishing, abilities that as sailors and fishermen they already possessed. The lack of knowledge of the English language did not hinder the newcomers for they worked with fellow countrymen who conversed with them in their native Croatian. This occupation was particularly fitting to the needs of the temporary immigrants who came here to earn a few hundred—later a few thousand—dollars and then return to their families back home. Also the required investment—before motorization—was nil, so that with the few hundred dollars earned as hired help, during the first four or five years, they bought the necessary equipment and were in business for themselves. Hundreds followed this occupation. They are discussed in detail in Chapter Four.

Although most of those who made their living from the sea followed the oyster-growing occupation, there were some who acquired engine-powered boats, bought large trawl nets, and went in search of shrimp. Although the seasons' earnings are not as predictable as those of the oystermen, they managed to make a living. Among those who chose shrimping to make a living were: John K. Barisich, Frank Curavich, Tom Cvitanovich, Ante Korach, John Korach, Steve Lucich, Ante Mihaljevich, Dominick Petricevich, Leo Protich, Nick Protich, Tony Protich, John Rudez, Joseph Stipelcovich, Vlaho Stipelcovich, Frank Stuprich, Mate Taliancich, Ante Tomasovich, John Vodopija, Joseph Vuljan, Nikola Vuljan, and Steve Zegura.

They also entered other occupations and opened various businesses (see Table II and Appendix I) with the restaurant business leading the list. Of the 263 business establishments owned and operated by the Yugoslavs at one time or another between 1840 and 1970—

that I canvassed—there were: ninety-five restaurants; thirty-seven fruit stands; thirty-two oyster dealerships; twenty-five saloons; fourteen groceries; twelve coffee stands; ten oyster bars; seven boardinghouses; three each of the importing houses, boat building shipyards, seafood shops, finance companies, ship chandlers, and soft-drink stores; two each of service stations, clothing stores, real estate firms, variety stores, tobacco shops, and freight-carrying companies; and one each of shoe store, billiard parlor, sail manufacturing plant, jewelry shop, and insurance agency.

Among the ninety-five restaurants, many were small family-type establishments though others became quite prominent in the New Orleans gourmet circles, competing with the best French and Italian eating establishments of the city. Gentilich's, Johnny's (John Marcev), Zibilich's, Crescent City (John Vojkovich), Chris' Steak House (Chris Matulich), Vienna Garden (Matt Franicevich), Bozo's (Bozo Vodanovich), Drago's (Drago Batinich), Visko's (Vincent Vuskovich), Lakeside Seafood (Drago Cvitanovich), and many other Yugoslav restaurants contribute to New Orleans' reputation for cuisine as much as the city's other world-famous restaurants. Many of these restaurants and other businesses such as grocery stores, coffee shops, and oyster dealerships are no longer in existence or are run by non-Yugoslavs. This is partly due to the parents' desire and insistence on professional educations for the second and the third generations.

Many also became farmers, an occupation they had followed on the rocky hillsides of the Adriatic seacoast. The early settlers such as John Vidacovich, Marko Givanovich, Charles A. Petrovich, and Luke Vucinovich became planters. A few became truck farmers, and many became orange farmers. N. Vasovich from Boka Kotorska was a pioneer orange grower. He started cultivating oranges as early as 1885 in the vicinity of the present town of Triumph, Plaquemines Parish. From World War I to the middle 1960s, when the repeated freezes and hurricanes almost obliterated the Louisiana citrus industry, many Yugoslavs were prominent as orange growers around Buras and Triumph. John Lulich, J. M. Sumich, S. Spanja, T. Garma, A. Franceski, Lulich Brothers, S. Pavlovich, J. Sumich, J. Marinovich, A. Pobrica, S. Cognevich, D. Cognevich, J. Cace, A. Maturich, George Pivach, and many others owned hundreds of acres under orange trees cultivation. John Lulich and George Pivach, in addition to providing some of the best Louisiana oranges, also pioneered the Louisiana orange wine industry. Their orange wine was sold throughout the country, and their trademarks became well known.

Some, like Mark N. Radovich and Alexander Bijelich, became captains on the Louisiana vessels and others became pilots guiding the sailing, and later steam, vessels up the winding Mississippi in all kinds of weather. Captains Nick Trojanovich and Steve Gusina were pioneers in this field. Born in southern Dalmatia they came to Louisiana in their teens and learned the seafaring trade. During the late 1800s they sailed out into the Gulf of Mexico near the river passes in small yawl boats with oars and small sails, risking their lives in all kinds of weather, fog, rains, and squalls and waited to meet the incoming ships. In those days there were no pilot organizations to regulate "who worked when," but each pilot was on his own, and the first man to reach a ship got the job of piloting her "over the bar." After the turn of the century the pilots formed their organizations which exist to the present day. Trojanovich and Gusina led in this. Both Gusina and Captain Mark M. Grusich served several terms as president. Following are the names of the pilots of Yugoslav background as they were listed by Captain Frank Jurisich: Captains Nick Trojanovich, Steve Gusina, Mark M. Grusich, George Zibilich, Albert Zibilich, all deceased; Frank Jurisich and Lawrence Jurisich, retired; and Lawrence Jurisich, Jr., Mark M. Grusich, and William Grusich, active.

While some piloted the vessels on the Mississippi others organized navigation companies and ran a freight and passenger service between New Orleans and Burrwood. Captain Peter Taliancich led the rest in this endeavor. In 1922 he organized the Victoria Navigation Company and had a 250-ton packet boat *Victoria* constructed to carry freight and passengers up and down the Mississippi. Later he was joined by Captains Marko Cibilich and Marine Gerica, and together they formed the Majestic-El Rito Freight Service. They employed several other Yugoslavs as captains and engineers. For several decades these boats carried freight and passengers between New Orleans and the many settlements in Plaquemines Parish. During the 1930s they freighted as many as five thousand sacks of oysters and two to three hundred boxes of oranges weekly.

After the pioneer immigrants established a foothold in Louisiana, the other immigrants, as they arrived here, naturally followed the trades and callings of their countrymen. Usually they were the sons, nephews, cousins, or acquaintances of those already here. The "settled" Yugoslav immigrants employed the newcomers in their business establishments. The newcomers, after working as hired help for a few years, either returned home, acquired managerial positions, became partners of their former employers, or started their own businesses. This chain reaction of employment and training has been practiced since the 1840s.

The immigrants were usually too busy earning a living to pursue a formal education beyond learning the English language. Some did learn skilled trades, and a few, with persistent effort, evening work, and personal sacrifice acquired a university education and entered professional fields. However, it remained for members of the second and the third generation to break the educational barrier and become business executives, lawyers, engineers, clergymen, physicians, dentists, and educators. Through the years the occupations of Yugoslav immigrants in Louisiana changed from the few simple service jobs at the beginning to the varied and desirable positions of today.

The Louisiana Yugoslavs and those of the Yugoslav descent are found in all walks of life. Many of them have reached a prominent position in public service: state legislator, district attorney, parish (county) sheriff, parish tax assessor, and a parish commissioner of safety. They have truly become a part of the mainstream of life in Louisiana and a part of this promised land and consider themselves as American as the descendants of the first arrivals to the American shores. Contrary to the claims of some of the latter-day sociologist, demographers, and writers, I found no evidence of the "unmeltable ethnics" among the members of the second-, third-, and later-generation Yugoslavs.

SOCIAL LIFE

When immigrants first arrive at American shores their social contacts are naturally limited to those of their own linguistic group. The language barrier is the limiting factor in their social life. Those who come at a somewhat advanced age have difficulty in mastering the language beyond the bare essentials, and consequently their circle of friends remains limited to fellow countrymen. For them the acculturation process is very slow and sometimes never takes place at all. The younger immigrants, on the other hand, master the language in a matter of few years, and enjoy an active and varied social life. Those who acquire an American education act, feel, and behave as native Americans.

The social life of the early South Slav immigrants centered primarily around the boardinghouses where they lived. Here a Slavic subculture existed, and they behaved, or could behave, as if they were back home. The language was Croatian, the food was cooked to their taste, and the beverage was wine—usually imported from Dalmatia. In the evening, after working hours, they played cards, told stories, sang patriotic, or love, songs, and listened to a boarder play a melancholy tune on his *gusle* (a single-string musical instrument popular in the Balkans) about a girl he left behind or about a brave warrior defending his homeland against the Turks to the last breath.

When the enterprising South Slavs in New Orleans opened saloons, coffee houses, and restaurants, these places, too, became centers of the immigrants' social life. A centrally located saloon became an unofficial headquarters where the immigrants met for a meal, a refreshing drink, and a friendly visit after a hard day's labor at the riverfront, shops, or after bringing a load of oysters from the Louisiana bayous. This was where many received their mail, conducted business, met newcomers to get news of their relatives, and parted with their friends returning to Dalmatia.

The social life of the South Slav oystermen, while away from New Orleans, differed from that of the city dwellers. They lived in camps isolated from organized civilization. If other oystermen were nearby, they visited each other in the evening and played cards or talked about oystering over a glass of wine. The family men, as a rule, stayed home in the evening but visited each other on Sundays. The wives' insistence on observing the Sabbath prevailed, and the husbands and their hired help did not work on Sundays. But bachelors and men whose families were in the old country worked seven days a week.

Before the advent of refrigeration and rapid transportation, no oysters were sold during the summer months. The hired help, primarily the young bachelors, left the camps in June for New Orleans where they remained until September or until the nine-month earnings were exhausted. They spent the three summer months as men of leisure or "playboys" and in September returned to the camps, broke and docile, to begin another nine months of oyster fishing. Many spent their money carelessly and too soon and were forced to borrow from their employers to see them through the last part of August. They continued this type of life until some fair maiden captured their hearts and prevailed upon them to start an oyster-growing business of their own.

On Saint John's Day (Sveti Ivan), June 24, the oystermen put their tools and paintbrushes away and took a holiday. This saint somehow became their "patron saint." The tradition of St. John's Day was brought over from Dalmatia. The celebrations were held in several large camps where the other oystermen with their families came by the boatload. They tied the boats alongside each other, sometimes extending as many as twenty to thirty boats out into the bayou. The day was spent in feasting, drinking, swimming, singing, and romancing, the latter under the watchful eyes of elders. In addition to the wide variety of seafood—oysters, shrimp, and fish—a lamb or a side of beef was barbecued on a spit, Dalmatian style. Nowadays since oyster fishing has become a year-round operation, St. John's Day is no longer celebrated.

During the summer months the oyster smacks and luggers (before motorization) participated in organized sailing races. Most of the races were held in Adams Bay where the participants were cheered by fellow oystermen and their families on boats alongside the racing course and by the city folk who were brought there by the large oyster freight boats. The captain-owners of these sternwheeler freight boats used the occasion to make an extra dollar during the slack summer season. Bets were wagered, and the winners were the "heroes of the day." One of the most exciting races was the annual race between Vlaho Jurisich's sailing lugger *Tegetthoff* and Salvatore D'Anthony's *Fourth of July* which was held on the Mississippi River. According to my Yugoslav informants the *Tegetthoff* usually won.

However, as motorization was introduced these races waned and by the end of World War I disappeared entirely.

During the last decade of the nineteenth century when tug-of-war contests were popular in New Orleans, the Louisiana South Slavs participated as a team. With their well-developed bodies (most of the participants were over six feet tall), wide shoulders, and strong muscles developed through a lifetime of pulling oars and nets on the Adriatic and tonging oysters and pushing and pulling boats on the Louisiana bayous, they had no trouble overpowering all opposition and becoming champions.

The tournaments were held in the Washington Artillery Hall in

New Orleans. The exhibitions were rather elaborate. An elevated platform, ninety feet long and six feet wide, was constructed in the middle of the hall. The cross boards on the platform were spaced a few inches apart so that the contestants could push their feet against the boards as they pulled on the rope. In 1892 several teams (American, Norwegian, French, Irish, German, Spanish, and South Slav) competed. Each wore a special team uniform. South Slavs wore blue shirts, black trousers, and black felt hats. The 1892 tournament lasted seven days, or rather seven evenings. The elimination contests were held during the week and on the last evening (Saturday) the first- and second-place winners were chosen from the teams with the most victories. Excitement ran high and bets were placed by the spectators on their favorite teams. The New Orleans *Times-Democrat* of February 7, 1892, described the main event of the final night of the contest as follows:

> The first pull of the evening was between the South Slav and German teams. When the men marched to the platform the excitement in the audience ran high and speculation was rife as to which team would prove victorious in the struggle. South Slav's eight representatives had met all teams save the German and had easily defeated each in turn, and it was but fair to conclude that that team would also be beaten. . . . Matters did not long remain in doubt for the South Slavic team with an "ough" their watchword, straightened out and the heavy-weights on the other side of the rope began to bump over the cleats in a manner that was decidedly painful to them and discouraging to their adherents. The outcome of the pull was only 48 seconds in the balance for at that time the South Slavs won easily securing the first prize without sustaining a single defeat.

The 1892 team of eight regular members and four substitutes was organized by Samuel M. Fucich who served as its captain. The members, whose weights are given following their names, were: Gregory Kacich Miosich, 188 pounds; Joseph Petrovich, 188; Jack Simich, 186; George Slavich, 193; John Radovich, 211; Matthew Drazeta, 200; Matthew Perisich, 207; and Michael G. Perovich, 230. Vincent Tian, 198; Mark Vanovich, 175; Anthony Protich, 178; and M. Martinolich, 173, served as substitutes in case any of the regular members could not participate. The South Slavic team so impressed P. T. Barnum with their strength that he offered to feature them on a tour of the United States, but they refused.

These contests were watched by the South Slavs of Louisiana with keen interest and proud satisfaction. After the tournaments the champions were feted by the city. Saloons and restaurants competed for their patronage, but they preferred the familiar hospitality of the establishments of their countrymen.

Once the Slavonian Association was organized, the members held organized all-male banquet fetes. These were usually anniversary and election-of-officers celebrations. As they acquired families the members included them in the association's social activities. All-day picnics were given where there were food, drinks, entertainment, and games for all—adults and children. Presently there are several organizational annual events which the Louisiana Yugloslavs attend.

The Slavonian Pleasure Club, organized in 1915 and dedicated to social activities of its members, their families, and friends is still active. The membership (all male) is by invitation only and therefore limited. It sponsors dinner meetings, anniversary celebrations, fish fries, excursions to nearby towns, usually Biloxi, Mississippi, which include a dinner at a gulfside restaurant, a ride on a cruise boat, and friendly conversation and group singing on the chartered bus.

The Yugoslav American Club was organized in May, 1937. Yugoslavs and those of the Yugoslav ancestry of both sexes and their spouses are eligible for membership. Its objects and purposes are: "To establish and maintain a Club House where the members can meet socially, together with their families and friends, and where topics of the day can be discussed: to maintain in the said Club House a library or reading room for the use of its members, wherein literature, books, periodicals, magazines and newspapers shall be kept; the said library to be at all times open to the use of its members."

It also sponsors activities of a social nature such as supper dances, seafood suppers, bingo games, and picnics. However, its aim of acquiring a home and equipping it with reading and recreational material never came about.

The Slavonian Association sponsors annual supper dances which are well attended by the Louisiana Yugoslavs and their friends.

They also take part in the socials given by the oyster organizations of Louisiana and together with other oystermen participate in the organizations' annual supper dances, boat parades, festivals, conventions and other activities.

Plaquemines Parish Yugoslavs are also active in the annual

Orange Festival which is held during the second weekend in December at the renovated Fort Jackson near Buras. This too is well attended by Plaquemines Parish and New Orleans Yugoslavs. An orange queen is selected among the beauties of the parish to reign over the festival activities. The king is usually one of the prominent parishioners. The first festival was held in 1947. Its queen was Miss Gloria Cvitanovich (now Mrs. Drago Batinich of New Orleans), and the king was Thomas Popich of Buras. Luke A. Petrovich was king for 1970 and Mato Farac for 1973.

Many Yugoslavs also hold membership in New Orleans carnival organizations (krewes) where they participate in the activities such as carnival balls, cocktail parties, supper dances, and parades. As officers, many take a leading role in running the organizations. Their daughters are selected as maids and sons as dukes; some even reign as kings and queens.

When they first arrived in Louisiana most of the Yugoslavs were bachelors. Through the years some returned to their childhood sweethearts and remained in Dalmatia. Others either went back to Dalmatia to marry and return, sent for their brides, or married South Slav girls already in Louisiana. A few married native girls of French, Irish, or Italian extraction. When they marry, they "marry for keeps." Divorces and separations occur, but in less than 1 percent of the marriages. Some Yugoslavs raised large families of six, eight, or ten children, but the majority had a family of four or five children. Presently they average three children per family.

However, many Yugoslavs did not marry, and remained bachelors all their lives. The early oystermen lived isolated lives in the camps away from the population centers and attended very few mixed social events. Also, for many years there was a shortage of young ladies of South Slavic stock, and many young oystermen whose English was rather limited and whose social contacts were few felt ill at ease in the company of the American girls. Out of curiosity I once asked an old friend, Dominick Petricevich, why he never married. He thought for a while, looked into the distance, sighed, and replied: *"Kad sam htio nisam moga, a kad sam moga nisam htio."* ("When I wanted to I couldn't, and when I could I didn't want to"). Perhaps this explains why many remained bachelors. They hesitated to contract marriage until they were on solid financial footing, and for some it took a little too long to get there.

The young immigrants of today, however, do not wait for this financial security; nor do they live in isolated camps. They either marry a Yugoslav girl or a native full-fledged American. Many marry within a year or two of arrival. Their English may be limited and coarse but apparently love conquers all.

Yugoslavs in Louisiana have typical American weddings. As a rule, they marry in a church with bridesmaids and all the trimmings, followed by a lavish reception. A wedding between a Yugoslav and an American is no different from an ordinary American Catholic wedding. However, when the bride and the groom are both Yugoslavs the wedding reception is somewhat different. The conversation is more in Croatian than English. Among the refreshments there is always some *hrostula* (Dalmatian pastry made with eggs, milk, sugar and flour). The band plays a dancing piece or two of Croatian music. If it is the score of a popular song, the guests may break into song and sing along. During intermissions the men form into a group and sing songs such as: "Lijepa Nasa," "Marijana," or "Oy Slaveni," and of course the fishermen's song, "Yedan Mali Brodic ("One Little Boat").

Weddings and baby showers also provide excellent means for the ladies to get together, socialize, and exchange the latest gossip. Other occasions for getting together are: christenings, birthday parties, anniversary parties, and business openings. All in all, Yugoslavs lead active social lives. Gregarious by nature, they welcome social gatherings or create their own. They like the great outdoors and spend their spare time fishing, hunting, or attending football games and other sports events. They visit each other and their "American" friends frequently and receive visitors graciously. They insist on serving refreshments, and one is advised not to refuse, because to do so will offend them, for it is an old Slavic custom that no visitor leaves a house without partaking of food or drink, or both. Whether within their own group or within the wider circle of friends and acquaintances, they are more participants than observers on the social scene.

LEARNING THE ENGLISH LANGUAGE

The pioneer South Slav immigrants settling in New Orleans quickly began learning the essentials of the English language. Many, as men of the sea, came to New Orleans with a smattering of English. The rapidity and the degree of accuracy of learning English depended on the need. Those who were employed on the New Orleans riverfront, on the Louisiana vessels, or other places learned enough of the language to hold their jobs in a matter of months. If they were satisfied with the jobs, they usually were satisfied with the bare essentials of a vocabulary necessary to perform job duties, and to maintain limited social contacts. On the other hand, if they were ambitious and wanted to move to better paying jobs and/or to more responsible positions, they applied themselves and either by self-study or by attending night school improved their English. Those who operated their own businesses also had to have an adequate mastery of the language, including the ability to read and write. They learned English to conduct their businesses properly just as they learned skills to operate them successfully. Both were needed to survive in the business world and to compete successfully with other businesses in the area.

Oyster fishermen whose contacts with the outside world were the fellow Yugoslavs who bought their oysters and brought the necessary provisions to their camps, however, did not have a pressing need to learn English. They conversed with each other in Croatian, and if they learned a word or two of English during one of their rare visits to New Orleans, they quickly forgot them once they returned to their regular work. Later on, after the motorization of the oyster vessels, when their contacts with the population centers became frequent, and when they acquired families, learning the language became necessary, and they learned enough to "get along." After delivering their oysters to New Orleans or other places they bought necessary provisions and returned to their camps. In New Orleans they usually frequented stores along Decatur Street, a block or two from the oyster landings. With dollars in their pockets, they made themselves understood. The following story perhaps best illustrates their ingenuity in communicating with storekeepers. The competitive spirit among oystermen has always been keen. If one acquired an engine for his boat or painted his camp, the other did the same. One oysterman, visiting his neighbor, noticed an improvement on the neighbor's camp and decided to install the same thing on his camp as soon as he could get to Decatur Street and purchase the equipment. Reluctant to admit his ignorance, he did not ask its English name. He went to a hardware store in the French Market area and with motions of his hands and halting English tried to make the clerk understand what he wanted. He pointed to the nets along the wall saying, "like dat." The clerk showed him all his nets from casting to gill nets, including the shrimp trawls, and each time the oysterman shook his head negatively with obvious frustration but remained determined to get what he wanted. Finally in exasperation he said, "You know, keep mosquitoes outside, breeze inside." The experienced clerk then realized what the oysterman wanted, and when he brought out a roll of window screen, which was just then making its appearance on the market, the oysterman victoriously exclaimed, "Dat's it, dat's it."

The immigrants coming to Louisiana from Dalmatia brought with them a simple vocabulary, in Croatian, which for them, as sailors, peasants, or fishermen, was adequate. So when they came to America and to a new and different life they were unfamiliar with the Croatian equivalents of some of the English words which they had to learn. This, and the English words which do not have Croatian equivalents, presented certain difficulties and slowed the process of learning English. These words, somewhat Croaticized, became a part of their everyday Croatian speech. It should be noted that when they learned English they did not abandon their native tongue but continued to use it among themselves—somewhat modified—to fit their needs in the New World. Their Croatian changed. It was no longer the pure Croatian they brought with them but was intermingled with words neither English nor Croatian, and a kind of hybrid vocabulary developed which is used to this day. Table IV lists a few examples.

If both parents are Yugoslav-born, then the language spoken in the home is Croatian, and the children naturally pick up the language of the household and learn Croatian. Up to a decade or two ago the children from many of these homes (especially if they were brought up in the oyster camps) knew very little English when they were enrolled in school. However, once in school they learned English rapidly, without an accent, and became bilingual: speaking Croatian at home and English outside the home. Since the introduction of television to American living rooms, the children in Croatian-speaking homes learn the two languages simultaneously. It is impossible to ignore the tube, and from Romper Room and Sesame Street preschool children naturally learn English. It is amusing to hear some of these preschool youngsters (two or three years of age, who do not realize that they are learning two different languages) speak both languages at the same

TABLE IV

THE HYBRID VOCABULARY

HYBRID WORD	CROATIAN	ENGLISH
bira	pivo	beer
bomiti	skitati se	to loaf
bordinauz	pension	boardinghouse
briza	povjetarac	breeze
deskokijavat		culling oysters
driliti	busiti svrdlom	drill
drodje		dredges
falta	mana	fault
gaf	pristaniste	wharf
gafe		oyster tongs
galun		gallon
jarda	dvoriste	house yard
imbarkavati	sijati kamenice	bedding oysters
kajig	magla	fog
kolektat	utjerati novac	collect
kokije	ljustura kamenica	oyster shells
kontri	izvan grada	country (rural)
kosta		coastal land between river levee and marshes
litra	funta	pound
livijeri		oyster beds
marketa	trziste	market
mitit	susresti	to meet
ostrigari	ribari kamenica	oystermen
palauz	kormilarska kabina	pilothouse
perca	motka za turanje	pushing pole
peruga		pirogue
perugica		little pirogue
pusati	turat	push
rendita	stanarina	rent
rijo	rijeka	river
roni	kanditirati	run (for office)
ronija	voziti	travel
sipiti	prodavati (kamenice)	ship oysters
skarat		oysters too small to market
skifich		small skiff
strit	ulica	street
talir	dolar	dollar
tratati	pocastiti	treat
uzati	upotrebljavati	use

time; that is, starting a sentence in one and finishing it in the other. As they grow older and their English improves and the Croatian worsens, it is not uncommon for them to reply to their parents in English when the parents speak to them in Croatian.

On the other hand, in the families where at least one parent is American-born, the children do not, as a rule, learn Croatian except for a few phrases such as: *kako si* (how are you), *dobro* (good, well), *dobra noch* (good night), and *zbogom* (goodbye).

Most Yugoslavs, after their arrival in Louisiana, make a determined effort to learn English. They purchase an English-Croatian dictionary and study the English equivalents. All goes well until they encounter idioms such as: *rain check, take French leave, behind the eight ball,* and *elbow grease.* They consult a dictionary and with disappointment realize that when they put together the meanings of the individual words they get altogether different meanings for the idioms. So they become frustrated and somewhat bewildered. As they progress they learn that the one who paints is called a painter, one who builds a builder, one who writes a writer, but when they call one who cooks a *cooker* they discover that they are not understood.

They read newspapers and periodicals and translate the meaning as they read but soon realize that the word-for-word translation sometimes gives them a different meaning from the one intended by the article. Consequently they conclude that to be understood properly and to understand and read the language correctly they need more than the bilingual dictionary. So, some of them attend night school, some special language schools, and others take private lessons from a professional English teacher or from an English-speaking friend. To meet the demand of the foreign-born, lately, some of the local schools have introduced courses such as "English as a Second Language," which are taught by competent instructors who understand their problems. There they learn how to write as well as speak. They discover the subject of spelling with which in Croatian they did not have to bother, for Croatian is a phonetic language that is "written as it is spoken." They learn a few rules such as "an *i* before *e* except after *c*" and acquire the dictionary habit to insure proper spelling. They learn that some letters have different sounds in different words and that one sound may be represented by different letters or a combination of letters. They try to learn the correct pronunciation from native speakers (teachers) and succeed rather well, but unless they arrive at an early age—below nine or ten—they find the *v*, the *w*, and the *th* sounds rather troublesome, never quite master the five pronunciations of *a*, and they never completely lose their Slavic accent. They leaf through an unabridged dictionary and discover that many words have the same meaning though one word may have several different meanings. They discover, for instance, that the word *run* has over 170, *roll* over 60, *face* over 50, and *put* over 40 meanings, and wonder how anyone ever learns it all. When their teachers assure them that no one person knows all the words in an unabridged dictionary, they experience a sense of relief and struggle on.

When they first begin to use English they have a tendency to think in Croatian and as they speak, translate the words. This causes errors in syntax and difficulty in understanding. However, as they acquire a more comprehensive vocabulary, there comes a time in the learning process when they start thinking in English and abandon the translating practice entirely. Consequently their syntax improves. How well they learn English depends on their age at which they arrived, educational background, environmental conditions, the nature of their work, the duration of study, and on the degree of their concentration. Some learn just enough to "get along" while others keep on studying until their knowledge of English is commensurate with that of natives with similar educational background, except for the accent.

The new—post–1950—immigrants are better equipped for a lingual adjustment in America than their predecessors. They are better educated, having attended a year or two of gymnasium before coming to Louisiana, and probably studied English there, since it is the most popular foreign language in Yugoslavia today, having replaced Russian, which was encouraged and studied immediately after the war. When they arrive they make a serious effort to learn English as soon as possible. In addition to formal English-learning courses at school, they have at their disposal various electronic devices such as recordings, disk records, and cartridges on which they can record and listen to their own recitals, or they can purchase tapes and recordings which are programmed with English lessons and their explanations in Croatian. They watch television, which is an undemanding teacher of English to the foreign-born, and one of the most convenient means of improving English, for it gives them an instantaneous pronunciation by native speakers with visual situations making the meanings of the words easier to grasp. Also they do not work quite as hard or for such long hours as the immigrants of decades ago and consequently are less fatigued and have more time to study the new language.

EDUCATION

The early South Slav immigrants who before settling in Louisiana made their living navigating the sea had some schooling while the mates and the captains received advanced education from the nautical academies in Dalmatia. They all knew how to read and write, many in more than one language. This served them well in the New World, especially those who served as officers on the Louisiana vessels and those who operated their own businesses.

Although there were few well-educated immigrants among the latter groups—post–1880—they were all literate. Most had at least a few years of elementary education. Compulsory elementary education arrived much earlier in Dalmatia than it did in other parts of present-day Yugoslavia. For instance, according to V. Holjevac in his *Hrvati Izvan Domovine (Croatians Outside Their Homeland)* the rate of illiteracy among the immigrants from the interior of Croatia during the latter part of the nineteenth and the beginning of the twentieth century were as high as 30 to 40 percent. On the other hand, out of over a thousand applications of the Slavonian Association that I examined, none made their marks (X); all signed their full names.

This rudimentary old-country education did not prepare them for any professions, but it did give them the essentials with which to learn English and to keep books at their places of business.

Limited in education, the first generation realized their shortcomings and made every effort to see that their children received the necessary schooling. They were, and still are, willing to go to any lengths to insure proper education for their sons and daughters. Many saved through the years to pay for a university education for their sons if they showed the ability to pursue it. The oystermen were willing to be separated from their families so that the children could attend schools in New Orleans during the nine school months. The early oystermen's lives, as described in Chapter Four, were lives of hardship, and parents insisted on educating their children to give them a chance for a better life.

This insistence on educating their children still persists, but the financial hardships have eased somewhat now that they have improved their economic status and helpful loans are available to college students who are willing to study.

The second- and the third-generation Yugoslav immigrants have done well in professional fields. For example the Salatich brothers, Peter and Blaise, became doctors at the turn of the century. Three of Peter Salatich's sons have followed in his footsteps, and one son is a lawyer. The family of Nicholas and Gladys Persich is another example of total family education. One of their four sons, J. Donald Persich, is a physician; the other three, Nicholas, Harold, and Roy are priests; and the daugther, Anna, is a professor and chairman of the department of medical technology at nearby Loyola University. Dominick Zibilich's sons, Robert and William, are attorneys, and J. Michael is a member of the clergy. The Bautovich brothers, Colenda and Thomas, and father and son Anthony and Joseph Juracovich also entered the medical profession. Others are in education, law, science, government service, and business.

The college students are usually successful and many graduate with honors. For example: Luke A. Petrovich was student-body president at Northwestern Louisiana College (now a university); Vinka Carevich edited the Loyola yearbook, the *Wolf*; Mary Ann Batinich was selected the best all-around coed of the 1969 class at Loyola; John M. Marcev, Jr., graduated with honors in engineering from Tulane University; and Linda Barbalich, a magna cum laude graduate of the Loyola College of Music, was awarded the coveted Phi Beta leadership pin. There are many others who have received honors, but the above should suffice to show that most of them are diligent scholars.

Many also do extremely well in the secondary schools, and some, such as Keith Cognevich, valedictorian of Chalmette High, 1971 class, and Wendy Vujnovich, salutatorian of St. Joseph Academy, 1972 class, graduated at the top of their classes and were awarded scholarships to local universities. Some, such as Jonathan Salinovich, a 1971 honor graduate of Delta Heritage Academy and an appointee to the Air Force Academy, pursue their studies in the military. Others, such as Marlene Glavina, a National Honor Society member who was listed in Who's Who Among Student Leaders in High Schools of America, 1968, become outstanding leaders in their schools.

The result of this effort by first-generation immigrants to educate their children is that second and the subsequent generations of

Yugoslavs are well represented in all major professions in Louisiana and many are leaders in their fields.

RELIGION

All Yugoslavs coming to Louisiana were baptized either in the Greek Orthodox or the Catholic Church. Those coming from the Bay of Kotor area belong to either religion, and those coming from other parts of Dalmatia are Catholics. The Bay of Kotor is where East meets West, and consequently the population is split between the two churches, one religion predominating in one town and the other in the next. Sharing the same towns and villages for centuries, they learned to live in peace and harmony with each other.

In their early youth all received the sacraments but somehow as they went out into the world they became lukewarm toward their religion and were very seldom seen in church. However, when they married, the ceremony took place in a church with a priest officiating. They baptized their children and sent them to parochial schools. They may have joined the Masonic orders, but they insisted on a Catholic education for their children. The wives and the children attended church regularly though the men went only on Easter and Christmas and for funerals and weddings—a typical Dalmatian custom practiced in Dalmatia to this day.

However, as the old-timers aged and retired, the influence of their Catholic-educated children and pious wives usually resulted in their becoming regular churchgoers.

Many members of the second and the third generation, such as Fathers John A. Tomasovich, Nicholas, Harold, and Roy Persich, became priests while several girls became nuns, devoting their lives to the service of God and the community.

The South Slav Catholics in Louisiana were never strong enough numerically to have found a church parish of their own as is the case in many northern communities but have always generously supported the parish church of their location. They attend these churches regularly, and many serve as ushers and in other capacities. In contrast to their predecessors they do attend church services regularly with their families.

Between the late 1890s and the early 1940s the Croatian Catholic priests from the churches of Pittsburgh, Chicago, New York, Cary, and other communities where the Croatians established their own parishes, came to New Orleans every few years and held missions—reminiscent of the Old-Country missions—and preached in Croatian.

In 1949 a Yugoslav priest, Father Joseph Gregor, C.M., came to New Orleans where he was appointed chaplain at Charity Hospital and started celebrating masses on Christmas Day, Easter, and on Mother's Day of each year, in Croatian. He organized a choir of young singers to sing Croatian religious hymns and Christmas carols during these services. With Dr. Thomas P. Bautovich, and later with Father Joseph Spanich, as an organist, they performed quite well.

When Father Gregor was transferred to Florida, Father Spanich took his place as an unofficial spiritual adviser to the New Orleans Yugoslavs.

In May, 1968, Bishop (now Archbishop) Marijan Oblak of Zadar, Yugoslavia, visited New Orleans, Biloxi, and lower Plaquemines Parish. He celebrated masses to packed churches in Biloxi and New Orleans. He remained in New Orleans for several days and was received with enthusiasm in many New Orleans homes. Several socioreligious gatherings were provided so that he could meet and get to know his compatriots personally.

Since October, 1971, Father Spanich has served as the pastor of the St. Pius X Parish, Crown Point, Louisiana, but he still finds time to celebrate masses, hear confessions, and conduct choir practice three times per year for his fellow Yugoslavs.

The services are held in the Charity Hospital chapel which the good sisters make available to Father Spanich and his "three-times-per-year parishioners." The choir sings Christmas carols on Christmas day, and other Croatian religious hymns on Easter and Mother's Day, while Father Spanich preaches in Croatian so that they are transported, in spirit, to their childhood days in village churches along the Adriatic.

CIVIL WAR PARTICIPATION

As stated in Chapter Two, there were, by 1860, between five hundred and six hundred South Slavs living in New Orleans and in Plaquemines Parish. Therefore, when the American Civil War broke out in 1861, many of them were established businessmen and bona fide citizens of Louisiana, who considered themselves Southerners.

Feeling it their duty to participate in this conflict, they organized military units consisting of South Slavs, or Slavonians as they then called themselves.

The active participation of the South Slav immigrants in the Confederacy was on both individual and organized bases. Anthony Cognevich organized his own company and, as was the custom in those days among the voluntary military units, was elected its commander and captain. Others organized two more companies: Slavonian Rifles I, and Slavonian Rifles II, and several individuals joined various outfits on their own and saw action during the war, some giving their lives for the Cause.

The Cognevich Company was a part of the Fourth Regiment of the European Brigade which was a part of the Louisiana Militia. The roster of the company, as taken from the National Archives of the Compiled Service Records of the Confederate Soldiers from Louisiana, appears in Table V.

The two Slavonian Rifles companies were also attached to the European Brigade. The First Company, as reported by the New Orleans *Daily Crescent* of May 4, 1861, numbered 118 men. Some of the men appearing on its roster were: Second Lieutenant John Ramadanovich, who also served as the company's standard-bearer, First Sergeant G. Svaglich, Third Sergeant D. Mikalich, Second Corporal N. Covacevich, Third Corporal N. Giurgevich, Fourth Corporal S. Vidovich, First Musician L. Mazanovich, and Second Musician G. Srisich. Out of 118 men, 14 were officers, commissioned and noncommissioned, and 104 privates. The following men also served in Slavonian Rifles, although I could not find in which company: Nikola Garbini, Frank Masich, Peter Masich, John Radovich, V. Radovich, Nikola Racich, Matthew Stiglich, Stephen Vidovich as privates; John Marunich as second lieutenant; and Joseph Svaglich as first lieutenant.

These three companies together with the companies of the other nationalities formed the European Brigade. They were stationed in and around New Orleans. While drilling in one of the city's squares they would present a picturesque assemblage in their many-colored uniforms. The commands of Captain Cognevich and Lieutenants Governovich, Jovovich, Mazurano, and Tovovich were probably given in their native Croatian, which would further add to the uniqueness of the group. One can picture New Orleanians observing with keen in-

TABLE V

Civil War soldiers from New Orleans who served in Cognevich Company, Fourth Regiment, European Brigade, Louisiana Militia, Confederate Army.

NAME	RANK	NAME	RANK
Luka Abovich	Pvt	Luka Glavina	Pvt
Thomas Antoncich	Pvt	Peter Governovich	Lieut
George Arnet	Pvt	Anthony Granich	Pvt
John Aurich	Pvt	Louis Grashich	Pvt
Peter Barbarich	Pvt	Anthony Greysich	Pvt
Ivo Beccir	Pvt	Joseph Grisich	Pvt
George Bejanich	Pvt	Luka Grisich	Corp
Peter Beleich	Pvt	Louis Grusich	Pvt
Marco Bendiss	Pvt	Peter Gugliemich	Pvt
Nikola Bendiss	Pvt	Matthew Guglievina	Pvt
Matthew Bosina	Pvt	Lazar Jovovich	Lieut
Anthony Breskovich	Pvt	Nikola Lovro	Pvt
John Buccarich	Pvt	John Lucass	Pvt
Luka Calugerovich	Pvt	Luke Luchetich	Pvt
Stanislav Calugerovich	Sgt	Mario Lucich	Pvt
John Catich	Pvt	Anthony Markovich	Pvt
Anthony Chernich	Pvt	Matthew Marina	Pvt
John Cherssanac	Pvt	Frank Mazurano	Lieut
Matthew Cherstell	Pvt	Ivan Memed	Pvt
Ellia Cheteovich	Pvt	Joseph Meysich	Pvt
Ellia Chezovich	Pvt	Matthew Michalich	Pvt
Anthony Cognevich	Capt	Nikola Mieskovich	Pvt
Anthony Comaich	Pvt	Bogdan Millinovich	Pvt
Matthew Constranich	Pvt	Nikola Minarich	Pvt
Matthew Cornvich	Pvt	Michael Mitrovich	Pvt
Jacob Covachevich	Pvt	George Murguretich	Pvt
Ellia Dabelich	Pvt	Natale Natupich	Pvt
Peter Donquich	Pvt	Jacob Nicaoelovich	Pvt
John Drakori	Pvt	Luke Nichicevich	Pvt
Nikola Fizovich	Pvt	John Perlenda	Pvt
Simun Fortunich	Pvt	John Pesinich	Pvt
Casimir Galovich	Corp	John Radich	Pvt
Ivan Ghergurovich	Pvt	Matthew Radovich	Lieut
Marko Ghergurovich	Pvt	Vincent Radovich	Pvt
Michael Ghergurovich	Sgt	John Radulovich	Pvt
Peter Glavich	Pvt	Kristo Rainovich	Pvt
Vincent Glavich	Pvt	George Rosmarich	Pvt

TABLE V (Continued)

NAME	RANK	NAME	RANK
John Saramania	Pvt	John Xipcovich	Pvt
George Savinovich	Pvt	Anthony Zasprizka	Pvt
Luka Skobelj	Pvt	Spiro Zaputorich	Pvt
Nikola Sherich	Pvt	Anthony Zar	Pvt
John Sharia	Pvt	Michael Zar	Pvt
John Shartan	Pvt	Frano Zellinich	Pvt
Nikola Stella	Pvt	Matthew Zemo	Pvt
Peter Stolich	Pvt	Luka Zibilich	Pvt
Stefo Tepssich	Pvt	Matthew Zibilich	Pvt
Lazar Tovovich	Lieut	Tepto Ziger	Pvt
John Tripiovich	Pvt	Stefo Zigovich	Pvt
Nikola Vouinac	Pvt	Floro Ziretich	Corp
Peter Vucalovich	Pvt	John Zureovich	Pvt

terest these companies as the European Brigade passed in review on the parade grounds on Sunday afternoons to the strains of martial music.

Immediately before and during the invasion of the city, by Admiral Farragut's naval forces in April, 1862, the European Brigade was called upon by New Orleans Mayor John T. Monroe to control the unruly crowds, prevent looting, and keep order in a restless, confused and panic-stricken city. This, we are told, they did admirably.

Nikola Danilovich, Mario Grozovich, and George Petrovich enlisted together on July 22, 1861, at the newly established Camp Moore at Tangipahoa, Louisiana. Grozovich, sailor by trade, was eighteen years old when he enlisted. He served in Company I, Tenth Louisiana Infantry, and was discharged at the cessation of hostilities. Danilovich, also a sailor, was twenty-three when he enlisted, served in Company I and Company G, Tenth Louisiana Infantry. He was captured at Gettysburg, Pennsylvania, on the second day of the battle, July 2, 1863. Paroled shortly after, at Fort McHenry, Maryland, he took the oath of allegiance to the United States and enlisted in the Union Army. Petrovich, the third member of this group, sailor-laborer by trade, was twenty-eight when he enlisted. He achieved the rank of corporal in Company D, Tenth Louisiana Infantry. From his records it can be seen that he participated in several battles. He was admitted to the

Confederate Hospital at Culpepper, Virginia, on September 25, 1862, and on September 29, he was transferred to the General Hospital. He fully recovered, reentered the active ranks, and participated in the Battle of Gettysburg, where on July 2, 1863, he was killed in action.

The South Slav oyster growers and fishermen, who at that time were concentrated around American Bay, Grand Bayou, Bayou Cook, and Bayou La Chutte, contributed to the war by supplying Fort St. Philip and Fort Jackson with fish and oysters.

An interesting incident took place sometime after the fall of New Orleans when the Delta waters were patrolled by the Union naval forces. One day late in April of 1862 three Louisiana oyster growers, Anthony Zibilich, Matthew Zibilich, and Luke Jurisich, were fishing oysters in Bayou La Chutte while their fourth partner Matthew Murina remained in a nearby camp.

That morning one of the oystermen washed his clothes and hoisted them atop the mast for better drying. Atop the mast was a red flannel shirt. Shortly after, they saw a Federal warship patrolling that area that apparently mistook the red shirt for the Confederate stars and bars, coming full steam in their direction. Realizing that the Federals mistook them for an enemy they hoisted sail and tried to escape to the shallow waters, but it was too late. The warship fired a warning shot off their bow. Fearing that the second shot might be more accurate, they "surrendered" and were taken aboard the warship for interrogation. They could not make themselves understood to explain their predicament because, although they had been in this country many years, they had not learned the English language. Living on the bayous away from civilization and American communities they did not need much knowledge of English. Needless to say, they were locked in the brig.

While conversing, probably cursing, among themselves they were overheard by one of ship's officers who, fortunately, was a Yugoslav and spoke the Croatian language, their native tongue. He interpreted for them, and soon the embarrassed captain released them. By this time the warship had rounded the mouth of the river and as it proceeded up the Mississippi it deposited them on the bank opposite their camp near the present-day community of Sunrise. From there they returned to their oyster reefs to pursue their peaceful occupation. The old oysterman who narrated this story to me assured me that after this incident the oystermen never hoisted their wash atop a mast to dry.

THE TWO WORLD WARS AND BEYOND

On the eve of World War I the homeland of the South Slavs in Louisiana—Dalmatia—was, with the rest of the Croatian lands, under the Austro-Hungarian yoke. As the fortunes of the war fluctuated they rejoiced when the Allies were victorious, and sad when they suffered defeat. They hoped for the defeat and the dismemberment of the Austrian Empire so that their brothers back home could become masters in their own land and determine their destiny as free people.

When the United States entered the war in April of 1917 the New Orleans South Slavs, or Yugoslavs as they began calling themselves, organized the Yugoslav League of New Orleans to help the cause of the South Slavs against Austria and especially to convince the Allies that Dalmatia was a Slavic (Croatian) land and that it should not be given to Italy as promised by them (the Allies) by the secret treaty of London to entice Italy to join the war on the Allied side. To prevent the Allies from giving Dalmatia to the Italians, the league sent numerous telegrams, appeals, and resolutions to President Woodrow Wilson, French Premier George Clemenceau, Yugoslav delegate Ante Trumbic, and other Allied leaders at the Paris Peace Conference. In February, 1920, the league issued, among other things a declaration which insisted upon immediate evacuation of Fiume (Rijeka) and other Dalmatian territory occupied by the Italians. The declaration was sent to the Paris Peace Conference. It was signed by the following Louisiana Yugoslavs: Ostoja Pavlovich, Spiro Pavlovich, Milos Pavlovich, Vaso Pavlovich, Jovo Vasiljevich, Stevo Vasiljevich, Stipan Vela, Donko L. Jurisich, John Sukno, Nikola Spremich, Ante A. T. Tomasovich, Grgo Keko, Marian Vela, Ivo Korach, Ivan Rudez, Kuzma Cibilich, Ljubo Porobilo, Nikola Kandich, Autun Busko, Gjuro Pavlovich, Simo Pavlovich, Spiro Pavlovich, Jr., Tony Zibilich, Gjuro Trazivuk, Ante K. Barisich, Tripo Ivovich, Stipe Zuvich, Mato M. Picinich, Ante Slavich, Ivan Morovich, Grgo Anticich, Ante Tomasevich, Vaso Rusovich, Antun Vidak, Petar Taliancich, Blagoje Pavlovich, Ilija Pavlovich, Tripo Pavlovich, Andrija L. Petrovich, Bozo L. Petrovich, Ante Marinovich, Ante Vujevich, John Hihar, John Lulich, Jero Andrich, Nick Popich, John Mihaljevich, and John Zaninovich.

The league also helped the Yugoslavs who suffered during the war by sending to them, through the Red Cross, over $8,000 to care for orphans, to equip a hospital in Dubrovnik, and to help rehabilitate the wounded.

The prime organizers of the league were: George Trazivuk, Basil Rusovich, Joseph Jurisich, and Dr. Peter B. Salatich, with Dr. Salatich serving as chairman and Jurisich as president.

The Yugoslavs in Louisiana helped the war cause wherever they could. They bought Liberty Bonds generously. Many enlisted in the United States Armed Forces, and several served on the front with distinction. Among those were Gregory Slavich and Dimitry Vidacovich.

Gregory Slavich was born in Sucuraj, Yugoslavia, on September 14, 1894, and came to Louisiana as a youth of fourteen on August 15, 1908. At first he worked as an oysterman in the Bayou Cook area but soon left the bayou and settled in New Orleans where he worked at various jobs and attended Soulé Commercial College.

He enlisted in the United States Army on August 30, 1917, served with the 114th Engineers Company "F," and saw action in the Meuse-Argonne sector and other theaters of operation. He was hospitalized in France and honorably discharged in May, 1919.

After discharge he continued his education in bookkeeping and accounting at Soulé College and Loyola University. In June, 1921, he married Clare Meyers by whom he had two children, Dorothy and John. He was employed by the United States Government as a custom official until his death on January 4, 1949.

Slavich was extremely loyal to his adopted country and its democratic principles, hence his voluntary enlistment in the army. He was active in the veterans affairs, especially the disabled veterans. He was one of the main organizers of the first active Disabled American Veterans chapters in New Orleans. He remained an active member of this organization and worked tirelessly for the good of the veterans until his death.

In recognition of his loyal military service and of his unselfish work for the disabled veterans, a disabled veterans chapter organized in June, 1949, the Gregory A. Slavich Chapter No. 27 Disabled American Veterans, was named in his honor.

Dimitry Vidacovich was born in Plaquemines Parish on September 25, 1890. His grandfather, John Vidacovich, came to Louisiana in 1839 from Hercegnovi, Bay of Kotor—now Yugoslavia. Dimitry was raised in lower Plaquemines Parish and enlisted in the United States Army on September 18, 1917. After a few months' training in the

States he was sent overseas and served in France in Machine Gun Company, 167th U.S. Infantry, Forty-second Rainbow Division. On July 26, 1918, he was killed in action at Le Croix Rouge while fighting the Germans. The Dimitry Vidacovich Post No. 193 American Legion, Buras, Louisiana, is named in honor of his memory.

After the Japanese attacked the United States at Pearl Harbor, many of the Louisiana Yugoslavs enlisted to serve in the armed forces. These were primarily the sons of the immigrants who came over before the First World War. They joined the war because they felt that their country, America, needed them. They did not speak with an accent as their counterparts of the First World War did, for as native-born Americans, they had American upbringing and education. They joined as privates, but many came out as officers. Needless to say, those who arrived from Yugoslavia between the two wars also joined. Hundreds of the Louisiana Yugoslavs served; they served in the navy, the army, the Air Force, the Marines, and the Coast Guard; they fought on the African front, on the Italian front, on the beaches of Normandy, in the interior of Europe, and in the malaria-infested jungles of the Pacific.

As sailors serving in the Pacific many, while on leave in faraway New Zealand and Australia, came in contact with their cousins and other relatives who had emigrated to these places years before and whom they never had dreamed of ever seeing again. They all served with honor, many with distinction, and several gave their lives.

In the meantime, civilians back home, working in defense plants, increased their oyster and shrimp production to meet the increased demand to feed the soldiers stationed nearby. Others whose boats were "drafted" by the government for the "duration" remained with their boats and served as captains or crew members while patrolling the Louisiana waters, thereby giving up their peaceful pursuits of making a living at shrimp or oyster fishing until after the war. The contacts with the relatives in the old country were severed when the Germans attacked, conquered, and divided Yugoslavia early in 1941. After the war when the Louisiana Yugoslavs learned of the devastation of the old country and of the privations that their relatives had endured, they generously sent money, food, clothing, machinery, tools, and medicine to help them.

During the Korean and the Vietnam conflicts they answered the call to serve their country. In Vietnam, for instance, Lieutenant Nicholas M. Balovich, Jr., was awarded the Bronze Star for services as a river-boat patrol officer, and Marine Corporal Joseph G. Sercovich was killed in action on January 17, 1966, at Da Nang, Vietnam. Many others served, and not a single Louisiana Yugoslav or anyone of Yugoslav background went to Canada or to Sweden to escape the draft.

CIVIC PARTICIPATION

Most Yugoslav immigrants acquire American citizenship as soon as it is legally possible. Those who intend to remain here permanently realize the need and the advantage of citizenship for full participation in the American way of life. Those who intend to stay only a few years acquire citizenship so that their children can someday come to the United States as citizens, if they so desire, and that they themselves may reenter America if they change their minds, once they return to Yugoslavia. As American citizens they have no trouble gaining reentry.

Their loyalty to the democratic principles of the American way of life is beyond question. They tend to be constitutionalists from the start. When they acquire citizenship they, as a rule, join the Democratic party and vote the straight party ticket and are in favor of liberal economic policies. However, once they acquire material goods and have something to conserve, they become conservative and may vote Republican in general elections while still retaining their registration as Democrats.

Almost without exception the Yugoslavs in Louisiana are law-abiding citizens. Their low crime rate has been noted by several writers on this subject. It is often emphasized by the local officials. In his speeches, the late Judge Leander Perez of Plaquemines Parish regularly commended those of Yugoslav background on their model citizenship. In dealing with each other and with the general public they are thoroughly honest and just and expect to be treated likewise. If differences arise among themselves, they tend to settle them without resorting to courts.

Their exemplary law-abiding behavior can perhaps best be explained by their strong family ties, community consciousness, and the fact that they take their duties and obligations seriously. Also they work hard and steadily to succeed in the New World and consequently

They gave their lives so that democracy may live . . .

U.S. Air Corps Lt. Matthew Barbier, Jr., pilot of B-24 bomber, killed in action on his fifth mission over Stuttgart, Germany, July 21, 1944.

Cpl. Vincent Dimitry Jurisich, died in France on July 12, 1944, from wounds received in the Normandy invasion.

Pvt. Slavko Milicich, killed in action in France, November 24, 1944.

HONOR ROLL*
UNITED SLAVONIAN BENEVOLENT ASSOCIATION
To Our Members Who Are Serving In The Armed
Forces Of The United States Of America

Anzulovich, Mato

Barbier, Mato, Jr.
Barbier, Frederick
Baricevich, John
Bautovich, Dr. C. F.
Biskupovich, Tomo
Bilich, Stipan
Bujacich, Jozo

Carevich, John
Cvitanovich, David

Franicevich, Mathew
Franicevich, Zvonimir

Gentilich, Nicholas S.
Gerica, Nikola
Glavina, Frank

Ivicevich, Vladimir
Ivosich, Ivo

Jovanovich, Luke V.
Jurisich, Alvin
Jurisich, Milenko
Jurovich, Frank
Jurovich, John, Jr.

Kopanica, Frank

Levata, Dr. Anthony N.

Marcev, Ivo P.
Marinovich, Milton
Matulich, Nikola
Milicich, Slavko
Muhoberac, Mato, Jr.

Parun, Benard
Parun, Peter
Pausina, Luka
Popich, Anthony J.
Porobilo, A. J.
Protich, Leo

Radetich, Nick

Seckso, Paul
Seferovich, Geo. H.
Seput, Gaspar
Slabich, Jozo
Slavich, Ante S.
Smokovich, Ante
Spanja, Chris
Spremich, Rudolf

Tadin, Nicholas
Taliancich, Joseph
Taliancich, Lawrence
Taliancich, Peter, Jr.
Taliancich, Sam
Tesvich, Luka, Jr.

Urlich, Marian D.

Vela, Emile
Vezich, Anthony A.
Vlahov, Harvey M.
Vodanovich, Geo., Jr.
Vojkovich, John
Vujnovich, Milos
Vuljan, Philip

Zibilich, August
Zibilich, August M.
Zibilich, Wm. Martin

* Facsimile of a plaque showing the members who served in World War II.

are too busy to "get into trouble." When immigrants arrive at American shores their strongest desire is to "get ahead," and they devote most of their energy toward this goal.

In the past—when so much paper work was not required for every transaction as it is today—in dealing with each other and with their business associates, they usually agreed to a business deal or to perform a certain task by merely giving their word. I have often heard it said, especially among Plaquemines Parish residents, that once a *Tako** gave you his word, you had nothing to worry about.

As was mentioned elsewhere in this study, the Yugoslavs have their ethnic organizations to help each other and to enrich their lives socially, but they also join other organizations. They join the Masonic orders, the Knights of Columbus, the American Legion and other service and trade organizations. As a rule, once they join an organization, they tend to be doers rather than mere observers. Many achieve high positions in these organizations. There are several 32nd degree Masons and many have held offices in their lodges. For instance, John R. Begovich served as worshipful master of William D. White Lodge 408, Free and Accepted Masons in Gretna, and Joseph J. Barbier (whose father came from Vrgorac) was a grand knight of the Gentilly Council 2925, Knights of Columbus.

Being gregarious by nature, they like and enjoy political activities. They talk and discuss politics for hours, and sometimes, when a heated discussion ensues, their short Dalmatian tempers flare. They participate actively in election campaigns for the man of their choice. The ladies give coffee parties so that their friends may meet the candidates, and the men invite the candidates to their places of business and contribute whatever they can afford or whatever they think their candidate is worth. Many of the second- and the third-generation members run for various offices, and some win. In Plaquemines Parish they have served on the police juries and levee boards for generations. Dewey Cognevich was the parish assessor for decades, and upon his death he was succeeded by another Yugoslav-American, Brian Bubrig.

* *Tako* is a nickname for the Louisiana Yugoslavs given to them by their French neighbors and fellow oystermen. When the Yugoslav oystermen met they greeted each other with *kako si?* or *kako ostrige?* (how are you? or how are the oysters?) Not given to bragging, they would reply, "*Tako tako*" ("So so"), and the French-speaking oystermen simply referred to their Slavic neighbors as *Tako*. The name stuck, and it is used to this day, mostly in a humorous way.

Alwynn J. Cronvich, whose great-grandfather came from the island of Cres in northern Dalmatia, is sheriff of Jefferson Parish. As chief law-enforcement officer of Jefferson Parish he improved the parish's law enforcement apparatus and in 1971 was a Merit Award recipient from the National Crime Prevention Foundation. Apparently his constituents approve of his progressive crime prevention methods, for in 1971 they again reelected him to the office.

Anthony J. Vesich, Jr., and Luke A. Petrovich are among those who achieved prominent positions in Louisiana public life.

ANTHONY J. VESICH, JR.

Vesich was born in New Orleans some forty-eight years ago. His grandfather, Anton Vesich, came to Louisiana from Trpanj, Dalmatia, towards the end of the last century. He attended parochial schools in New Orleans and upon graduation from high school entered Loyola University and was graduated from its law school in 1951. He has been practicing law in New Orleans for the past twenty-two years. In 1956 he was elected to the Louisiana House of Representatives and served as a representative for sixteen years. During that time he authored and coauthored many bills that were advantageous to the city of New Orleans and to the state. He was instrumental in establishing Louisiana State University at New Orleans; in increasing the pay for police, firemen, county and municipal employees, and schoolteachers; in securing funds for the restoration of the Cabildo and other historic buildings; in establishing the Code of Ethics for the state; and in the construction of the domed stadium for New Orleans. In 1972 he was elected as a delegate to the Louisiana Constitutional Convention.

He is a member of the New Orleans and Louisiana State Bar associations. A lifelong member of the United Slavonian Benevolent Association, he helped to rewrite its charter and bylaws during the reorganization of the association in 1963. He is married to the former Rita Curtis and has two children. He is a navy veteran of the Second World War.

As a legislator, an attorney, and as a delegate to the 1973 Louisiana Constitutional Convention, Vesich has devoted most of his adult life toward a better government for his fellow Louisianians.

LUKE A. PETROVICH

Luke A. Petrovich, whose father, Andrew L. Petrovich, came

Luke A. Petrovich

Anthony J. Vesich, Jr.

Sandra Vujnovich presenting flowers of welcome to Archbishop Marijan Oblak of Yugoslavia upon his arrival at New Orleans International Airport in May, 1968.

from Duba and mother, Catherine Turich Petrovich, from Kuna, Dalmatia, was born in Olga, Plaquemines Parish, on November 16, 1929. He received his early education in the public schools of the parish, his high school diploma from Buras High School in 1946, and a B.A. degree from Northwestern State College (now a university) in Natchitoches in 1951 where he demonstrated his leadership abilities by becoming president of the student body during his senior year, president of the Lambda Zeta fraternity, and president of the Inter-fraternity Council. While at Northwestern he was a two-year letter-man on the college debate team and represented the state of Louisiana in the Georgetown Invitational Debate tournament. He also won the state Peace Oratorical contest, and placed ninth in the nation of over five hundred contestants.

Upon graduation from Northwestern he taught school for one year at Buras High School, then entered Tulane University and received his law degree in 1955. While at Tulane he served as president of his senior class. He was a member of the staff publication, *Student Lawyer*, and a member of the Phi Delta law fraternity.

In 1960 he was appointed attorney for the inheritance tax collector for Plaquemines Parish and in 1962 he was elected to the office of Public Safety Commissioner for the parish. He is still serving as a commissioner, and with distinction.

Ever since graduating from Tulane Law School, Petrovich has served Plaquemines Parish in one capacity or another. He is genuinely interested in the progress and improvement of his parish and to this end has dedicated most of his energies and time. His complete dedication to the welfare and safety of the people of Plaquemines Parish was demonstrated beyond any doubt during the devastating Hurricane Camille. To make certain that everyone was evacuated to the safety zones, he remained on duty until it was too late to retreat to safety and consequently was forced to spend the entire night of August 17, 1969, atop a building at Boothville, experiencing two-hundred-mile-per-hour wind and rain and high water all about him. In spite of all this, the very next morning he was on duty directing rescue operations and making plans with the rest of the parish officials for the restoration of the destroyed areas. The grateful people of Plaquemines Parish have bestowed upon him many honors for his unselfish service. One of these honors was being chosen to reign as king of the 1970 Plaquemines Parish Fair and Orange Festival.

Well liked and respected by his fellow parishioners, he is in constant demand to serve as chairman or master of ceremonies for various undertakings and functions. To these many demands he has responded generously.

Gregarious by nature, he is a member of the Twenty-fifth Judicial Bar Association; Knights of Columbus, fourth degree; the Plaquemines Parish Lions Club; and a lifelong member of the United Slavonian Association, and many other clubs and organizations.

GEORGE PIVACH

More than any other Yugoslav immigrant, George Pivach of Triumph and Belle Chasse, Louisiana, represents the type of immigrant who left his native land as a youth and with hard work and persistence succeeded in the New World.

Pivach was born on April 16, 1894, in the small town of Podgora on the shores of the Adriatic Sea. Here Mount Biokovo rises steeply from the sea leaving little land suitable for cultivation. Hence this region was unable to support a rapid increase of population during the end of the last and the beginning of this century, thereby forcing many of its youth to emigrate.

After completing six years of elementary schooling, Pivach joined his father, Mitchel, in fishing and sharecropping of olives, grapes, and figs. However, within a few years he left for America arriving in Louisiana in April of 1911 on his seventeenth birthday. Upon arrival in Plaquemines Parish he went to work fishing oysters for fifty cents a day for John I. Sumich and Company. By 1914 he became part owner of the Champion Oyster Company. For many years this company was one of the largest oyster-producing enterprises in Louisiana.

During World War I his soldier-father died, and the responsibility of providing for the family fell on young George. In the ensuing years he devoted all his time and energy to cultivating and selling oysters. In 1926, however, he took a few months of well-deserved rest and returned for a visit to his native Podgora where he married Simica Sumich. They returned to Louisiana in 1927. Also, during 1926 he and his brother Tony and Peter Cvitanovich, Anthony Lulich, John Lulich, Anthony Garma, Sam Spanja, John I. Sumich, and John M. Sumich purchased several hundred acres of land in lower Plaquemines Parish near Fort Jackson. This land had some citrus trees on it, and the eight partners planted hundreds of additional orange trees there.

In 1929 the company (Pivach and his partners) divided the land, and each proceeded on his own. By this time the orange trees which they planted began to bear fruit, and Pivach quit the oyster-growing business to devote more time to orange farming. He introduced many scientific methods to orange growing and his oranges won several first-prize awards. During the early 1930s he and several other growers started making orange wine. Soon Pivach was producing thousands of gallons of orange wine annually and selling it under the "GP" (George Pivach) brand all over the country.

His energies and business acumen, however, were not satisfied with these activities, and during this time he built and operated a dance hall and a saloon. Subsequently he also acquired extensive real estate in New Orleans, built and rented housing complexes for the oil-field workers coming into lower Plaquemines Parish, owned boats and draglines that assisted the search and development of petroleum, became president of the Gulf Loan Company, the Home Loan and Thrift Company, the Pivach-Perino Realty Company, and the Gulf Credit Corporation.

He and his wife, Simica, have one son, George, Jr., and two daughters, Magdelene Pivach Perino and Eleanor Pivach Elliot. His successes, as enumerated above, were many, but so were his sorrows. Among his disappointments were the death of his first-born son, Mitchel, at the age of nine months; loss of money and property through bank failures; the freezes of 1951 and 1962 which completely destroyed his orange groves; the loss of his home, his winery and packing warehouse in a fire in 1962; and the loss of his home and possessions as well as the homes of his two children during Hurricane Camille in 1969.

A man of undaunted courage and patient persistence, Pivach was disappointed by these reverses but not defeated. After Hurricane Camille he left the Triumph-Buras area, where he had spent fifty years of his life; he bought land in Belle Chasse, Louisiana, and constructed a spacious home near his children and grandchildren where he spends his retirement years. But even in his retirement he does not rest completely. Although approaching eighty he is still busily engaged in clearing the woods near his home, planting trees, caring for those he planted since he moved into his new home in the spring of 1972, directing his business interests, and complaining about the fact that he cannot do as much as he was able to in his younger days.

Group of Yugoslavs from the Triumph-Buras area, *circa* 1925. From left to right, front row: John Lulich, John I. Sumich, John M. Sumich, and George Pivach; back row: Tony Pivach, J. Monte, Anthony Garma, Anthony Lulich, Peter Cvitanovich, and Simo Spanja.

George Pivach inspecting his orange wine bottling plant, Triumph, Louisiana, *circa* 1938.

MICHAEL A. BACCICH

Captain Michael A. Baccich was born in Dubrovnik on February 22, 1859. He completed his elementary education there and soon after, at the age of sixteen, joined the crew of the merchant sailing vessel *Stefano*, a nine-hundred-ton brig owned by his uncle. On his first trip in September, 1875, the *Stefano* was wrecked, and young Baccich narrowly escaped death. The ship carried a cargo of coal from Cardiff, Wales, to Hongkong. The crew consisted of fifteen sailors, a captain, and Baccich.

The trip was uneventful until, near the western coast of Australia, the captain ordered the helmsman to turn the vessel northwest. The helmsman misunderstood and turned northeast toward the coast where it hit a submerged rock and was wrecked in rough seas. The captain was killed outright, and the crew clung to the wreckage or swam to shore. Six sailors drowned before reaching land. A few days after the rest of them waded ashore, eight more sailors died from exposure, hunger, and thirst, leaving Baccich and another sailor named Jurich as the only survivors.

They walked to the interior where they found a tribe of aborigines by whom they were well treated. Their food consisted of sea-turtle meat. When the aborigines caught a turtle they feasted; otherwise Baccich and Jurich went hungry with them. After four months of this primitive living, they were rescued by an English vessel which was fishing pearls in the Indian Ocean.

Meanwhile, back home in Dubrovnik all his relatives thought Baccich was dead. When he returned to his native city they looked upon him as some kind of a ghost. Under those circumstances he felt uneasy and went to Rijeka where he completed the studies at the Nautical Academy. Upon graduation he assumed command of a new ship, the *Resurrection*, which his uncle had built to replace the wrecked *Stefano*. After two years as a captain of this vessel he docked in New Orleans in 1880 and decided to stay there.

Although his education, training, and experience up to that time prepared him to be a sea captain, he adjusted well in the New World and soon became a prosperous merchant operating a grocery and general store, first with Andrew Cietcovich, then with Vlaho Salatich, and by 1890 on his own.

His store at Decatur and Ursuline streets soon became an un-

Mrs. Mary Lulich, Anthony Lulich, and Mitchell Lulich at their orange farm in Buras.

Gloria Cvitanovich Batinich, 1947 Plaquemines Parish Fair and Orange Festival Queen.

Matthew J. Farac, 1972 Plaquemines Parish Fair and Orange Festival King.

official headquarters for the Yugoslavs then living around the French Market area and for oystermen who brought their oysters up the Mississippi to New Orleans market and docked their boats, only a stone's throw from the store, at the foot of Dumaine Street.

When the great hurricane of October, 1893, devastated the Yugoslav community of Bayou Cook and vicinity, Baccich hired a steamer and provisioned it from his store, at his own expense, and sent it to the Bayou Cook area to search for survivors and supply them with groceries and needed goods. We can easily understand his compassion for the hurricane victims when we remember his ordeal of being shipwrecked.

At the turn of the century he gave up the grocery business and entered the real estate field, first as president and one of the founders of the National Realty Company and later as president of the Gentilly Terrace Company. This firm developed the Gentilly Terrace area. After his withdrawal from the Gentilly firm he formed a partnership with his son George under the name of M. A. Baccich and Son. He headed this company until his retirement in 1933. He died two years later, on December 12, 1935.

He was married to Angelina Cvietcovich, and together they raised a family of six daughters and one son. He was active in civic affairs all his life and worked tirelessly to help build and improve his adopted city. Baccich Street in the Gentilly section of New Orleans is named in his honor as a lasting memorial to his many accomplishments.

4

Dalmatian Fishermen Become Louisiana Oystermen

OF THE MANY CONTRIBUTIONS made by the Yugoslavs to Louisiana, the most outstanding is the development of the oyster industry. It was mostly through the ceaseless, arduous, and indomitable effort of the Yugoslav fishermen from Dalmatia that the primitive method of gathering oysters was changed to the highly skilled, profitable, useful, and beneficial industry which today employs thousands of persons and provides New Orleans and the rest of the country with a succulent and healthful food. They developed the art of cultivating oysters to a science. Their reputation for good business practices, quality of the oysters, and truthfulness in dealing with the oyster dealers and consumers is beyond reproach. This formidable reputation was not earned overnight but rests on more than 125 years of experience in oyster growing and cultivating in the bayous of Louisiana.

Oysters grow in abundance in the Louisiana coastal waters, where the fresh water of the Mississippi, Atchafalaya, Sabine, and Pearl rivers mixes with the seawater of the Gulf of Mexico. The mixture of the river water with the seawater provides the proper water salinity for the propagation of oysters. The first Louisiana planter and the early historian of the state, Antoine Du Pratz, in his *Historie de la Louisiana*, published in 1743, tells us of the abundance and deliciousness of the oysters in the Louisiana bayous. When the white men arrived on the Louisiana shores and found the tasty oyster they recognized it as the cousin of the European oyster. The earliest oyster consumers were the people who lived at the water's edge and picked the oysters as they needed them for their daily consumption. As the population increased, fishermen living near the oyster-growing areas realized the commercial potentialities of the oyster. Soon they were selling oysters with other fish.

THE YUGOSLAVS ARRIVE

During the 1840–1850 decade many Yugoslavs arrived and remained in New Orleans. Among these were many who made their livings as fishermen in the Adriatic Sea before becoming sailors on the sailing vessels that brought them to New Orleans. Many of them did not, or could not, find employment in New Orleans and went on down the Mississippi River to fish for a living in lower Plaquemines Parish. The rich delta country with its many bays, bayous, and inlets provided ample supply of fish, shrimp, and oysters.

They settled at Grand Bay near the present-day town of Olga and later in Bayou Cook, Grand Bayou, Bayou Chutte, and the Adams Bay area located a few miles southwest of Empire. After the Civil War, as their numbers increased, they fished oysters in other bays, lakes, and bayous of the Mississippi Delta. Here they built their camps which at first were simple one-room structures built on four corner pilings, their floors raised about six feet off the marshy ground for protection from high tides and hurricanes. These camps resembled the habitats of prehistoric lake dwellers more than those of civilized society. Later on, as the camps were improved the Bayou Cook area actually became a substantial settlement, only to be completely destroyed by the 1893 hurricane.

Among the first Yugoslavs who started methodical cultivation of oysters during the mid-1850s in the bayous of Louisiana were: Anthony Cibilich, Nikola Cibilich, Joseph Jurisich, Luke Jurisich, Matthew Murina, and Anthony Tomasovich from the village of Duba near Trpanj on the Peljesac Peninsula; Nicholas Matulich and Steven Matulich, from Postire on the Brac Island; and Peter Barich, Frank Benushi, Ilia Catovich, Nicholas Cartovich, Joseph Churlich, John Cornavich, P. Escovencovich, M. Finici, Anthony Franovich, Andrew Juraditich, Frank Juratich, Andrew Jurich, Anthony Liandir, George Lusich, John Martovich, Frank Matovich, Peter Merlich, Bosko Musselivich, F. Novasina, Anthony Ozmanovich, Luke Pastrovich, Anthony Payitich, Frank Pergovich, John Petrovich, Marko Petrovich, Peter Petrovich, Nicholas Suich, Nicholas Tanovich, John Vukovich, and Peter Yankovich, who were from the area stretching from and including the Bay of Kotor to the estuary of the Neretva River; that is, from the same general area as the early Yugoslav immigrants arriving in New Orleans a few years before.

CULTIVATION OF OYSTERS BEGINS

Anthony and Nikola Cibilich, Joseph and Luke Jurisich, Tomasovich, and many others came from the Peljesac Peninsula where, near Mali Ston in the Bistrina Bay, the best Adriatic oysters have been cultivated by the suspension method for centuries. The Austrian nobility, vacationing in summer palaces on the Brioni Islands and on the coast of Istria near Opatija, had these oysters shipped to their tables. So when these Dalmatian fishermen, who at first probably made their living primarily from fishing, picked a few oysters along the Louisiana shores at a low tide and shipped them to New Orleans, they remembered the successful cultivation of oysters in the old country, and decided to try to do the same with the Louisiana oysters on a somewhat larger scale and by a different method.

They found that the area east of the Mississippi River had an abundance of natural reefs where the oysters grew and multiplied at a rapid rate and thereby exhausted the food supply before maturing. So the Dalmatian fishermen thinned out some of these reefs and from them fished the so-called "natural reef oysters" which were good for cooking. They also discovered, through persistent and careful observation and experimentation, that if these overcrowded, flavorless, natural reef oysters were transferred to the west side of the Mississippi River and spread out over a wider area where the water salinity was in the right proportion, the current steady, and the microscopic food supply plentiful, the skinny seed oysters matured to fully grown mollusks in a few months, developed a round and a well-proportioned shell, and most important of all, acquired that tangy taste for which this type of oysters soon became famous. Here then was the beginning of the Louisiana oyster cultivation as it is practiced to the present day, and the development of a dual method of oyster fishing: natural reef oysters for cooking and canning, and cultivated oysters for raw, half-shell consumption. These cultivated oysters soon were in great demand by their New Orleans customers and were served in all better New Orleans restaurants, oyster bars, and hotels. The Bayou Cook, Bayou La Chutte, and Adams Bay areas were especially suited for growing this type of oyster, and the better tasting Louisiana ones, Bayou Cook oysters, became a generic term. Even today this area produces a sizable supply of the New Orleans counter-stock oysters.

TOOLS ARE INTRODUCED

At the beginning of oyster cultivation, the method of gathering oysters was very primitive. The Yugoslav oystermen picked the oysters out of the water with their bare hands while wading waist-deep, separated the mature marketable oysters from the clusters, dead shells, and small immature oysters, placed them in skiffs which were rowed or sailed over to the favorable areas, and deposited them in water again. Their bare hands soon bled profusely from handling the jagged shells. When they had prepared enough oysters, they took them out of the water, scrubbed them, and sold them to the upriver plantations or took them to the New Orleans market. They planted the small seed oysters in the water near their camps. In the early days they "planted" these oysters one by one, spacing them a few inches apart to give them room to grow. They enclosed this area with wooden boards to protect the oysters from predators, such as drumfish, and from poachers. Because this was slow, tedious, and backbreaking work they experimented with tools and implements to gather the oysters and bring them out to the surface in larger quantities. They probably used ordinary garden rakes to scoop the oysters in small piles and later (probably during the cold winter months) crossed two of these rakes in a blacksmith's tongs fashion to get the oysters out of the water without getting wet. Eventually they were constructed by blacksmiths and professional tong makers by hinging two rakes—similar to the garden rakes but with teeth curved to form a "basket"—about two feet from the bottom, so that in operation they worked like the blacksmith's tongs; hence the name. The length of the handles varied from six to sixteen feet, depending on the depth of the water. Since the tongs enabled the oystermen to get the oysters out of the deeper waters and into the boats without getting wet, the men were no longer restricted to "fish" the oysters in shallow waist-deep waters and only in tolerable temperatures, but could extend their oyster gathering to a larger area, and during the whole year including the freezing winter months, and tap new sources heretofore unavailable.

As they obtained larger quantities of oysters from water bottoms by tongs, they naturally turned to other implements to handle these

Typical late-nineteenth century oyster camp and lugger, *circa* 1895.

Bird's-eye view of modern-day oyster camp.

Photo courtesy Kuzma Tesvich family

oysters; the shovel was a logical tool for this. At first they used the shovels only in loading and unloading the oyster shells and the clam shells which they spread on muddy bottoms as a base where the cultivated oysters were kept, while the marketable oysters were still handled by hand. A story is told that one day while the oystermen were transporting the ready-to-market oysters by hand-filled baskets so as not to damage the oysters, from their skiffs to the boats across the levee, rain began to fall. (The skiffs were in a canal near the levee while the freight boat was in the river.) To speed the loading process one of the oystermen, Mato B. Zibilich, grabbed a nearby shovel and started to fill the baskets with oysters, "Hey stop that," yelled the captain. "You will kill all the oysters." To this Zibilich replied: "If any of these oysters arrive dead in New Orleans, you do not owe us a penny." "O. K., O. K.," answered the captain, "but be careful." The rest is history. The oysters were not damaged, and from then on the shovel, slightly modified, became a standard part of their equipment.

At the turn of this century the oyster dredges made their appearance. Leopold Taliancich, in 1905, installed the first pair of oyster dredges on an oyster boat, and a new method of fishing oysters was initiated which is in use to the present day. The oyster dredges are V-shaped iron frames, with ring-mesh sacklike enclosures, about three to four feet in length. When in use they are connected to a boat, with chains attached to the smaller ends, one to each side of a boat, and dragged along the oyster reef bottom by a boat that circles around at a moderate speed. For many years the dredges were hoisted aboard by manually operated winches, an improvement over tongs but still a difficult task. In 1913 John and Anthony Zegura installed the first power-operated oyster dredges on their lugger *Venus*. This was done by running a central shaft from the main engine to the front part of the boat and connecting the winches to it. This type of operation is used to the present day.

THE OYSTERMEN PROSPER

The living conditions of the early Yugoslav oystermen in Louisiana bayous were very difficult; they were constantly annoyed and plagued by mosquitoes and other insects; their lives were in danger from hurricanes of which they had no warning; their diet was very simple consisting primarily of fish, oysters, shrimps, and hardtack; their days were long, filled with hard physical labor from dawn to dusk; their oyster crop was often disappointing, periodically ruined by oyster conch, drumfish, and hurricanes; their health frequently deteriorated from constant exposure to dampness and improper diet; but the most difficult part of this life was the eternal loneliness for their loved ones, their wives or sweethearts, their womenfolk.

However, despite all of these hardships they stuck it out and succeeded. Slowly but surely they made progress; they improved their camps and built larger and faster boats. They prospered economically, saving their hard-earned dollars prudently and scrupulously so that after a decade or two of fishing oysters some of them accumulated enough to return to the old country. Some stayed and improved the ancestral homesteads with their American savings. Some married their childhood sweethearts and returned to Louisiana. Others remained in Louisiana and married native Louisiana girls of French and Irish ancestry.

While some of them returned to Dalmatia and others left the oyster work for less backbreaking occupations, their numbers were constantly replenished by relatives and friends from the villages along the Adriatic so that the population of the Yugoslav oystermen never remained stagnant but was always in a state of change. The news of the successful and profitable oyster cultivation in Louisiana by Yugoslavs spread northward along the Adriatic Coast. Many of the new arrivals of 1860s and 1870s, and later, were from the area north of the Peljesac Peninsula, the Makarska Littoral, and from the nearby island of Hvar.

ADDITIONAL YUGOSLAVS ARRIVE

Among the Yugoslavs from Dalmatia who joined their countrymen in fishing oysters in Louisiana during the 1860s and 1870s were: Frank Bandich, Peter Bandich, Elias Barbarich, Mark Bendich, Peter Bendich, Joseph Camovich, Joseph Cascarich, George Catach, Simon Catach, George Catanovich, A. Ceheovich, Ignacio Cognovich, P. Cogurovich, P. Conivicich, Nikola Cossich, Elias Cussevich, Felix Darbich, Louis Dascovich, L. Dracotonovich, Vincent Dulsich, Nikola Franovich, George Grandovich, Anthony Granich, Ivan Granich, Spiro Gobelich, M. Gusmanovich, Michael Ianovich, Anthony Iasprich, Andre Iaduk, Hyacinthe Illisich, John Istanovich, Luka Itirinich, Ivan Jucurovich, Paul Jurivich, Adam Lapovich, Luka Lidotich, Peter Littovich, Leo Lusich, Bosko Maloscich, Oscar Mandich, Ivan

Margodich, J. Markovich, Peter Markovich, S. Markovich, Joseph
Mascovich, Joseph Masich, Stefan Mastich, R. Matovich, H. Matta-
vich, Thomas Meladin, K. Meryovich, S. Meryovich, Nikola Mladi-
neo, Adam Millanovich, Bogdan Millanovich, C. Millanovich, Joseph
Millovich, Thomas Millovich, Dominick Monaspina, Elias Mundich,
Joseph Mundich, S. F. Mundich, Anthony Munich, Bosko Mustanich,
P. Munanovich, J. Ochevich, A. Ochiglevich, M. Pablovich, N. Pari-
vaporich, Marko Patovich, Vincent Pederich, Peter Pedrocorach, Ilia
Pendo, Samuel Pendo, Michael Perovich, Anthony Petanovich, Pe-
rani Petrovich, Vlaho Petrovich, S. Petterovich, Peter Picolich, Peter
Pilotich, Luka Portovich, James Radovich, Lazar Radovich, S. Rado-
vich, Vlaho Rana, R. Rastovich, Bosko Rastianich, Nikola Ruffanich,
Vincent Sansovich, Thomas Sapatovich, Peter Taliantich, Gaspar
Tertorich, V. Tomasich, Ilia Tosich, John Ubirichich, Kristo Ubiri-
chich, Stefan Urich, Steve Vasovich, Sam Vidacovich, Lazar Viscovich,
Anthony Volich, and Marko Zar.

OYSTER CAMPS ARE IMPROVED

As the heretofore lonely Yugoslav oystermen became family men,
their lives changed for the better. Their camps were no longer one-
room structures with coarse boards for a floor but contained a kitchen,
a bedroom or two if there were children, and a front porch across the
entire length of the camp. Some still built their camps in the middle
of their oyster "bedding grounds" isolated from each other, but those
who fished oysters in and around the Bayou Cook, Adams Bay, and
Bayou Chutte area built their camps near each other for mutual protection and companionship of their families when the oystermen were
away delivering harvested oysters or obtaining a fresh supply of seed
oysters. As the number of camps increased in the Bayou Cook area, it
acquired a regular communal village type of life similar to the farming and fishing villages along the Adriatic Coast. Children were born
and raised there (many an early United Slavonian Benevolent Association member lists Bayou Cook as his birthplace), wives gossiped and
raised their families; a one-room school was intermittently conducted
where the rudiments of three Rs were taught, and on Sunday, their
day of rest, a priest would visit the community and a mass would be
said where they prayed fervently, for their lives and livelihood depended on the elements.

During the parching and humid Louisiana heat of the summer

months, oyster production and sales came to a standstill; the men took time out from reconditioning their luggers and skiffs to haul some marshy and humid soil to the rear of their camps and make a garden for their families. There the wives planted, with loving care, some cabbage (perhaps a Dalmatian variety which was smuggled aboard the ship that brought them), lettuce, tomatoes, potatoes, and a fig tree to remind them of the Adriatic vegetation. On the front porch of the camps they constructed long wooden troughs and filled them with soil where the wives planted flowers: a few carnations, a few geraniums, and always some sweet basil, *bosiljak*, all brought over from Dalmatia. This was a far cry from the flowers on the terraces and verandas in their native villages, but it served as a substitute for the Old World atmosphere and made their homesickness bearable.

The married fishermen now lived a more contented and comfortable life. Their clothes were washed and mended, their meals were properly cooked, and when needed their mates went with them on the boats and helped at the helm or at some other less arduous task. They were raising their families. Now they had a purposeful and a useful existence. Needless to say, not all of them lived with their families. Some were single and others had their families back home.

COMMUTING BETWEEN LOUISIANA AND DALMATIA

Many Yugoslavs who had families in Dalmatia commuted back and forth on an annual basis. In May they would tie their boats, leave them in care of friends or relatives, and depart for their native villages on the Adriatic. Here they would spend the summer months with their families, refurbish their vineyards and olive groves and mend their fishing nets and in late September, after the wine harvest, return to Louisiana for another eight months of oyster fishing. If two or three partners worked together they alternated in visiting their families. Some would leave in May of one year and return in September of the following year. Their share of the profits would be waiting for them.

This type of commuting was popular from around 1880 to the eve of the First World War. As stated previously in this study, there were two types of immigrants: the permanent ones and others who came to earn a few thousand dollars and return to their families or sweethearts. Naturally the latter type did the commuting. Traveling back and forth every May and September fitted well with the oyster fishing in winter months and the work in vineyards and olive groves in summer months. The frequent trips were inexpensive: a steamship ticket from New York to Trieste during the 1880s and 1890s was only $25. Many an oysterman's United Slavonian Benevolent Association's membership record reads: "May 1887, took leave of absence; September 1887, re-instated; May 1890, leave of absence," and so on. The years differed for members but the sequence of entries was the same. The last entry usually revealed whether they finally settled in Louisiana or returned to Dalmatia for good.

To a lesser degree this intercontinental commuting continues today, but much less frequently. The stays are longer: two or three years in Yugoslavia for every six or seven years in Louisiana. There is one substantial difference, however: the father acquires an American citizenship as soon as he can so that his children may follow in his footsteps and come to the United States whenever they wish. Their neighbors in Dalmatian villages usually refer to these children as *mali Amerikantsi* (little Americans).

PROCEDURES IN PREPARING
THE CULTIVATED OYSTERS

Between 1850 and the early 1950s the task of preparing oysters from the time the seed oysters were removed from the natural reefs to the final delivery of the finished product to the city dealers required long hours of hard labor and constant care and supervision of the oysters. To illustrate this let us follow a typical Yugoslav oyster grower of yesteryear in preparing his counter-stock oysters for the market. (After the installation of engines and dredges sometime in the early 1900s, some of the hard labor outlined below was removed, but the steps and the method remained the same until the early 1950s.)

1. He traveled a full day sailing, rowing, and pushing his oyster smack or lugger to reach the public reefs on the east side of the Mississippi River.

2. He tonged the seed oysters from water bottoms from an average depth of three to six feet to his boat. If the boat were of a large size (lugger) he tonged the oysters in a specially constructed skiff and transferred them to the boat. Regardless which method he used, it usually took all day to load the oyster boat.

3. He sailed, rowed, and pushed his boat, now fully loaded, to his private oyster bedding grounds; a trip requiring another full day of hard labor.

4. He carefully shoveled the oysters overboard onto his bedding grounds, spreading them evenly so that they would not be overcrowded. The boat or skiff was held in place by poles driven into the bayou bottom, each pole passing through a rope loop attached to the bow and to the stern. As he spread a sufficient number of oysters over a given area, he moved the boat away from the spread oysters a distance equal to that which he could throw them with the shovel; this planted the oysters a square at a time. This he continued until the boat was empty. Again, if the boat were too large to maneuver over the reefs, he transferred the oysters to the skiff which he towed behind the boat for this purpose.

5. He left the oysters there from ten to eighteen months until they were fully grown and ready to be harvested. He then tonged the oysters into an oyster skiff.

6. He pushed the skiff to a landing by his camp where he "culled" the clustered oysters. The marketable oysters were placed in three different piles according to size: large, medium, and small. The oysters that were too small to sell—the discards—he placed in a fourth pile to be replanted. The oyster shells, which varied from 10 percent to 90 percent of the total, depending on the mortality rate of that season, he wheelbarrowed to the shore to build a "beach" around the camp, or he planted them as a base for a new reef.

7. The marketable oysters were thrown overboard on a specially prepared hard-bottom reef, in separate piles according to size.

8. The oysters that were too small to sell he transferred to the bedding grounds and replanted them for further growth.

9. A day or two before he took the oysters to the market he tonged the culled oysters and loaded them into his boat.

10. He sailed the boat up the Mississippi River to New Orleans or sold the oysters directly to the passing lugger, "the freight boat," which took them to the New Orleans market.

11. Upon arriving in New Orleans, he sold the oysters, collected the money, and, finally realizing the fruit of his arduous labor, returned to his camp.

Among those who entered the oyster-fishing field between 1880 and 1920 were the following Yugoslavs: (To avoid repetition, names listed on pages 120–121, which cover the time included in this period, do not appear below.) Jerome Andrich, Anthony N. Antunica,

Matthew Antunica, Thomas Anticich, Anthony Antunovich, John Antunovich, Anthony M. Anzulovich, Matthew B. Bakalich, Nicholas Barach, Gajetan Barbalich, Matthew Barbier, Anthony K. Barisich, John Barisich, Jack Begovich, John Bekavac, Rado Bendich, Kristo Benovich, Jack Bilich, Donko Bjazevich, Anthony Bjelancich, Nicholas Bogdanovich, Milan Boronja, Visko Bronzini, Marin Busko, Baldo Butirich, John M. Butirich, John Cace, Marko A. Cibilich, Dominick Cvitanovich, Nicholas Cvitanovich, John Crnjak, John Deskovich, Nicholas Dimak, Matthew Djuka, Matthew Duba, Andrew Dujmich, Anthony Farac, Nicholas Ficovich, Joseph Francicevich, Matthew Frankovich, Andrew Giurisich, Simo Glavocich, Nicholas Gojkovich, Anthony Grzina, Baldo Hajtilovich, Marine Hihar, Vincent Ilijich, Steve Ivichevich, Tripo Ivovich, Frank Jasich, Paul Jasich, Joseph Jurakovich, Savo Juncevich, Nicholas Jurich, Frank Jurisich, Joseph J. Jurisich, Jack Kopanica, Marko Kopajtich, Anthony Kos, John Kos, Dominick Kovacevich, Baldo Kovacich, John Krstelj, Steve Kristicevich, Anthony M. Kuluz, Matthew Kuluz, Visko Kuluz, Matthew Kumarich, Joseph Kurucar, Peter Kuselich, Marko Lolich, Anthony Lulich, John S. Lulich, John Maras, Anthony Markovich, Simo Markovich, John P. Marinovich, Nicholas Marinovich, Dominick Martinolich, John Mazuran, Danko Merkovich, Anthony Mestrovich, Nikola Mihocevich, Nikola Milicich, Bozo Mijoch, Nikola Miscich, Donko Mrkotich, Anthony M. Mrlais, Joseph Murina, Kuzma Murina, Ilija Mustur, Anthony A. Nesanovich, Jack Nesanovich, Anthony Nikolac, George Okiljevich, George Parun, Novak Pavlovich, Baldo Perivancich, John Perovich, Nicholas Persich, Dominick Petricevich, Vlaho Petrovich, Anthony Poluta, John Poluta, Matthew Poluta, Peter Poluta, Anthony Popich, John Popich, Nicholas Popich, Anthony Protich, John P. Rozich, George Rudolf, Matthew Ruvo, John Salatich, Nicholas Salatich, Anthony Salinovich, Risto Sarich, Nicholas Satara, Cedomir Seferovich, John A. Seput, Anthony Sesa, John Skalko, Vincent Skurich, Anthony F. Slavich, George J. Slavich, Gregory Slavich, Donko Spaleta, Karlo Stela, John Stuk, Matthew Stuk, Andrew Taliancich, Leopold Taliancich, Peter A. Taliancich, Anthony Tesvich, John S. Tesvich, Kuzma F. Tesvich, Luke S. Tesvich, Matthew V. Tomasovich, Mato Trinaestich, Anthony Tripkovich, John Vasiljevich, Matthew Vela, Steve Vela, Savo Vecerich, Bozo Vodanovich, George Vodanovich, Vincent Vodanovich, John Vodopija, Matthew Vujevich, George Vujnovich, Joseph

Oyster luggers unloading oysters at the Mississippi River levee at the foot of Dumaine Street, New Orleans, *circa* 1899.

Photo courtesy Glenn E. Martina

Oyster luggers *Enterprise, Desoto, New Petrograd,* and *Frisco* at the Esplanade Street wharf on the Mississippi River, *circa* 1938. Having delivered the oysters to New Orleans dealers, the boats are awaiting their owners to take them to the Louisiana bayous for another load of oysters.

Vukasov, John Vulich, Peter Zaninovich, Nicholas Zecevich, Matthew Zelencich, Anthony L. Zibilich, Fred Zibilich, George D. Zibilich, John B. Zibilich, Luke A. Zibilich, Matthew Zile, and Philip Zuvanik.

OYSTER REEF OWNERSHIP

To protect their oysters and identify the location the oystermen leased the water bottoms, at a set fee per acre, from Jefferson, St. Bernard, or Plaquemines Parish depending on the location. Since 1902, however, when the Louisiana Oyster Commission (the predecessor of the Louisiana Wild Life and Fisheries Commission) was established, the oysters-water bottoms have been leased from the state of Louisiana.

The private oyster bedding grounds are marked by signs erected on poles stuck in the muddy bottoms. The signs usually bear the owner's name or his initials preceded by the word *oysters*. At first, oyster poaching was a troublesome problem, but when the poachers learned that the Slav oystermen took the idea of private oyster beds seriously and were willing to use their shotguns to protect the oysters, poaching decreased to a minimum. However, the owners are not able to guard all their reefs which may be scattered throughout several areas, bays, and bayous and oyster poaching is still a problem.

Through the past hundred years numerous stories have evolved on this subject. Some are sad but most are humorous. Zeljko Franks remembers one afternoon during the late 1930s observing a strange skiff on a distant reef owned by his late father Joseph Franks and the late George Vujnovich. After bringing this to Captain George's attention the two of them rode to the scene on a fast boat. Catching the poacher, a slight acquaintance with a large pile of oysters in his skiff, Captain George asked him angrily: "Don't you know that you are stealing my oysters?" Knowing that he would not be prosecuted for the oysters that he took to eat for himself and his family, the poacher replied: "But, Captain George, this is for me and my family for supper." Taken aback momentarily, Captain George looked at him, then at the large pile of oysters, and exclaimed: "You show me a pot big enough to cook those oysters and you can have them." The man realized that he could not top that one, defeatedly dumped all but a handful of oysters over the side and, with a promise never to return, left the area.

CHANGES IN LIVING CONDITIONS
AFTER THE 1893 STORM

Until 1893 the center of oyster cultivation was the Bayou Cook area. There were other areas of oyster production, but this was the place where most of the oyster people lived. The estimated population of Bayou Cook area at this time was about four hundred persons. Here they lived a contented family life until their lives were suddenly changed by the hurricane of October, 1893. The horrors and the sufferings of that storm are described in Chapter Five.

When the survivors recovered from the shock of the storm's ravages, many quit oyster fishing for good. Some moved to the higher ground along the river and became farmers, some moved to the Mississippi Gulf Coast—Bay St. Louis and Biloxi; others moved to New Orleans and found employment there or opened small businesses. Oyster bars, saloons, and restaurants were often the business occupations followed by the storm's survivors. Cedomir Seferovich, one of those who lost his wife and a child in the storm, abandoned his reefs and went to New Orleans and opened an oyster saloon. Some returned to their native Dalmatia and resettled there. However, most of the survivors remained in the oyster business. They built new and better boats and new camps but not on the same sites. They avoided crowded settlements and built their camps-homes at a site surrounded by their oyster reefs. Their families remained with them, but their lives took a new direction after the storm. Some settled their families on higher ground at Empire, Buras, and Olga where the families were safer and the children could go to primary schools. Others did not want their children to go through the hardships they themselves had known and decided that a new way of life lay in education which the city of New Orleans provided. As soon as the eldest child reached school age, the oysterman took his wife and the children to the city and placed them with relatives; or he rented a small house, usually half of a shotgun double, located within walking distance of the oyster landing on the Mississippi. The husband showed the family the location of the grocery, the butcher shop, the nearest drugstore, and the vegetable market and returned to his camp and oyster fishing. The children attended school faithfully, although sometimes grudgingly if both parents were from the old country and the household language was Croatian. English, for them, was a new language and the first year or two presented environmental and communicative difficulties. The new bayou pupils were at first ridiculed and bullied by the neighborhood children and schoolmates. But this was of short duration; it ended when they were provoked into fist fights with the strongest bullies who would usually scream, "Enough!" after the first few seconds, for they were no match for the young country boys who had strong muscles developed by healthy outdoor living and net and oar pulling in the Louisiana bayous. After the first such encounter the boys, and the girls alongside them of course, were accepted on equal terms, notwithstanding their "foreign" ways which soon disappeared as they entered the mainstream of New Orleans life.

Many of the oystermen, after they acquired motorized boats, made weekly trips to the city to bring oysters to market and to visit with their families. This went on for the eight to nine months out of the year which fortunately coincided with the nine-month school year. During the summer months the family would pack and move to the camp. Here the children had a prolonged country vacation and the families were together. Commuting continued widespread until the Second World War and still persists, to a lesser degree. I still remember with fondness many a pleasant and a carefree summer I spent fishing, boat riding, swimming, and enjoying the outdoor life at the family oyster camp on Lake Grand Ecaille during my early teens.

MARKETING AND TRANSPORTING OYSTERS

From the beginning of the oyster cultivation in 1850s until the oyster vessels were motorized during the first decade of the twentieth century, the Yugoslav oystermen's most time-consuming activity was transportation. It robbed them of their precious fishing time and sapped their energy.

At first they used the regular fishing skiffs and later designed and constructed low-decked, shallow draught, one-masted, lateen-rigged sailboats from thirty to forty feet in length, similar to the *leuti* with which they fished sardines during their youth off the Dalmatian coast. Many were built at the shipyards at Olga, and later at Empire and Buras by the Dalmatians who brought the boat-building skills with them from their native towns and villages. Korcula, Ston, cities in the Bay of Kotor, and other coastal towns along the Adriatic were for centuries world renowned for their boat-building skills.

These oyster smacks were propelled by sails, oars, and, in shallow waters, by pushing poles that were specially designed for this purpose. The boats had long narrow "walkways" along each side so that the oystermen walked from bow to stern pushing on the poles thereby moving the boat forward. They "walked" from one end of the bayou to the other. They placed flat boards on the inside of the boats so that they could scoop the oysters with a shovel and spread the oysters over their reefs. These vessels were usually owned and manned by two men —brothers, cousins, or close relatives who worked as partners, equally sharing the profits and the hardships. Since the boats did not have any equipment except the very basic rigging, they did not cost much (three to five hundred dollars), and most of the oystermen were able, in a few years, to purchase their own boats, so that very few Yugoslavs, at that time, worked as hired hands but operated and worked their own vessels. This fitted their enterprising spirit well, for they were an extremely rugged and individualistic people; their pride and independent spirit did not tolerate orders about their daily work, at least not from each other. The boats carried patriotic names such as: *Louisiana, America, George Washington,* and names which reminded them of the old country such as: *Galeb (Sea Gull), Slaven, Dalmacia, Dubrovnik, Vila (Nymph),* and *Danica (Morning Star).*

As the years passed by, they improved their boats, and built them larger and more seaworthy so that by 1870s and 1880s several Yugoslav oystermen owned luggers that carried from 150 to 200 barrels of oysters. Others built two-masted schooners. These boats were used primarily to transport the seed oysters from the public reefs to their private bedding grounds and to bring the marketable oysters to New Orleans. Of the two operations, transporting the seed oysters from the east side of the river to the west side was more dangerous; it required more time, effort, and excellent seamanship. Before the opening of the Empire and the Ostrica Locks during the early 1900s, this was done by a long, indirect, and tedious route. They would load the boats with the seed oysters from the public reefs on the east side of the river. During the months when the river level was high, they would enter the Mississippi at the Baptiste Collette Bayou (about five miles below Olga), cross the river and at the Jump, near Venice, enter the Grand Pass and go southward to the Gulf of Mexico then turn in a northwesterly direction, enter the Bastian Bay at Grand Bayou Pass, cross the Bastian Bay and proceed to Bayou Cook, Bayou Le Chutte, Ferrand Bay, Ferrand Bayou, or Adams Bay, transfer the oysters to a smaller skiff, and bed them. The smaller boats, which could not dare the open seas, usually followed this route.

Some of the oystermen from the Buras area, I am told, would enter the river at Baptiste Collette Bayou, sail the few miles up the river, tie along the levee, wheelbarrow the oysters across the levee to the skiffs waiting in a canal, and, while the skiffs' crews bedded the oysters, return to the natural reefs for another load of seed oysters.

If the river level was low so that the Baptiste Collette Bayou was impassable, the larger luggers and schooners would sail clear around the mouth of the Mississippi River, sometimes taking advantage of the bays and passes on the route, depending on the wind and the currents. The straight-line distance was not more than fifteen to twenty miles, but the actual distance traveled was over one hundred miles. Needless to say, this was a long, dangerous route, filled with contrary currents and tides, which required the best of seamanship.

A special brand of seamen evolved who prided themselves on taking a fully loaded boat across these treacherous waters in record time. Some of these Yugoslavs sailed on the boats that brought them here; others learned their navigating skills from their fathers along the Adriatic coast. After all, the Dalmatians have been renowned sailors for centuries, and they soon adapted their skills to the low-decked, shallow-draught Louisiana oyster boats. Many of them excelled at this, took out their captain's papers, and hired themselves to the oyster companies or partnerships to transport their oysters, while others bought luggers and schooners and used them solely to transport the seed and the marketable oysters for profit. Many a hair-raising experience was lived through by these captains and their crews as they raced their boats across these perilous waters. They raced with each other and daringly took desperate chances to deliver the oysters in a record time. An *esprit de corps* developed among them and they became the elite of the oystermen. Many a time they would encounter high winds, and rough seas with waves splashing across the decks of their oyster-laden boats and, if the pumps could not keep up with the incoming water, be forced to dump the oysters overboard to avoid sinking A one-way trip would take from one to two days, depending on the winds and the tides. Sometimes when they became becalmed due to a lack of wind the trip would take longer. If it took too long, some of the oysters, depending on the temperature, would spoil before they

Capt. Ralph Pausina and his crew dredging for oysters.

Oyster luggers awaiting their turn to pass through the Empire locks to deliver the seed oysters to the oyster bedding grounds, *circa* 1938.

Photo courtesy Joseph M. Jurisich

arrived at the bedding grounds with the seed, or to New Orleans with the marketable oysters.

During the sailboat era the Yugoslav oystermen either brought the oysters to the market in New Orleans or sold them to the lugger-men who transported them to the city. Either way they were at a dis-advantage. If they took the cultivated oysters to the market they lost almost a week's time making the roundtrip and selling the oysters. This time could have been used to work their reefs and prepare addi-tional oysters. If the winds were favorable, they may have cut the traveling time by a day or two and rested a little on the way. The up-river trip usually took two days, sometimes more. When the wind died down they hired a pair of mules to pull the boat along a canal or the levee; or they may have pulled it themselves to save a few dol-lars. Sometimes they would just give up and hail a passing tugboat to be towed to the city. The fee for this, in the early days, ranged from twenty-five to fifty dollars, which usually represented their profits, de-pending on the size of the boat or the number of boats pulled. If be-cause of a favorable wind, too many boats arrived at the market at the same time, they were at the mercy of the buyers who dictated the price. The oystermen had no choice but to sell at any price, for time was against them; the oysters could not keep forever. On the other hand, if the winds were contrary, the trip may have taken too long or the weather may have turned warm, then the oysters arrived opened and spoiled. When this happened they would silently shrug their shoulders and, in their stoical Slavic way, give a wharf boy a dollar or two, instruct him to shovel the oysters over the side, and return to their camps, the trip a total loss.

Later on as the number of boats and the tugboats on the river increased, the oyster boats met the tugboats at designated places, such as Olga, or Socola Canal, and from there were pulled to New Orleans. The return trip was accomplished on their own. This was much easier, the boat was empty, and the current was with them.

Luggermen either bought the oysters from oystermen at their bedding grounds or met them at river landings across from canals es-pecially dug to bring the oysters as near the river as possible. Usually these canals had a large shed where the oysters were unloaded and carried in baskets of a particular size—so that a tally could be kept by the captain—over the levee to the waiting luggers. There were many such canals on both sides of the river. Socola Canal, above Port Sulphur, Jurjevich Canal, and the Valer Canal near Ostrica, and the Nestor Canal below Pointe a la Hache are some of the canals that were used for this purpose.

If the Yugoslav oystermen sold the oysters to the luggermen, they had to sell them at a much lower price than they would get in the city. The oysters were sold by the barrel. Curiously there were two different barrel measures. Oysters sold or bought at the bedding grounds were measured by the "bank" or "fisherman" barrel while those sold in New Orleans were measured in "market" barrel. The fisherman barrel was equal to one and one half the market barrel. That is, the fisherman barrel held three present-day sacks of oysters, and the market barrel two sacks. Around 1880 the fisherman barrel sold for one dollar at the bedding grounds, though in New Orleans the market barrel sold for two dollars. Later the prices in New Orleans and at the bedding grounds and the river landings were equalized, but the two different measures remained so that the luggerman's profit was the extra one-half market barrel that he obtained out of each bank barrel. That is, regardless of price, which fluctuated, he was assured of 50 percent gross profit on his investment.

The natural-reef noncultivated oysters were brought to the Old Basin Canal and to Bayou St. John and there sold from between fifty cents to eighty cents per barrel. The cultivated oysters were brought to the inclined landing in New Orleans at the foot of Dumaine Street. The landing, which could accommodate up to two hundred boats was known locally as the Picayune Pier or the Lugger Bay. The small boats would ground their bows on the landing, the exact spot depending on the height of the river.

Until the motorization of the oyster industry, when the oysters could be delivered at a predictable time, the oystermen sold directly to restaurants, oyster shops, and shucking houses who sent their wagons to the oyster landings to buy the amount they needed. The buyers haggled with the oystermen or the lugger captain-owners about the price, going from one boat to the other. To insure delivery some preordered their supply, especially the larger restaurants and the shucking houses, while others, hoping for an excess of oysters at the market, would take their chances. When oysters were plentiful they bought them cheap, and when scarce the buyers paid dearly or could buy none at all.

The following list contains the names of some of the boats and the names of their owners. These boats operated in the Louisiana waters during the first two decades of the twentieth century and later. Since this was the transition period from sailboats to motorization, about half were sailboats while the rest were former sailboats with engines installed sometime after 1902 or newly constructed motorized boats. A few were sternwheelers while the others were propeller driven. For this list I am indebted to Marko A. Cibilich who fished oysters in the Louisiana bayous during this era.

Boat	Owner
Dalmacia	Blaise Anticich
Antunica	Anthony Antunica
Example	Gajetan Barbarich
Austria	John Barbier
Protector	Bendich Brothers
Robinsoe	Peter Bendich
Sufran	L. Bilich and George Slavich
Irresistible	Matthew J. Bilich
Carolina	Miho Biskupovich
Joseph Brajkovich	Joseph Brajkovich
Two Sons	Bubrig Brothers
Independence	Marko Dezina
Gladiator	Anthony Dimak
Andro D.	Andrew Dujmov
Karmela	Frank and Bosko Franicevich
Charlice	Rado Hihar
Andjelina	Savo Juncevich
Radeski	Miho Jurich
New Atlas	Anthony L. and Vlaho L. Jurisich
Fourth of July	Vincent, Joseph, and John Jurisich
Gem	Vlaho J. Jurisich
Flying Star	Vlaho and Donko Jurisich
Bon Pere	Peter Kopanica and Marine Delo
Nick and I	Miho and Nick Kresich
Two Cousins	Anthony Kristicevich
Jozefina	Anthony Kulisich
Dalmacia	Kuluz Brothers
Grand Duke	Marijan Lalich
Supirija	Vincent Lenac
Two Brothers	Jacob Mihaljevich
Mihaljevich Brothers	John Mihaljevich
Louisiana	Joseph Mihaljevich
Two Brothers No. 2	Matthew Mihocevich

I Am Go	Matthew Mihocevich
Young Eagle	Anthony and Luke Morovich
New Year	Matthew Muhoberac
Venus	Simo Murina
New Brilliant	Anthony Negodich
Trpanj	Matthew Nesanovich
Three Brothers	Matthew and Steve Parun
Zenta	Vincent Pausina
Three Brothers	Spiro, Milos, and Gus Pavlovich
Superior	Andro and Bozo Petrovich
Rising Star	Peter A. and Peter V. Petrovich
Champion	George Pivach, John Sumich, John Lulich,
New Champion	Dominick Taliancich, John M. Sumich,
Young Champion	Tony Lulich, Peter Cvitanovich, and Sam Spanja
Mali Brilliant	Poluta Brothers
Flying Dutchman	John Radetich
Samson	Peter Rozich
Evening Star	Anthony Rudolfich
New York	Salatich Brothers
Sunrise	Vincent Seput
Rogers later renamed *Petrograd*	Simo Slavich and Kristo Murina
Cupido	Donko Stuk
Adriatic	Simo Anthony Tomasovich
Traveler	John, Joseph, and Marijan Vela
New Princess	Anthony Vezich and John Zaninovich
Lion	Simo Vidos
North Star	Bozo, George, and Vincent Vodanovich
Leader	Matthew Vuskovich
Princess	Vincent Vuskovich
Young John, Venus	Anthony and John Zegura
Duba	Steve Zegura
City of New Orleans	Steve Zegura
Happy New Year	Bozo Zibilich and Anthony Tomasovich
Elmeri	Jack, Matthew, and Peter Zibilich
Miho	Miho Zibilich
Steve Z.	Steve Zuvich

The first Yugoslav oysterman in Louisiana to install a motor on his boat was Miho Zibilich on the *Miho* in 1902. Others soon followed, for although it represented a sizable investment, forcing many to borrow money or to form partnerships, they realized the enormous advantages of rapid transportation and assured means of arrival on time for a perishable industry such as theirs. (However, the smaller fishermen kept their sailing vessels, and it was not until 1920 that the last of the quaint sailing smacks disappeared from the scene forever.) Now they were not only able to transport the oysters in a shorter time, but, more important, they could predict and control the time of arrival with the oysters at the market. This enabled them to make a definite commitment to the city dealers for delivery on such and such a day if not the hour. The dealers, in turn, to assure delivery, started giving definite orders for a definite amount of oysters on a certain day, the day usually being Thursday, for Friday consumption. Now the Yugoslav oystermen could rest during traveling time and arrive at their destination refreshed. They were freed from the exhausting drudgery of rowing and pushing their vessels.

Equipping a sizable oyster lugger with an engine, winches, and other necessary equipment meant a large investment before any substantial oyster growing could be undertaken. As a result, the small individual oystermen were replaced by larger operators, partnerships, and companies, who hired experienced oystermen and newcomers to work for them. Consequently the small individual oyster fisherman disappeared from the scene. The new launches were from fifty to sixty feet long and could carry from six hundred to nine hundred sacks of oysters.

As a result of the introduction of the oyster dredges, the opening of the Ostrica and the Empire Locks, and the general motorization of the oyster industry—all of them came about the same time: during the first half of the first decade of the twentieth century—oyster production increased tremendously so that loading and unloading the loose oysters with baskets consumed too much time. The luggers' and the river packets' captain-owners urged the introduction of sacks, to be filled by the oyster fishermen. The oystermen agreed to this, purchased the empty sacks, and shipped their oysters in them. Instead of oysters being sold loose and measured by the barrel, they were sold by the sack, one market barrel equivalent to two sacks. The state defined and legalized the sack measure, and the fishermen obtained the state-approved metal basket measure for the amount of oysters that went in each sack.

At first, the city oyster dealers insisted that the fishermen sew the tops of the sacks rather than simply tie them. The fishermen balked at this, complaining that it took too much of their time and that it was unnecessary. Also, because many dealers failed to return the empty sacks, friction developed between dealers and fishermen, and a sort of a "sack war" ensued. The fishermen reasoned that they could not go around the city picking up the empty sacks but that the dealers could do this when delivering oysters and would be more apt to do so if the sacks were theirs. Finally, this was resolved peacefully. The dealers agreed to supply the sacks and did not insist that the fishermen sew the sacks but simply tie them at the top. All this speeded up the process of oyster production and delivery, and as a result the city was "flooded" with oysters. In 1906 the fishermen were getting between 45 and 50 cents per sack; by 1913 this dropped to 22½ cents per sack.

After the First World War the oyster boat landing was moved from the foot of Dumaine Street to the foot of Barracks Street. The oysters were brought here directly by the oystermen in diesel powered launches which most of them owned.

Several of them with larger boats also carried freight for other fishermen who chose not to make the trip to the city or who did not have enough oysters to justify it. Some of the owners used their boats exclusively to carry oysters for other oystermen. Instead of buying the oysters from fishermen and reselling them to the dealers, they simply delivered the dealers' orders and charged "freight" to the fishermen by the sack, which usually varied from 10 to 20 percent of the price.

However, during those years most of the oysters were brought to the city by the oystermen themselves. I remember, during the late 1930s, several such trips on a loaded boat, the *Royal Queen*, owned by George Vujnovich and Joseph Franks, with over six hundred sacks aboard, and the decks awash. The boat would be loaded with the prepared oysters on Wednesday of each week. The loading would start at about 5:00 o'clock in the afternoon and last well into the night; the boat's spotlights were used after dark. When the boat was fully loaded, or when the order was filled, the boat, with a two-man crew, would leave for an all-night trip to New Orleans. It would reach the Mississippi River through the Harvey Canal just at dawn.

The boats tied up at the Barracks Street wharf, either at the wharf or alongside other oyster luggers that had arrived there first. The oysters were unloaded by stevedores, who carried sacks on their shoulders, and placed them by each dealer's designated area to await his trucks for the distribution through the city. As the dealers received the oysters, they would place an order for the coming week by supplying the oystermen with the necessary number of empty sacks. Usually no words were necessary; the tags on the bundles told the story. This weekly cycle continued from September to the middle of May each year.

During this period—from the First World War to the early 1950s —on any Thursday during the oyster season more than a dozen boats could be seen unloading oysters at the Barracks Street wharf in New Orleans. *"Kako si?"* and *"dobro jutro"* were heard just as often as, if not more than, "How are you?" and "Good morning." Some of the Yugoslav boats and their owners, bringing oysters to New Orleans were: *Betsy Ross*, owned by Peter and George Vujnovich; *Capt. Peter*, Peter Taliancich; *Dakota*, John Popich; *De Soto*, Luke Tesvich; *New Atlas*, Anthony and Vlaho Jurisich; *Enterprise*, Anthony Nikolac and John Antunovich; *Franka* and *Capt. Simo*, Simo Slavich and Sons; *Imperial* and *Frisco*, Vlaho Petrovich; *Indiana* and *New Petrograd*, Baldo Pausina; *Irresistible*, Matt J. Bilich; *J. V. Franks*, Zeljko and Zvonko Franks; *Royal Queen*, George Vujnovich and Joseph Franks; *Young John*, Bozo Zibilich; *Capt. Mike*, Marko Vujnovich; and *Dixie*, Matthew Barbier, Anthony Morovich, and Luke Morovich.

The boat crews, if they had families in the city, lingered for a day or two; otherwise they left immediately, to begin preparing oysters for the following week. The return trip was usually made by two or three boats going in the same direction and secured alongside each other so that the oystermen socialized and compared business notes during the six-to-eight-hour trip.

The Barracks Street wharf was closed during the early 1950s, and the oyster delivery to the city by the individual oyster boats— a hundred-year practice—came to an end. Since then, through the present-day, the dealers' trucks meet the oystermen's boats at several points: at Port Sulphur, Empire, Buras, Violet, Hopedale, Myrtle Grove, and Chef Menteur Pass. Oystermen bring the oysters that are sold for canning directly to a factory, which is usually located on a canal or bay to permit the boats to dock by its loading platform.

The Mississippi River packet boats, which ran a route between New Orleans and Burrwood, stopped along the way wherever there was something to load or unload, brought a substantial portion of oysters to New Orleans from lower Plaquemines Parish. They operated on the river from the 1890s to 1960. During the seventy-odd years of their operation, there were several packet boats that plied the river, from the first steamer, *Grover Cleveland*, to the diesel-powered *New Majestic*. Other boats were: *Reliance, Hercules, Majestic, Independent, Louisa, Ozone, America, Victoria*, and *El Rito*. In September, 1960, they, too, abandoned their dwindling routes to the swifter and more economical trucks.

MANY CONSIDERED OYSTER FISHING AS A TRANSIENT OCCUPATION

Until a generation ago, when the oyster industry became highly mechanized, many Yugoslav oystermen considered it to be a transient occupation at which to earn and save enough money to return to the old country or to open a saloon, a restaurant, an oyster dealership in New Orleans, or to buy rental property and retire on the income. Some did save enough to buy extensive rental property in the city and retire at a relatively early age. They became a "separate class" so that they were called by the other Yugoslavs the *rentijeri* (rentiers). Others left the oyster fishing unexpectedly when some disaster such as hurricane or fire struck and destroyed their means of livelihood. For example, Anthony Gentilich left oystering and entered the restaurant business after his boat, the *Molat*, was wrecked against the Bay St. Louis, Mississippi, bridge during the 1915 hurricane. The Vodanovich brothers, Bozo, George, and Vincent, came to New Orleans, and each opened a restaurant after their boat, the *North Star*, burned to the water level in 1918 at Bayou Lazere.

The Yugoslav oystermen adapted easily to the city and its commercial life. Here they applied the same formula as when they fished oysters: hard work, thrift, honesty, and perseverance, and they succeeded. Some prospered considerably, some struggled on, but very few returned to the oysterman's life.

THE PRESENT-DAY YUGOSLAV OYSTERMEN

The present-day Yugoslav oystermen still get most of the cultivated oysters from seed oysters that they obtain from legally protected public reefs and transplant to their private bedding grounds. There the oysters mature and acquire the flavor of the cultivated ones. However, instead of transplanting the seed oysters some oystermen plant old shells or clam shells on their reefs where the conditions for natural oyster propagation and growth are favorable. The drifting oyster spat (the spawn of an oyster), as it sinks to the bottom, attaches itself to the hard surface of oyster or clam shells and in eighteen to twenty months becomes a fully mature oyster ready for marketing. About 20 to 30 percent of the cultivated oysters are grown in this manner.

During the months when the natural state-owned oyster reefs are open to the public, many oystermen dredge and immediately cull and sack the oysters of marketable size and sell them to dealers. A good portion of oysters for shucking and cooking comes from these reefs.

The method of getting the oysters out of the water and preparing them for the market has changed drastically. The auxiliary skiffs have disappeared from the scene. When mature, the oysters are dredged to the deck of the boat, immediately culled there, and brought to the nearest boat landing near a highway to meet the waiting trucks; a simplified, straightforward and time-saving operation. Gone are the days of transporting oysters from the water to a skiff, back to water, then to a skiff again, and finally to a boat. Almost never seen are oyster tongs which the oystermen used for over a hundred years to get the oysters out of the water. By the early 1950s they were entirely replaced by the more efficient dredges.

Several of the more enterprising Yugoslav oystermen have recently installed on their boats conveyor-belt machinery to transfer the oysters from where the dredges are emptied to the load-carrying area. They have also installed high-pressure water nozzles to "push" the seed oysters from the boat deck into the water, a comparatively effortless method of bedding them. This is a far cry from the primitive hand-picking and planting method of the 1850s.

Camps and the oyster reefs of the Yugoslav oystermen are located in the Louisiana estuarine areas in Jefferson, St. Bernard, and Plaquemines parishes. Among the English- and the French-sounding names of the bays, lakes, canals, and bayous such as *Lake Washington, Anderson Bay, Bay de la Chenniere, Pierre Bay*, are also Croatian names. A few miles south of Pointe a la Hache on the east side of the Mississippi River there is a *Fucich Bayou*; across from Boothville a *Jurjevich Canal*; four miles north of Ostrica a *Cuselich Bay*; a few miles south of Port Sulphur a *Bilich Bay*; between South Pass and Southeast Pass near the mouth of the Mississippi a *Cognevich Pass*; on the east side of the river a few miles north of Main Pass a *Yuratich Bend* and a *Yuratich Bayou*; and a *Morovich Canal* near Empire.

Presently there are not as many Yugoslavs engaged in the oyster

Cultivated Louisiana oysters on their way to the New Orleans oyster bars.
Photo courtesy Matt Farac

Oystermen and their ladies take time off to promote the oyster industry, June, 1952. From left to right: Joseph Franks, Stanley Pausina, Sam Carevich, Celina Popich, Lilian Moreno, Katie Pausina, Baldo V. Pausina, Zeljko Franks, Helen Franks, Peter Vujnovich, and George Vujnovich.
Photo courtesy H. L. Peace Publications

industry as in years past, but they still grow, cultivate, and sell a large percentage of Louisiana oysters. The majority of them are growers and cultivators. The following list, though not an all-inclusive one, presents a cross section of Yugoslavs and those of Yugoslav ancestry engaged in the oyster industry: the M. J. Bilich family, Mato Farac, M. S. Franicevich, Zvonko Franks, John E. Jurisich, Joseph J. Jurisich, Joseph M. Jurisich, Luke V. Jurisich, Mitchell Jurisich, Kuzma Murina, Captain Baldo and Ralph Pausina, Kuzma Petrovich, Luke Petrovich, Ivo N. Popich, Popich Brothers, Gerald Rusich, Nikola Skansi, Anthony and Frank Slavich, the Taliancich brothers, Anthony Tesvich, Luke Tesvich, Peter S. Tesvich, John Vezich, Peter Vujnovich, John Zaninovich, Ante E. Zibilich, Bozo Zibilich, Bozo Zibilich, Jr., Jack Zibilich, Mato and Milenko Zibilich, and Matthew D. Zibilich. As in the past, their numbers are still replenished by the cousins, relatives, and acquaintances from Dalmatia, for the Adriatic fishermen still make good and industrious oystermen, and America continues to be a land of opportunity to newcomers.

The typical Yugoslav oyster grower of today lives a far different life from that of his predecessor. He owns and operates one or more of the large, speedy, diesel-driven, machinery-equipped boats containing modern, comfortable living quarters, stainless steel kitchens, refrigeration facilities, two-way radio, and many other up-to-date navigational devices. He employs several workers who may be fellow Yugoslavs or native Louisianians. He operates from a comfortable, structurally sound, fully furnished multibedroom camp. He lives with his family in a three-to-four bedroom brick, centrally heated and air-conditioned home in New Orleans, Port Sulphur, Empire, or Buras, and commutes in a late model sedan at least once per week.

He belongs to the United Slavonian Benevolent Association, to the Louisiana Oyster Dealers and Growers Association, to one or two carnival organizations, participates in local civic affairs, and keeps in touch with his congressman and his legislators to inform them of his feelings about legislation that may affect his livelihood.

Friction that existed between the oyster growers and the dealers in the past has entirely disappeared. The majorities of both groups belong to the same above-mentioned trade organization where, in harmony and cooperation, they work together for the common good: the promotion and improvement of the oyster industry.

5

Battling the Elements

THE GULF OF MEXICO AREA, including south Louisiana, has been plagued with tropical cyclones, called *hurricanes* in this part of the world after the Caribbean word *hurakan*, meaning high winds. The first recorded Gulf hurricane occurred in 1462, according to records kept by the Maya.

Louisiana fishermen and coastal residents living along the bayous and the exposed shores were used to a certain amount of bad weather, and they took the ordinary storms in stride. The Yugoslavs, who brought considerable sea experience with them, also became accustomed to the Louisiana squalls and minor hurricanes. During a storm they suspended their fishing operations and waited for it to pass. Afterward, they repaired the damage and resumed their normal work.

However, every now and then—some say every generation, some bayou dwellers say every nineteen years, and some say that whenever God wills it—a devastating hurricane comes along and leaves destruction and desolation in its wake. The hurricane that destroyed the summer resort of Last Island (now called Isle Deniere or Denieres for there are now two islands) about eighty-five miles southwest of New Orleans and killed three hundred persons on August 18, 1856, was such a hurricane. Lafcadio Hearn made this storm famous with his imaginative description in his novel *Chita*. Another hurricane occurred on October 4, 1886, when over fifty persons were killed in southwestern Louisiana. There were many other hurricanes that were remembered for a year or two. But the hurricane that struck the south Louisiana coast on the night of October 1, 1893, was to be remembered for generations. It killed over two thousand persons in Louisiana, among them over two hundred South Slavs living in Bayou Cook and vicinity. From then on, whenever "the storm" was mentioned, whether by the oystermen in Louisiana or the returnees in Dalmatia, everyone knew it referred to the 1893 Louisiana hurricane. Other severe hurricanes were to follow: in 1915, in 1947, and, more recently, Audrey, Betsy, and Camille, but none of these can compare in the loss of life to the 1893 storm.

In 1893 the main concentration of the Yugoslav oystermen's camps on the west side of the river was in Bayou Cook proper. There were also camps in Bayou Ferrand, Ferrand Bay, Bayou Chutte, Bayou Courant, Grand Bayou, and Adams Bay, but the area was known as the Bayou Cook country.

The camps along the bayou shores were the oystermen's homes, where they lived all year with their families and raised their children. They had no other homes in New Orleans or on the high ground near the river as oystermen do today. The camps were well constructed. They rested on pilings driven deep into the ground and stood about six to eight feet off the marshy ground for protection from high tides and storm floodings. The four corner pilings were usually heavier than the rest and were driven deeper into the ground. They extended through the building to the roof. There were few doors and windows, and they were well constructed to withstand heavy winds and rains. This type of camp served them well and survived many a storm. As a storm approached—as they invariably did with some frequency during the hurricane season—the oystermen would gather their families, bring the chickens and maybe a piglet or two, if they were raising them for Christmas holidays, and other perishables into the camp, secure the luggers and skiffs with extra ropes, or anchor the heavier luggers in the middle of a bay away from destructive objects on the shore, bring an extra supply of water from the cisterns into the kitchen, secure the doors and windows, and hope for the best. During the storm, to pass the time, the men played poker or mended nets and the women crocheted or mended clothes. They weathered many an ordinary storm in this fashion.

THE HURRICANE OF OCTOBER 1–2, 1893

The hurricane of October 1–2, 1893, came from the Antilles unrecorded by the Cuban or the Miami weather station so that no warnings were given to the Louisiana residents. (Telegrams were in general use for this purpose by 1893.) It came upon them like a thief in the night, robbing them of their homes, their belongings, their dear ones, and in many cases their own lives. It came with winds averaging 140 miles per hour and a tidal wave estimated at twenty feet, leveling everything in its path.

October 1 was a Sunday, a day of rest and get-together for the folks of Bayou Cook and vicinity. They spent the day socializing, and some, remembering that it was the Sabbath, said a prayer. Toward evening menacing black clouds darkened the skies, followed by gusty rain, increased winds, and rising tides. By the time darkness fell the experienced oystermen realized that a hurricane was blowing somewhere in the Gulf, and, without alarming their families, they hoped and prayed that it would pass them by as many storms had done before or that it would blow itself out during the night, without doing heavy damage to their homes and luggers. But it struck the Bayou Cook area at about eleven o'clock that night. The tidal wave flooded the marshes, crushed the camps, smashed the luggers, and destroyed everything in its path. Many were drowned by the wave; others were killed or injured by the falling and flying timbers. In the confusion of the onslaught of wind and water, all in complete darkness, families were torn apart, children separated from their parents, and parents from each other. The hysterical cries of desperate mothers and fathers and frightened children calling out for each other mingled with the howling wind, rain, and rushing waters. The storm raged through the night, and when daylight came it revealed a sight of destruction, desolation, and death. The lumber from the wrecked camps was mixed with logs, torn trees, smashed boats, boats' rigging, furniture, and other debris floating on the surface of the murky water. The strong wooden pilings remained fast, pinpointing above the water the locations of the camps and happy homes which they supported a few hours before. Here and there human forms could be distinguished, some dead, others dying, and some clinging to the pilings and the debris, hoping and praying to be rescued. Most of the living were rescued before nightfall and, with the dead, were taken to higher ground. Not all the bodies were recovered, however, and not all the living and the injured were saved. Many, before the rescue parties could reach them, were swept away into the Gulf by receding waters.

All of the oystermen were seasoned sailors, and many, before settling in Louisiana to fish oysters, had navigated the oceans of the world and experienced storms on the high seas. Unhesitatingly many of them credited their survival on this night to a miracle. As they narrated later, they prayed fervently—reciting prayers they learned from their village priests—to St. Nicholas, patron saint of sailors, and to the Almighty; they made promises of sacrifices and became "believers." After the storm they attended church regularly, to which they had been complete strangers.

By midday Monday the water had receded sufficiently for the oystermen to stand and walk on the marshy ground. Most of the survivors were brought, or found their way, to Fred Stockfleth's store at Tropical Bend. Some walked through the marshes in water up to their waists while others came by skiffs, small boats, and anything that would float. The store was located on the high ground near the levee so that they were able to stand and rest on dry land. Stockfleth's generosity was boundless. He freely distributed his food and clothing stocks to the hungry and shivering survivors. Dead bodies from all directions were also brought here for identification and for delivery to relatives and authorities for burial. Every square foot of Stockfleth's space was occupied either by the living or the dead. Several survivors praised the generous man to the New Orleans newspaper reporters: "He is a true Christian, may God bless him for all he has done for us," and "I'll never be able to repay his kindness to me but I shall try," were typical expressions of appreciation.

From Tropical Bend they boarded the Fort Jackson train to New Orleans where they were helped by relatives, friends, the United Slavonian Association, and by the New Orleans storm-relief agencies.

Much could be written of the sufferings and the experiences of the coastal residents during that night. However, I shall confine my story to the experiences of the Yugoslavs, describing several incidents, some heroic, some miraculous, and many tragic. There were parents who unselfishly risked their lives to save their children; sons who left the safety of secure pilings to swim after their foundering parents; a sister who sacrificed her life by releasing her life-saving hold on her brother, who was having difficulty swimming with her clinging to him; and a mother, who, standing in water up to her shoulders, miraculously saved her small children by holding their heads above water all night.

The full impact of the hurricane was not known in New Orleans until Tuesday evening when the steamboat *Neptune* arrived from the scene with Kuzma Murina and several others on board who survived the storm by tying themselves to wooden pilings and who told a tale of horror, death, and destruction.

In the confusion of the first few days, many were reported dead who later turned up alive. Letters concerning the tragedy were dispatched to wives, mothers, and relatives in distant Dalmatia. The letters contained the names of those reported dead and those reported missing by the first arrivals from the scene. As the tragic news reached Sucuraj, Duba, Igrane, Ston, and other towns along the Adriatic a haunting sadness came over the people who had relatives and friends on the Louisiana bayous. Young wives, who overnight became widows, went into mourning, donned black clothing, and wailed through the village streets for their husbands. However, several of them were "widows" for only a few days, until other letters arrived telling them that their husbands were rescued, safe and sound. Then they—some embarrassingly—regretted their premature mourning. (I remember, in Sucuraj during the late 1930s, several of those "widows," who were by then old and gray, telling the wives whose husbands were in Louisiana, as they anxiously waited for the latest news about Louisiana hurricanes, not to despair or prematurely assume the worst as they did in 1893.)

Ivan Lupis, a Croatian writer of note, who was then living in New Orleans, wrote:

> *U gradu New Orleansu se za strasnu nesrecu saznalo tek Utorak vecer....* The people of New Orleans learned about the tragedy only Tuesday evening. That same night urgent help was organized: boats were hired, loaded with food, water, clothing, and medicine and sent "down the coast" to save the living, collect the injured, and bury the dead. Urgent assistance was essential to save the survivors who were suffering from hunger and thirst, and especially those left on isolated spots through the marsh, distant from habitation. . . . The United Slavonian Association spared no effort or funds to help its countrymen: members and non-members. A like example of brotherly generosity is not found anywhere in the history of our immigration. The first rescue boat that started down the Mississippi to help the suffering was a steamer hired by the association. No one questioned the cost but all worried about saving the living, bringing the injured to New Orleans, clothing those who lost all, and housing those whose homes were destroyed. All the oystermen who were in the city during the storm boarded the rescue vessels to search for their wives, children, relatives, and friends. . . . The association rented a large hall and

converted it into a makeshift hospital for the sick and the injured and a refugee center for the homeless. The association's physician took care of the sick and the injured and the association's pharmacy supplied the medicine, while the officers and the members bought and collected food and clothing.

As soon as the officers of the United Slavonian Association learned about the tragedy, they called a special meeting to decide on the best way to help their stricken countrymen. The *Daily Picayune* of October 4, 1893, reported the meeting as follows:

> There was a special meeting of the United Slavonian Benevolent Association yesterday. President R. J. Abramovich in the chair to consider the distress existing among fellow countrymen in the stricken district, many of the sufferers being brother members.
>
> It was resolved to charter a tugboat, place it in charge of a relief committee, load it with provisions and clothing and go to the assistance of the afflicted. One of the missions of the boat was to find bodies of drowned members and give them a decent burial.
>
> The *Annie Wood* was chartered yesterday and left at 4 o'clock in the afternoon. The relief committee is composed of Joseph Jurisich, Financial Secretary; John Popovich, Grand Marshal; S. Lalosevich, and V. Ilich and several others. The committee is not limited as to funds or restricted in any way, the only instruction being to "help."

Another meeting was held on October 7, 1893, where Jurisich reported on his trip to the stricken area. He reported that they distributed all the food, medicine, and clothing and estimated the South Slav dead at 250. All the bills that the committee contracted were approved to be paid, and the members were thanked for their work.

For several days after the storm the lugger landing at the foot of Ursuline and Dumaine streets was a beehive of activity. As the remaining luggers arrived at the landing they were swamped by relatives and friends who searched anxiously for their dear ones. Those who recognized their fathers, brothers, sons, or relatives sighed with relief and thanked God profusely while others screamed with anguish when told that their fathers, brothers, or sons were drowned. All this was going on in their native Croatian so that the *Daily Picayune* and the *Times-Democrat* reporters searched for interpreters among those who spoke English. Joseph Tomasovich, a barkeeper of the Luggermen's Exchange Saloon acted as interpreter between the reporters and the non-English-speaking oystermen.

The survivors sought help in New Orleans where they arrived by boat and train. Some stayed with relatives, others with whomever gave them shelter. Joseph Jurisich and Blaise P. Salatich put their houses at the disposal of the surviving oystermen, and each had as many as fifteen beds occupied by their countrymen.

As the rescue crafts returned to the city the survivors gave additional details of the storm. Many narrated their personal experiences though others were too overcome with the tragedy and declined to talk about it for months, some for years.

Tony Tomasovich reported to the *Daily Picayune* of October 4, 1893: "All camps in Bayou Cook and Grand Bayou have been swept out of existence." He estimated the loss of life to be about 150 in Bayou Cook and Grand Bayou.

Fred Zibilich sent a letter to his brother in New Orleans by the first rescue boat. In it he said:

> *Ovdje je gubitak zivota bio strasan....* The loss of life here was terrible. After the storm it looked as if none of the fishermen nor their families in Bayou Cook and vicinity survived to tell about the hurricane and its destruction of everything. Finally it was determined that about twenty persons saved their lives who tell tales of horror and death. There is not a family of our countrymen that has not lost one or more of its members. Some families are wiped out completely. I was not at the camp and could not help anyone. My wife drowned. I do not know about the others nor what happened to them. No words will describe the horrors of death and destruction. There is not a camp that is not destroyed and most of them were carried away by the water.

This hurricane delivered a severe blow to the Louisiana oyster industry from which oystermen did not recover for several years. It was a tragedy of major proportions for the Louisiana South Slav community. Lupis calls it: "The greatest disaster that befell the Croatian immigration." The number of dead was never correctly established, but it was estimated by various sources to be from 150 to 250 persons. Because all the bodies were not recovered, an exact count could not be made. An official census did not exist before the storm, nor was one made after the storm. (I could find no record of any.) The papers ran the names of the reported dead as they were sent in by their reporters from Buras, Empire, and Tropical Bend. The following list of the South Slavs dead was compiled from these reports: Clement

Antonovich, John Barbier's infant daughter, John Barkovich, John Barich, 20 years old; Nikola Barish, 23; Steven Barich, Mrs. Ida Benadvich, John Bendich, 8; Peter Bendich and wife; Michael Berich, Mrs. Bosco Boscovich and two children; Mrs. Michael Franatovich and three sons; John Frankovich, Matt Frankovich, Tony Frankovich; Nikola Franovich, 45; Basile Franovich, 12; Joe Frelich and family; Mrs. John Giasich and daughter; Mrs. Paul Giasich and two sons; John Jakovich, Vincent Jasprica, Jasen Jurelich and two children; Frank Juretich and five children; Joseph Kersanac, Joseph Koschina, Savo Kosich, Mrs. Bosco Lupis and four daughters; Nicholas Milicich, John Mecevich, 52; Luke Mehovich and two children; Luke Micovich and three children; John Milich, Mrs. Jacoam Mircovich, John Mjesicevich, John Nulich, C. John Pecovich, 25; Tony Perovich, Tony Petrovich's wife, son, and a nephew; Baldo Petrovich, 45; Mrs. Luke Petrovich and four daughters, 8, 6, 4, and 3; Mrs. Tony Rudolph and two children; Mrs. Baritola Salatich and two daughters; Mrs. George Seferovich and two girls; Anthony Stiepovich, 50; Nicholas Stiepovich, 16; Joseph Stipelcovich, Peter Stipelcovich, John Stuk, 17; Peter Sukno, John Tabovich, Matthew Tascovich, Steven Tomasovich, Anthony Tontich, Matthew Tuscovich, Mrs. Bosco Vucassovich and two children; John Vincich, Luke Viscovich, John Vokich, Luke Vonvich, Luke Vucinovich, Hyacinthe Yuratich's wife and two children, his father, and his sister and her three children; and Tony Zibilich.

Those who were saved by clinging to pilings remained there all night and part of Monday until help arrived or the water receded enough for them to stand and walk on the ground. Among those saved in this fashion were: Kuzma Murina with thirteen fishermen; Raphael Vukich and his wife; Luke Zibilich, John Seput, Luke Petrovich and his two helpers; Dominic Markovich and his two oystermen whom he dragged half dead to posts and tied there; John Keko, Matthew Zibilich, Bosko Lupis, and many others.

Vincent Pausina was in Bayou Cook during the storm at his oyster camp. When he saw water coming in he took an ax and cut holes in the floor to break the force of the water. When the water rose higher he climbed to the roof. Shortly after, the camp was swept away, and he grabbed a corner post to which he clung from 11 o'clock that evening until after daybreak next morning when the water receded to waist-high depth. He waded to the wreckage of another camp where he saw Tony Negodich who could not make out where they were due to the complete destruction of the camps, wharfs, and boats. With part of a skiff they made their way to Steve Zuvich's camp, which partially survived, and were given food and drink.

Luke Zibilich was camped with his lugger in Bayou des Huertes, near the Grand Bayou. About eleven o'clock the hurricane wind approached from the Gulf carrying with it a giant wave so high that, in Zibilich's words, "it crushed and carried away the oyster camps and swamped and tore apart the luggers." During the storm Zibilich sprang to a high piling and secured himself to it with a rope and remained in that precarious position until 9 o'clock the next morning. When the water subsided he waded to his stranded lugger, which luckily was still navigable, and together with John Seput, who had an almost identical experience, began picking up fellow oystermen and their families whom they found clinging to posts or floating about on the debris. In a few hours time they thus saved thirty persons whom they took to Bayou Cook, where they met the luggers *Venus* and *Atlas* with survivors aboard. They took all of them to Stockfleth's store at the Tropical Bend where they were clothed and fed, and some of them boarded the Fort Jackson train for New Orleans.

John Stuk, a seventeen-year-old youth, was at his brother's camp in Grand Bayou and as soon as he heard the storm approaching he made his way to Tony Negodich's camp nearby. He swam to the camp and was pulled up by Negodich. As the water rose higher and higher Stuk jumped up to reach a ceiling beam to lift himself up, but as he did so, he was bitten by a floating water moccasin. He held on for a while, but the venom weakened him so that he let go and was swept away in the swirling waters where he perished.

In the meantime Negodich was trying to help his frightened wife up to the rafters but a huge wave sent him into a corner of the camp and when he surfaced she was gone. He succeeded in scaling a pole and in getting upon the roof of the camp clutching the clothes of his child between his teeth. They were eventually rescued by a passing lugger and taken to the tracks of the Grand Isle railroad.

Mrs. Eleonora Pelegalli Barbier, the wife of Captain John Barbier, was in her camp in Grand Bayou with her five children, whose ages ranged from one to nine years, while her husband was in New Orleans delivering a load of oysters. When the high winds and tides struck the camp around eleven o'clock the children became panicky and screamed with fear. The wind tore the camp apart but somehow a part of the flooring of one corner remained fast. The remainder of the camp, the walls, the roof, and the furniture, was carried off by the hurricane. Mrs. Barbier managed to collect her children about her on the corner where they remained all night. The water level soon rose to her shoulders, but with superhuman effort she held their heads above the water. However, the baby, her youngest, was torn away from her by one of the huge waves and she never saw the child again. The pilings and the fragmented floor held, and after an all-night ordeal they were rescued by a passing vessel.

When the other oystermen, who survived the hurricane, surveyed the site later, they insisted that no one could have survived the high winds and high water standing on that corner of the camp, least of all a woman with four small children. Many could not explain her survival by any natural means but credited it to the intervention of the Almighty. "A miracle," some whispered, while others shrugged their shoulders and said that it was the mother's loving instinct to save her children from the clutches of the cruel elements that gave her the strength to endure such an ordeal.

Luke Vucinovich, a planter at Homeplace, was visiting his friend John Mjesicevich in Bayou Cook for a weekend of friendly fishing. Both perished in the storm while Vucinovich's house at Homeplace was damaged very slightly.

Nick Salatich had a newly constructed strongly built camp in Bayou Chutte. When the storm came he and his family put on heavy winter clothing, secured the doors and windows, and waited. When the first big wave hit the camp it tore the door off its hinges and the water began to rise along the floor. Part of the roof went next. When the water level became dangerously high Salatich lashed himself and his family to the roof rafters. About two A.M. the house blew away as if cut by a giant knife. Miraculously, the rafters remained together, and the family floated on them, tossed back and forth by the heavy seas, for hours. On Monday when the water subsided Salatich and his family cut the ropes which bound them to the rafters and waded ashore, saved.

Captain Matthew Duba, Frank Oldrich, and George Oldrich were on the lugger *Flying Dutchman* at Simon Island in Grand Lake. About 10:30 Sunday night the lugger was capsized by a heavy wave.

The same wave that capsized the lugger swept Frank Oldrich away with it and he was never seen again. Captain Duba grabbed onto the mast of the capsized vessel and George Oldrich to the keel. Both held on for their life, all night long. Neither knew that the other was holding on to the same boat until morning when daylight came and they saw each other. When the boat was grounded, as the water receded, they knew that they were saved.

Luke Petrovich, whom the paper called "educated Slav," narrated the following story to the *Times-Democrat* reporter:

> Sunday night my wife, four children and I were in our house in Bayou Cook. As the storm raged outside we knew not what to expect. Suddenly as if the heavens had fallen there was a deluge of rain. It fell in sheets so thick that we gasped for air. Before I knew what had happened my house was swept away by the waters of the bayou which rose fifteen feet in an instant. Crying out to my wife to save herself, I grasped my youngest child, a girl of three years, and tried to get out of the filling building. My daughter was torn from me by the seas and the wind and I was carried away by huge waves. I saw my wife but once. This was about eleven p.m. All other camps nearby were swept away. For four and a half hours I swam with the current. On and on I swam on the waves which tossed me about like a cork. I grabbed a picket as I passed by it but the wind and the seas tore me away from it, lacerating my hands.
>
> Once as I sank, my body struck against a picket at top of which a young lad, Felix Buras, was clinging. He grasped me by the hand and pulled me up where I hugged the picket. When the waters receded I made my way to Fred Stockfleth's store where I received food and clothing. My wife and four children were drowned forever.

Jakov Urinovich was at Bayou André where everything was swept away by the storm. He grabbed a floating log and clung to it for two days until he was rescued by the New Orleans' *Daily Picayune*'s rescue boat *Anna McSweeney*.

Natale Boget, who as a sailor had once been shipwrecked and cast away on the Black Sea, lashed himself to a log and so drifted all night tossed by the waves. He later said that the storm in the Black Sea was nothing compared to this hurricane.

Nicholas Viskovich swam, with an aid of a board, twenty miles from Grand Lake to Bayou Cook where he was pulled out of the water by a seaching party on the morning of October 6.

Stephen Tulica and his family of fifteen lived in Bayou Chaland. The storm destroyed most of the camp but one corner where the kitchen was located. He moored a small skiff to the pilings supporting this part of the camp, placed his family in it, and clung on to the sides of the skiff. As the waves filled the skiff with water the children bailed it out. They kept this up through the storm and the entire family was saved.

Marko Bendich, sixty-two years of age, saved his wife and seven children by remaining in the attic of his camp. The camp was partially destroyed but they managed to stay above the water.

Nikola, John, and Matthew Ficovich, living in Bayou Chutte, were on the lugger *St. Eugenia* in Grand Lake. During the storm the lugger was capsized, but they managed to climb on the hull. While drifting in the storm the lugger was turned completely over, 180 degrees, but somehow they managed to straddle the hull and drift ashore.

Christopher Kosich, B. L. Petrovich, and C. Locovich were in Bay Champagne on the lugger *Young Victoria*. The hurricane came upon them while they were asleep. All except Petrovich were saved by clinging to the mast of the boat.

In Adams Bay, Davario Yuncevich was fishing oysters with Anthony Tontich and Peter and Joseph Stipelcovich on the lugger *Andelina*. The lugger capsized at the very beginning of the hurricane and they were thrown into the water. Yuncevich, thrown to the bottom of the overturned boat, was soon washed off and just as he was sinking he grasped a log and managed to keep afloat until he was rescued by Peter Peterson. All others aboard the *Andelina* were lost.

Nick Geritich, John Serantich, and Tom Ratanovich, who fished oysters in Bay Cyprian, came to New Orleans after the hurricane and said that since they lost everything, they would never return to oyster fishing again. At the height of the storm Geritich was in his camp with his wife and two children, and Serantich and Ratanovich. As the water rose they cut holes in the floor of the camp, but the waves battered the camp constantly until it finally fell to pieces. Geritich and his family tried to reach a nearby tree but as they drifted near the branches the family was pulled under by the undercurrent and disappeared under the waves. Geritich managed to surface, and he dived for them repeatedly but to no avail. Finally, as his strength was giving away, he tied himself to a tree where he spent the night. When daylight arrived his camp and his lugger were gone. His two companions were miraculously saved, and together they waded the receding waters looking for his family. They found bodies but not those of his wife and children.

The lugger *Three Brothers* had a crew of four: Miho Zibilich, Savo Kosich, Tom Tomasovich, and an unidentified sailor. They were fishing oysters off Razor Island. After supper, Kosich and Tomasovich unsuspectingly retired below the deck in the forecastle part of the boat for the night. At the onset of the hurricane huge waves filled the boat and overturned it on its side with the mast and the rigging dragging alongside. Captain Zibilich realized that the trapped men, who frantically rapped on the side of the forecastle, would soon drown unless he did something fast. Tying a rope about himself he felt his way, in complete darkness, down into the hold feet first, feeling for Kosich and Tomasovich. All this time he was screaming to them: *"Capajtemese, Capajtemese,"* ("Grab on to me, Grab on to me.") They grabbed on to his legs, and in this fashion he lifted himself and the men to the deck. But a moment later Kosich was swept away by another huge wave and drowned. The lugger, driven by winds and waves, impaled its mast in a sandbar. The heavy seas finally tore the mast and most of the deck off the boat. The men clung to the hull, which became grounded on nearby Razor Island. When the water subsided they set about exploring the conditions of the island. Out of five camps, many skiffs, and luggers, only a part of one camp remained. Here they found four of their friends shivering from exhaustion and cold, but alive, and they reported that all other oystermen of the island were drowned. (Among those reported dead were Matthew Kumarich and Matthew Kuluz, who were later rescued.) Zibilich reached the lugger landing in New Orleans on the evening of October 4 on the *Eclipse* and narrated the above.

Dominic Markovich and his partner Captain Gajetan of the lugger *Good Bye* tied the boat to the wharf in front of their camp in the Bayou des Huertes and hoped to weather the storm in the camp. At about eleven o'clock a huge wave crushed the camp to pieces. In confusion each man grabbed a post and clung on to it all night, neither knowing that the other was saved and nearby. The same wave that crushed the camp also ripped all the rigging off their boat, but the ropes by which it was secured to the pilings held. Several times, in the early morning hours, they tried to work their way to the vessel. Captain Gajetan, being younger and stronger, finally reached the boat by half swimming and half dragging himself along the ropes. Markovich tried the same but was too weak from the all-night ordeal and was swept under the water. He surfaced twice at some distance from the boat and the ropes, both times hearing words of encouragement from his partner who tried to help him but could not reach him. Luckily when he came up for the third time he surfaced directly under the ropes, and, by summoning all the strength left in him, grabbed onto them and worked his way to the boat.

Many near miraculous escapes and many hardships were experienced by the sturdy oystermen during this hurricane, and one of the most outstanding was the survival of two immigrants from Sucuraj, Matthew Kumarich and Matthew Kuluz. They had a lugger named *St. Nicolo* and a camp on Razor Island in Grand Lake and worked as partners. That Sunday evening they retired to their camp to weather the storm but soon realized that this was not a mere storm but a hurricane. As the water rose they tore up some of the floorboards to let the water rise into the camp without severing the camp from its foundation. But the water rose rapidly, and they climbed to the rafters hoping that it would rise no higher and that the camp would withstand the wind and waves. About midnight the camp was torn to pieces, and they were thrown amid the debris, some of which each managed to grab onto. As they were carried from the campsite they spotted an overturned submerged skiff and caught hold of it. When the morning came they realized that they had drifted out into the Gulf, miles from Razor Island. They held on to the sides of the skiff hoping a rescue boat would save them. They drifted with the skiff in open Gulf waters for four days, the hot sun beating down on their peeling skin, which was further irritated by the salty waves washing over their sore bodies. They encouraged each other as best as they could under the circumstances. Thursday passed, and sometime during the night Kumarich exclaimed: *"Hvala Bogu, eno svijetlo"* ("Thank God, there is a light"). They recognized the Southwest Pass lighthouse. As they drifted nearer, expecting to touch the bottom at any moment, the wind suddenly shifted, and they were once more driven out to the sea.

Alternating between complete despair and faint hope, they knew that neither could hold on much longer, but as experienced sailors they also knew that their only hope lay in staying with the submerged skiff. Drifting thus for the fifth day, early Friday morning their feet touched the bottom and soon after, exhausted and half dead, they pulled themselves ashore. Some distance away they saw a light on a boat and Kuluz, weak as he was, managed to swim to the boat and explain their situation. The lugger took them to the rescue vessel *Louisiana* by which they were taken to the Grand Isle railroad which took them to New Orleans. The rescue committee of the Slavonian Association took charge of them and supplied them with shelter, food, clothing, and medical care. The *Times-Democrat* reporter interviewed them at Michael Baccich's store on Decatur Street. Bewildered and unsure of their future, the other oystermen were glad to see their compatriots Kuluz and Kumarich whom they thought lost. Kumarich, the larger and sturdier of the two, survived the ordeal without noticeable change, but Kuluz was not recognized by his own friends, so much had he suffered. His weight had decreased from 165 pounds to 132 pounds in six days. Kumarich later returned to his native Sucuraj where I knew him in my childhood and where he died in old age. Kuluz continued fishing oysters in Louisiana waters. Later, his sons moved to nearby Biloxi where they established an oyster canning factory.

After the storm passed and the waters abated completely, most of the oystermen returned to the sites of their homes. They constructed new camps and larger, safer, swifter boats, and they rebuilt and restocked their reefs. Augmented by the upcoming Louisiana-born youth, and newcomers from Dalmatia, the oyster industry of Louisiana, by the turn of the century, acquired its pre-hurricane production level, and in a few more years far exceeded it. There were other storms, some as fierce as the one of 1893, but never again was the loss of life so great to the Yugoslavs. As communications improved and as the warning systems were developed, human safety could be controlled by obeying the weather authorities.

6

The United Slavonian Benevolent Association

"BIRDS OF A FEATHER FLOCK TOGETHER," goes an old proverb, or as the Yugoslavs would say, *"Svaka ptica svome jatu leti."* So it was with the Yugoslav immigrants in New Orleans and other cities in the United States. Upon arrival, they naturally sought out each other and lived in the same boardinghouses, if single, and in the same neighborhoods, if they had families. They ate and socialized in the same restaurants, cafés, and coffee shops, preferably in those owned by fellow country-men. Consequently, close relationship developed between individuals of the same nationality. They depended on each other for social activities, in finding employment, and for financial assistance during hard times. Eventually this led to the formation of sociobenevolent organizations.

If we examine the names in the City Directories from the late 1840s to 1865 and the United States Censuses of 1850 and 1860, we notice that very few New Orleans Yugoslavs' names appear more than once. This shows that they were very mobile groups migrating from one area of America to another or returning to their native Dalmatia. For many California or St. Louis, Missouri, Yugoslav immigrants, New Orleans was a port of entry, or a place for a short stay. However, by the late 1860s more Yugoslavs were forming families, and by the 1870s there were many more "permanent" immigrants. That is, they did not return to the old country after earning a few hundred dollars but settled in New Orleans and Plaquemines Parish.

When one of these "American formed" or transplanted families was left without a breadwinner, and if the family were destitute, the cousins and the friends of the deceased would care for the widow and the children as best as they could. Also they would give the deceased a Christian burial. If one of their less fortunate countrymen fell sick, they naturally would pitch in and help. As human nature would have it, some helped more than others, and by the 1870s they realized a pressing need for a benevolent organization to insure assistance in need on an equitable basis.

The coastal areas of southern Dalmatia, primarily Dubrovnik and vicinity, where most Louisiana Yugoslavs were born and raised, were rich in the tradition of fraternal brotherhoods, *Bratovstine*, which prospered in that area for hundreds of years. As early as 1200 the citizens of the Dubrovnik Republic had their fraternal and occupational brotherhoods whose main functions were to give a decent Christian burial to their members, to help the widows and orphans of the deceased brethren, and to help brother members when they were sick or out of work. During the sixteenth century the City Republic of Dubrovnik had thirty-three such brotherhoods whose function, in addition to those mentioned above, was "to look to the moral and spiritual behavior of their brothers."

They knew the main aims and functions of such an organization, so it was a matter of getting together to start an organization and to get a committee to draft the rules and regulations. Also, by 1870 most of the other nationalities in New Orleans had already formed their benevolent and cultural organizations; some more than one. The French had the *Societé Française de bienfaisance et d'assistance mutuelle*; the Germans had the German Association, 1st and 2nd districts respectively, the German Emigrant Aid Society, and the German Workingmen's Association; the Italians had the Italian Society, and *Società Italiana di mutua beneficenza in Nuova Orleans*; the Spanish had the Spanish Benevolent Union Society; and the Portugese had the *Lusitanian Portugese Association*. Each national group organized for mutual benefit during its transitional period.

The restaurants, coffee houses, and saloons, which provided the means for social gatherings, played their parts in forming benevolent organizations. They were natural meeting places to discuss the mutual problems. After the Civil War there were many such establishments owned and operated by Yugoslavs along Decatur, Chartres, and nearby streets. The most prominent one seems to have been the saloon and café located at 233 Old Levee Street, now Decatur Street. (233 was located between Dumaine and St. Philip Streets. The decimal system of numbering houses by assigning a different hundred to each block between through streets did not appear in New Orleans until 1894.) This saloon, which was called the New Bazaar Café and Hall and owned by Luke Jovanovich, was the main meeting place of the New Orleans Yugoslavs. It was here that in early 1874 concrete steps were taken to form a benevolent organization.

THE FOUNDING OF THE ASSOCIATION

In April of 1874 a group of New Orleans Yugoslavs—Anthony Sortan, Chris Vucassovich, Nicholas Garbini, John Rusin, John Sortan, Andrew Cvietcovich, and Anthony Bajurin, under the able leadership of Michael Drascovich—issued a call for a meeting to be held in the New Bazaar Café and Hall saloon on May 1, 1874, to discuss the founding of an organization for mutual assistance. And so, as we read in the minutes of that founding meeting, the *United Slavonian Benevolent Association* had its beginning. Forty-eight Yugoslavs answered the call, met, and laid the foundations for the present association. They included the word *united* in the name of the organization to show that they were united and determined to preserve their Slavic heritage. The United Slavonian Benevolent Association of New Orleans is the second oldest Yugoslav organization in the United States; the first such organization, the Slavonic Illyric Mutual Benevolent Association, was founded in San Francisco in 1857.

The original minutes of the founding meeting of May 1, 1874, have been preserved, and since this is the oldest such document in the history of the Yugoslav immigration in America, it is of historical importance to the transitional period of immigrant groups from a foreign way of life to full Americanization. Therefore the minutes are hereby reproduced: first in the original Croatian and then in the English translation, without grammatical corrections.

New Orleans, Svibnja 1vi, 1874.

Na odgovor od zvanja oglasenog od Gospode séduce crez: Mico Draskovich, Anton Fucich, Krsto Vukassovich, Nikola Garbini, Ivan Rusin, Joko Sortan, Anria Cvietcovich, Anton Bajurin, seduca gospoda sastasese u New Bazaar Hall No. 233 Old Levee Str: Bogdan Abramovich, Nikola Mladineo, B. L. Fucich, Todor Tripkovich,

The United Slavonian Benevolent Association emblem. The woman (representing the association) points to modern-day Yugoslavia to remind members of their Old World heritage.

Slavonian Association's tomb in St. Louis Cemetery No. 3, New Orleans.

Luka Skobelj, Ivan Giona, Simon Picinich, Marko Popovich, Petar Skalamia, Joko Krsanac, Lazar Radovich, Frano Tovarac, Ivan Radovich, Petar Rassica, Mato Stiglich, Luka Jovanovich, Spiro Vuskovich, Ivan Strbinich, Nikola Veljacich, Joso Kutzum, Bozo Mustahinich, Mato Dercelja, Ivan Apoloneo, Ivan Barbara, Anton Ban, Rade Abramovich, Ilia Pendo, Joso Koskina, Filip Picoli, Baro Soljacich, Giuro Gusina, Vicko Antulovich, Vicko Radovich, Joko Ramadanovich, Abro Sangaleti, Frano Masich, Stefo Abramovich, Stefo Surdich, Bozo Mijoch, Tomo Antoncich.

Gosp. Mico Draskovich, poslied zovijuci skupstinu u red, kaza da predlog ovog Sastanka jest za ustrojiti Sjedinjeno Slovinsko Drustvo od Dobrocinstva, koje ce providjeti svaku pomoc za nas narod, tojest za drazbenike ovog Drustva u slucaj bolesti, uzdrzati sirocad i udovice od onih Druzbenikah koji budu umriéti i provodieti jedno pristojno miesto za ukopati one druzbenike, koje Providnost s'nje Atajanstvem bude razdiéliti vjecito od nas. Bijuci po misao od gospode gore recene dase ovo drustvo mora ustrojiti od Slovinca sami, stiém predlogom biti cemo slozni u slogi i u tvrdoj ljubavi, koja stanovito mora prebivati izmedju Zemljaka od jedne otacbine u inostranoj zemlji.

Potom Gosp. Draskovich uvede Gosp. Anton Fucich, koji pita svu gospodu prisutnu, jesuli zadovoljni ustroiti Drustvo sa Imenom predlogom imenovano od Gosp. Draskovicha sva gospoda u jedan glas povikase dasu zadovoljni ustroiti Slovinsko Drustvo od Dobrocinstva, i da potvrgjivaju imenovanje i predloge Gosp. M. Draskovicha. Potome Gosp. M. Draskovich imenova Gosp. Iva Radovica za prvoga Predsjednika ovog Drustva, kojie jednoglasno bio potvrgjen od sveg prisutnog Druzbenikah i metnut napred sastanku. Gosp. M. Popovich ucini zanes dase moraju odabrati Glavari ovog Drustva jednoglasno, kojice sluziti jedno godiste kako sto nam zakoni kazu. Gosp. Predsjednik Ivan Radovich imenova sleduce Urednike crez: Nikola Garbini, Joso Kutzum, Anton Bajurin, Joko Sortan, Luka Jovanovich, kojisu bili svi jednoglasno potvrdgjeni od svieh druzbenikah.

Poslied gore recene rabote seducese stvari odlucise jednoglasno, crez Odluceno, da ovo Drustvo morase nazivati u sve nje dojduse vrieme Sojedinjeno Slovinsko Drustvo od Dobrocinstva od Grada New Orleans, Drzave od Louisiane, i da ovo Drustvo nemora imati ali nositi nikakvog drugog Barjaka vec samo onog od U. S. Amerike, i da nema primati u ovom Drustvu nikog inostranog kao Druzbenika, i da na Sastanke ovoga Drustva nemorase govoriti ili knjige drzati u ikakvi inostrani jezik vece samo Slovinski, i da Glavari ovog Drustva morajuse sastajati dva puta nedjelno za urediti Zakone, Ustav i Djelo

od Utelovanja, da receni moraju biti spravni do prvog opceg izvan-
rednog Sastanka koji cese sadrzati u Sabornicu Talijansku na 4 ure
p.m.
    Sjednica se zatvorni na 7½ p.m. Ivan Radovich, Predsjednik, C.
Vucassovich, Tajnik.

New Orleans, May 1, 1874

In response to a call issued by the following: Messrs. Michael
Draskovich, Anthony Fucich, Chris Vucassovich, Nicholas Garbini,
John Rusin, Joseph Sortan, Andrew Cvietkovich, and Anthony Ba-
jurin the following persons met at the New Bazaar Hall No. 233,
Old Levee Street: Bogdan Abramovich, Nicholas Mladineo, B. L.
Fucich, Theodore Tripkovich, Luke Skobelj, John Giona, Sam Pici-
nich, Marc Popovich, Peter Skalamia, John Krsanac, Lazar Radovich,
Frank Tovarac, John Radovich, Peter Rassica, Matthew Stiglich,
Luke Jovanovich, Spiro Vuskovich, John Strbinich, Nicholas Velja-
cich, Joseph Kutzum, Chris Mustahinich, Matthew Dercelja, John
Apoloneo, John Barbara, Anthony Ban, Rudolph Abramovich, Ilia
Pendo, Joseph Koskina, Philip Picoli, Baro Soljacich, George Gusina,
Vincent Antulovich, Vincent Radovich, John Ramadanovich, Abro
Sangaleti, Frank Masich, Stephen Abramovich, Stephen Surdich,
Chris Mijoch, Thomas Antoncich.
    Mr. Michael Draskovich, after calling the assembly to order, said
that the purpose of this meeting is to form a United Slavonian
Benevolent Association which will provide assistance for our people,
that is for the members of the association, in case of sickness and will
look after the orphans and widows of those members who will die
and will furnish a proper and decent place for burial for those members who, by the will of the Holy Providence, will forever be separated from us. The idea proposed by the above persons is that this
Association should be formed of Slavonians only. With this sugges-
tion we shall agree and we will have unity and love which must always
be present among countrymen of one fatherland in a foreign country.
    Then Mr. Draskovich presented Mr. Anthony Fucich who asked
all those present if they were willing to organize an association with
the name proposed by Mr. Draskovich. All present unanimously cried
out that they were willing to organize the Slavonian Benevolent Association and that they approve the name proposed and suggestions
made by Mr. Draskovich. Then Mr. Draskovich nominated Mr. John
Radovich to serve as the first president of this association. He was
then unanimously approved by all the members and was presented to

the assembly. Mr. M. Popovich made a motion that the officers of this association shall be chosen unanimously, who will serve for one year as the By-laws dictate.

Mr. President, John Radovich, nominated the following officers: Nicholas Garbini, Joseph Kutzum, Anthony Bajurin, John Sortan, and Luke Jovanovich who were unanimously approved by all the members.

After the fore-going took place the following items were agreed upon: that this association must forever be called the UNITED SLAVONIAN BENEVOLENT ASSOCIATION of the City of New Orleans, State of Louisiana; that this association shall not have nor carry any other flag but only that of the United States of America; that it will not accept into its membership any foreign persons; that at the meetings of this association the business shall not be conducted nor the books kept in any other language except Slavonian; that the officers of this association shall meet twice weekly to compose the By-laws, Constitution, and the Act of Incorporation; and that the said documents shall be ready by the first special general meeting which will be held at the Italian Hall at 4:00 P.M.

Meeting adjourned at 7:30 P.M.

/S/ John Radovich, President   /S/ C. Vucassovich, Secretary

THE ORGANIZERS

Within a few days of the founding meeting, six more South Slavs: Ilija Berberovich, Luke Petrovich, Vlaho Petrovich, Steve Puh, John Rikorski, and Gaspar Slabowski joined the organizational movement so that when the association was incorporated on May 12, 1874, there were fifty-four charter members.

As in every worthwhile undertaking, there must be leaders to provide the initiative and furnish the driving force necessary for the success of an enterprise, and so it was with the formation of the United Slavonian Benevolent Association. The leadership was provided by the following eleven prominent individuals who actively campaigned for the establishment of the association, initiated the founding meeting, wrote its rules and regulations, and served as its officers during the trying days of its formative years:

Michael Drascovich stands out as the leader of this group. He issued the call for the founding meeting, presided over it, was its main speaker, suggested that the organization be called the United Slavonian Benevolent Association, and adroitly led the actions of the meeting to their successful conclusion. He served as treasurer of the association from 1875 through 1876. An independent businessman, who

46.

Dilo od Utělovanja
od
Sjedinjeno Slovinsko Družtvo
od Dobročinstva
od
New Orleans

Děržava od Louisiane
Župa i Grad od New Orleans

Věka Bud Poznano, da na ovaj
dvanaeste dan od Svibanj, u godinu od
našeg Gospod, jednu hiljade osamsto
i sedamdeset i četiri i od Nezavisnosti
od Sjedinenih Děržavah od Amerike
devedeset i osmi.

Isprid mene, Andrew Herc Jr.
Javni Biljeznik u i za Župu i Grad
od New Orleans, Děržava od Louisiane
shodno pověren i povlastjen, na prisutje
od svědoka ovděk niztar imenovani
i podpisani.

Osobno doslisu i prikazalise
se, několica sobstvi čigovi imeni
jesu ovděka podpisani, i koji oči-
valise da poslužujuci se od providjn-
jah od zakonah od ove Děržave, dotične
za ustrojenyi od Društah za Imjinstvi,
Znastvene, Bogostovne, i Milosěrdne
odluke, i buduci jedni za stěci i
nougrati za njih-isti i za njihove Sudružtve-
nik i Nasljednike, sve pravo, oblast i
povlastiče od Tělina biła i politički u
zakonu, oni jesu progodili i ugodili
i pred ovaj prisutnik činu pogodbu

Partial Act of Incorporation of the
United Slavonian Benevolent
Association in Croatian (left) and
English (below).

47.

Act of Incorporation
of
The United Slavonian Benevolent
Association
of
New Orleans

State of Louisiana
Parish and City of New Orleans

Be it Known that on this
Twelfth day of May in the year
of our Lord one thousand eight
hundred and Seventy four,
and of the Independence of the
United States of America; the
ninety-eighth.

Before me Andrew Herc Jr.
a Notary Public in and for the Parish
and City of New Orleans, State of Louisiana
duly commissioned and qualified; and in
the presence of the witnesses hereinafter
named and undersigned,

Personally Came and Appeared; the
several persons whose names are here
to subscribed, who severally declared,
that availing themselves of the provisions
of the Laws of this State; relating to
the organization of Corporations for
Literary, Scientific, Religious and
Charitable purposes, and being desirous
of acquiring and enjoying for Themselves and
their associates and Successors, the rights
powers and privileges, of a body corporate

started in 1865 with a coffee house at Chartres and St. Peter streets, which he later converted into a saloon, he employed several young Yugoslavs as bartenders, who, under his tutelage, attended that initial meeting and became members of the association. He was born in Konavli, present-day Yugoslavia, which is but a stone's throw from Boka Kotorska and Dubrovnik where most of the other organizers were born.

Anthony Fucich was also very active in the organizational movement. He too was a member of the group that issued the call for the first meeting, and there asked the members if they were willing to form such an organization. He differed from the rest of the organizers in that he was not their "neighbor" in the old country but was born and educated on the island of Losinj in northern Dalmatia. At the first meeting he was elected vice-president of the association. He was an independent businessman and owned and operated A. Fucich and Co., a wholesale fruit company, "importing dried and fresh fruits." In 1874 it was located at 11 South Front and 14 Fulton streets.

Krsto (Chris) Vukasovich, from Boka Kotorska, also worked as a bartender at the same New Bazaar saloon. At the organizational meeting he assumed the office of the recording secretary and held that office until 1876. A year and a half later he was again elected to keep the records of the association and did so until his untimely death at age 29, in 1878. It is to his detailed recording skill that we owe the existence of the historic record of that founding meeting.

Nikola Garbini, from Hodilje near Ston, was an independent fruit dealer at 26 Jefferson. In 1875 he was elected vice-president and remained in that office until 1879.

John Ramadanovich was also from Boka Kotorska. He owned and operated a restaurant at 77 Royal Street. In 1874 he assumed the office of grand marshal which he held until 1878.

Marko Popovich, who was born in Lustice, Bay of Kotor, on July 22, 1834, owned and operated a coffee house and the Popovich's Grocery store at 3 Ursuline Avenue. At that initial meeting he was elected treasurer of the association, relinquishing this office to Michael Drascovich in 1875. At his place of business he employed several fellow Yugoslavs. Later on he became a director of a New Orleans homestead association, and for many years was one of the city's prominent citizens. He survived all the other organizers and died at the age of eighty-nine in 1923.

Luke Jovanovich, in whose saloon the founding meeting was held, was from Hercegovina near the Dubrovnik border. He arrived in New Orleans during the 1860s. For a time he was a clerk in Marko Topovich's grocery and later in Popovich's store. In 1872 he became an owner of the New Bazaar Cafe and Hall, which saloon soon became the headquarters for the Yugoslav immigrants. It was a large saloon employing several fellow Yugoslavs as bartenders. He served as recording secretary of the association from 1875 through 1877 and as financial secretary from 1877 to 1882.

Anthony Ban owned and operated a clothing store at 201 Decatur Street at the time the association was founded. In the Plaquemines Parish census of 1870 he is listed as a farmer with a wife, Genevieve, and five children.

Gaspar Slabowski, only nonbusinessman of this group, was a police officer, a corporal, stationed in the Third District. Born in Dubrovnik, he was vice-president of the association from 1882 to 1890.

John Radovich and Radoslav Abramovich were the other two leaders who helped organize the association. Their biographies appear later in this chapter.

From these notes on the leaders of the organizational movement we can see that, with the exception of Slabowski and Vukasovich, they were all independent businessmen. On a small scale, yes, but still subservient to no one in their daily living. Consequently they were well suited to provide the needed leadership for the young organization. Their businesses were in close proximity to each other which facilitated the frequent contacts needed to put the association on its feet.

RULES AND REGULATIONS OF THE ASSOCIATION

The By-Laws and Charter Committee must have worked overtime, for on May 12, only eleven days after the organizational meeting, the United Slavonian Benevolent Association was incorporated according to the laws of the state of Louisiana.

They drew a charter, which was certified by John McPhalin, district attorney from the First Judicial District of Louisiana; recorded in Society Book No. 118 in New Orleans on May 13, 1874, by C. Darcantel, deputy recorder; and notarized on May 20, 1874, by Andrew Hero, Jr., notary public.

The charter provided for the basic organizational structure; it gave the association corporate status. In its first article it stated the association's purpose as "the moral and material improvement of its members, to aid them in sickness and need, to contribute to the support of their widows and orphans, and to bury their dead." This purpose, which is almost identical to the aims and purposes of the Dalmatian fraternal organizations, *Bratovstine*, remains unchanged to the present day.

The second article created the Board of Directors; the third stated that the domicile of the organization shall be New Orleans; the fourth specified the number of officers, the duties of the board of directors, the number of meetings and means of calling them; and the fifth prescribed the method of dissolving the organization if and when that became necessary. The constitution and bylaws provided, in detail, the mechanics by which the aims and purposes of the association were to be achieved.

The life of the charter was for ninety years. Therefore, before its expiration, the association (in 1963) was reincorporated by amending the existing charter. A young attorney, who is also a member of the association, a third-generation Yugoslav, Anthony Vesich, Jr., handled the legal details.

The constitution and bylaws were amended as changing conditions dictated. In 1884, 1910, and in 1923 they were completely rewritten and readopted. In 1963, to eliminate needless repetition and duplication, the provisions of these two documents were combined into a single document: the bylaws.

The administrative duties are vested in the officers and the members of the Board of Directors, but the governing and legislative powers are reserved for general membership meetings, which take place four times per year. The Board of Directors has the right to propose changes in the bylaws, but only the general membership can adopt them. Thirty days must elapse between the introduction of legislation and its adoption or rejection. Any decision, however minor, made by the Board of Directors does not become final until approved by a general membership meeting. This was and is done by a simple act of accepting the minutes of the board meetings. Since the decisions made by the board are mostly administrative—any controversial subjects are referred to the general meetings—the minutes were, and still usually are, "approved as read."

MEETINGS

Most of the everyday business of the association is conducted at its Board of Directors meetings. The board meets monthly except when the general membership meetings are held. The general membership meetings are held quarterly: in January, April, July, and October of each year. All of these meetings are held on the first Sunday of the month. Sunday afternoon is not an ideal time, but the daytime meeting permits the Plaquemines Parish members to drive to New Orleans, attend the meeting, and return, without the hazards of the late night driving.

Since the association does not own a hall, the meetings have been held in the assembly rooms of other organizations. In the early days the facilities of an Italian organization were rented for this purpose. However, since the early 1920s the association has met in the Benevolent Knights of America Hall. Despite the falling membership, attendance is good, especially the annual election meeting.

Originally three general membership meetings were held in May of each year. May was a convenient month to hold large gatherings; the cold winter temperature was over, and the humid summer heat was still a month or two away. Also this time was convenient for the oystermen whose season, before the advent of rapid transportation and refrigeration, ended in May. The first meeting, an annual business meeting where the annual reports, financial and others, were read, was held on the first Sunday in May. Second Sundays in May were reserved for election of officers, physicians, druggists, and committees. The installation of officers, which in the early days was rather elaborate, was held on the third Sunday in May.

The election meetings were usually smooth and short, but every now and then strong opposing candidates would seek the presidency, and some heated campaigns would develop. Then the campaign for presidency would start weeks ahead of election, and the candidates would visit the business places of members urging them to attend the meetings and vote for them. At the meetings speeches were made on behalf of the candidates, extolling their virtues and enumerating their past accomplishments. By the time the speeches were over and the 150-to-200 ballots counted, several hours had elapsed, and the members departed, tired and thirsty, having experienced an example of American democracy at work at the personal level. They usually retired to a saloon (after 1933 to a restaurant) of a fellow member where the president-elect invited all for a refreshing victory drink.

At all of these meetings the business of the association was conducted as needed, but more important, the meetings were also social gatherings for the New Orleans members and the members who lived and worked tens of miles apart throughout the Mississippi River Delta. This worked well while most of them were bachelors or members whose families were still in Dalmatia, but as they became family men attending meetings for three consecutive Sundays in May, especially after the universal adoption of Mother's Day on the second Sunday in May, proved burdensome and impractical, so by the 1900s this was reduced to two Sundays. The annual business meeting was still held on the first Sunday, but the election and installation meetings were combined into one and held on the second Sunday in May. This continued until 1963 when all three functions were streamlined and taken care of at one meeting which was rescheduled for the first Sunday in January. It so remains to the present. Also in 1963 the business year was changed from May of one year to May of the following year to the calendar year.

Originally the Croatian language was used exclusively in conducting the meetings and in the record keeping. During the early 1960s the secretary was permitted to record the minutes in the English language. All reports, bylaws, the charter, and other documents are still written in both languages. However, since the 1950s most of the business at the meetings is conducted in English for the benefit of the second- and the third-generation members who are unable to speak Croatian.

MEMBERSHIP

The bylaws specifically stated that only male Yugoslavs and their male descendants could become members. They further stated that each applicant must be recommended by two members in good standing, that the applicant must be of good character, good health, and that each application, where personal statistics were enumerated, must be accompanied by a physician's certificate. Only then was the application considered, and after a thirty-day layover the applicant was voted upon. Three black ballots were sufficient to reject an applicant. These provisions are still in force. In the early years any male child of a member could be admitted after six months of age, but in 1910 the

Drago Cvitanovich inspecting the main dining room of his Lakeside Seafood Restaurant in Metairie, Louisiana.

John M. Marcev's Johnny's Restaurant (established 1934) on North Rampart Street was for many years the gathering place of Louisiana Yugoslavs.

Shrimp boat *F.J.G.* owned by John K. Barisich being loaded with ice before departing for another shrimp-catching trip.

lower age limit was raised to seven years and the upper was set at forty-five.

Dues were payable monthly. Any member who owed three months dues was suspended and after six months of nonpayment, was expelled. If he ever tried to be readmitted he had to pay all the elapsed dues or be readmitted as a new member. Presently the dues are collected on an annual basis.

Bylaws were very severe with those in trouble with the law. Members convicted by courts were to be immediately expelled and "never to be re-admitted as a member thereof." However, in the hundred-year history of the association there was never a need to enforce this provision.

When the association was organized in 1874 four categories of membership were established: active members who paid full dues; minor members (those under eighteen years of age) who paid one half regular dues; honorary members, who earned their status by some meritorious deed for the association and paid no dues; and the exempt members who also paid no dues. The exempt status was bestowed upon regular members after twenty-five consecutive years of active membership. Of course, for the first twenty-five years there were no exempt members. But by 1910 they realized that to have a regularly growing number of nonpaying members was a financial burden on the association. So that year the dues for the twenty-five-year members were fixed at one-half the regular dues. However, they were still called "exempt members." In 1963 this category of membership was abolished, and all regular members over eighteen pay full dues.

During the long life of the association, the membership has always consisted of a cross section of the Yugoslav immigrants and their descendants in Louisiana. However, not all immigrants joined. Based on my personal census, on the records of the association, and on the reminiscences of old-timers, about 40 to 50 percent of the immigrants became members. The percentage of the second generation is somewhat less and that of the third is insignificant. The names, dates of becoming a member, and places of origin of most of the members (some records are lost) who joined the association since its inception are contained in Appendix II.

AID TO THE SICK AND BEREAVED

One of the main reasons for the existence of the association is to provide needed aid to its sick members. From its organization to the late 1930s this aid was complete. Based on the records of the association's treasury, we can safely state that it has contributed over a million dollars to its members and their dependents during the century of its existence. The earlier bylaws stated: "The sick members shall have the right to the service of the physician of the association, medicine and five dollars weekly from the treasury of the association during their illness, or, if desired, to go to any hospital selected by the association."

During the organization's early decades the association's physician was paid a salary for his medical services to the members, their wives, widows, and orphans. Later this was changed to a certain amount for each office, home, or hospital visit; and several physicians, who were selected by the association, served the members. This system is still in force. A similar method is used for the medicine and hospitalization. The druggist is reimbursed by the association up to a certain amount for each prescription; the members pay the balance. When the members are hospitalized, the association reimburses them a specific amount for each day plus a certain allowance for medicine and laboratory services. In the early days the association paid all of the hospitalization expenses; today its share is from 10 to 15 percent of a typical hospital bill.

Until a few years ago, the association, in addition to paying for medicine and doctors, helped support its sick (nonhospitalized) members by giving them a weekly cash allowance. It also gave similar financial assistance to its needy members. This financial assistance sustained many a member and his family when he was out of work due to illness or to temporary unemployment. After the Second World War, as the members prospered, and as other forms of financial assistance became available, the weekly cash allowance to sick members was discontinued. However, if a member is considered to be in financial need, the association gives him financial aid to sustain him in his hour of need.

When a member dies the association, through its contracted funeral director, will, if it is so desired by the family of the deceased, provide complete services with interment in one of its tombs. If the member has no family, the association takes charge of all arrangements. This is most beneficial to the immigrant members who die leaving no close relative and thereby are assured a Christian burial by fellow members. When the family of the deceased handles the funeral arrangements the association reimburses the family the amount contracted with its funeral director.

Fellow members are officially notified of a death and the funeral arrangements through the city newspapers and are expected to attend the services, be ready to serve as pallbearers, and render other assistance. This does not mean that attendance is compulsory, and members are not fined, but if able, most of them do attend.

In addition to paying the partial cost of the funeral, the association pays the widow the so-called "death benefit"; the amount depending on the current membership. Each member is assessed a fixed amount for this purpose, to which a fixed sum is added from the treasury of the association. Also when a widow is in dire financial need the association provides periodic financial assistance.

The duty to "bury their dead" was always one of the main and most sacred functions of the association. To underscore this the founders, only two years after the formation of the association, constructed an imposing tomb in the St. Louis Cemetery on Esplanade Avenue for the use of its members and their dependents. In the days past, when most of the funerals were conducted from the deceased's residence, the members took a much more active part than today. The original bylaws of 1874 spell out in detail the ceremonies and procedures to be observed by the members during the funeral services. Again this is reminiscent of the Dalmatian brotherhoods whose main function was the ceremonial burial of its members. To quote the funeral section of the 1874 bylaws:

> It being one of the most sacred duties of this association to give a decent burial to all its deceased brothers whenever Providence in His mysterious dispensation shall remove a fellow member from our midst; it shall be the duty of all members to be present for that purpose; with all the decency possible and in black suits, and they shall be notified by the Collector for that purpose. Any member of whom it shall be proved that he is able to attend the funeral and neglects to do so, shall be reprimanded for the first time, and for the second, he shall pay fifty cents fine, and the third and each time thereafter he shall pay one dollar fine to the treasury of the association.
>
> It shall be the duty of the members, when the Society shall arrive at the residence of deceased brother to be silent, and at the indicated order of the grand marshal, the members shall form in two

open lines to receive the body of the deceased; and from that moment until the deceased shall be consigned to his last resting place no member shall have loud conversation with each other nor smoke during this sacred rite that we owe one to another.

In the minutes of the founding meeting, in the charter, in the constitution and in the bylaws, we notice repeated references to the *Holy Providence*. Coming from the fishing and seafaring—either Catholic or Greek Orthodox—communities along the southern Adriatic they were imbued with centuries-old religious convictions. They accepted death as inevitable and in the association's bylaws prescribed in detail the procedures for Christian funeral and burial. Perhaps the best example of their feelings about death is their main tomb in St. Louis Cemetery on Esplanade Avenue, on which they did not place the universal Christian sign of death—the cross—but the baptismal font which signifies rebirth.

FINANCIAL ASSISTANCE
NOT PRESCRIBED IN BYLAWS

The help given to association members and their dependents took many forms. The minutes of the association contain many references to financial assistance not prescribed by the bylaws. As an example, at the meeting of December 4, 1921, it was decided that the association would give each orphan five dollars for Christmas. This was in addition to the financial assistance that many were receiving. Two hundred and forty dollars were distributed in this manner for Christmas of 1921.

The December 3, 1922, minutes contain a report of member Ante Carevich that he met a member of the association who needed a haircut, a meal, and some tobacco and that he gave the member three dollars to pay for these things. The association reimbursed and thanked Carevich for his good samaritanism.

Five dollars to each orphan or three dollars to a needy member are not large sums, nor are they important in themselves, but they show that, above all, this is a humanitarian organization. There are many entries such as the two cited above. The members received help when they asked. No embarrassing questions were asked. If a member requested help he was considered needy; his word as one of their own was "good enough." During my survey of the association's records I found no unfair advantage ever taken by any member of this trusting policy, and this practice still continues.

During the life of the association the Louisiana coast has been hit with several devastating hurricanes, and after each the association extended its helping hand to the victims. For example, when the hurricane of 1893 hit Plaquemines Parish (described in Chapter Five), the association rose to the occasion. President Abramovich called an emergency meeting and named Joseph J. Jurisich chairman of the relief committee. Its entire treasury of four thousand dollars was placed at the disposal of the committee, and 75 percent of it was spent to rescue the survivors and bury the dead. There were no questions asked as to whether the victims were members or not; all were helped alike. The association hired and equipped with food, medicine, and clothing a fast steamer, *Annie Wood*, and dispatched it, with the oystermen who were in New Orleans at the time, to the stricken area to search for bodies and for survivors.

During the 1915 hurricane the association once more helped those who suffered material damage from the storm, financially and with food and medicine. And on May 18, 1927, it assessed each of its 302 members one dollar and donated the proceeds to the American Red Cross to assist the victims of the Mississippi River flood.

During the Great Depression of the 1930s the association generously helped the less fortunate members, whose numbers, reflecting the national trend, increased during those lean years. The leaders of the association used to, and still do, point with pride that not a single member of the association received government relief assistance during the depression. The average Yugoslav immigrant considered, and still does, that receiving public assistance for no work done, is a form of begging, and begging for able-bodied men is frowned upon by them with shame. During those trying depression years the association again earned the right to *benevolent* in its name.

Hurricane Betsy struck the Louisiana coast on September 9, 1965, and did hundreds of millions of dollars damage. Even with the modern warning methods and rapid transportation the death toll was heavy. However, most of the Yugoslav oystermen and their families did evacuate to higher ground and only one Yugoslav oysterman, Gregory Keko, was lost to the storm and presumed drowned. The association, to help those whose property was destroyed, canceled its supper dance for that year and donated the entire proceeds of its raffle (three thousand dollars) to the Plaquemines Parish Relief Association. In addition to this, it helped many of its members and their families, who suffered storm losses, with substantial financial donations.

Again in 1969, when the hurricane Camille swept the coast, the association came to the aid of the storm's victims; it donated three thousand dollars to the Plaquemines Hurricane Relief Association and gave financial aid to the widows of the association's members and to the members who sustained material loss by the storm.

SOME VITAL STATISTICS OF THE ASSOCIATION

The original membership of fifty-four founders of 1874 was quickly augmented by new members. As the other Yugoslavs realized that the newly formed association was a successful undertaking; that during their sickness and need it gave them financial shelter; that it helped even after death by giving financial assistance to their widows and orphans, they joined the young association in large numbers. Unfortunately, some of the records of the first half century of the life of the association—from 1874 through 1920—were not preserved, and we do not have accurate numbers of members and other pertinent information. The records simply disintegrated, I am told, from lack of proper care and are forever lost to us. However, we do know, from a copy of bylaws published in 1910 that in that year there were 210 members on the rolls of the association. In 1922 there were 318 members (including the minor members); in 1925, 331; in 1928, 350; in 1930, 337; in 1940, 325; in 1950, 288; in 1960, 224; and in 1970 there were 190 members on the rolls.

Whereas the membership peaked in 1928, then declined, the treasury, the other index of growth, showed a steady increase. At the end of 1874 the association—after only seven months of its existence—was worth $910.15; in 1884, $1,184; in 1894, $4,454; in 1904, $14,611; in 1914, $18,232; in 1924, $23,855; in 1934, $25,819; in 1936, $16,240; in 1940, $20,721; in 1950, $52,157; and in 1960 it was worth $78,647.

From 1874 to 1970 the treasury increased each decade except during the 1930–1940 decade when it dropped from $27,000 in 1930 to $16,000 in 1936 and did not reach its 1930 amount again until the mid-1940s. The reason for the drop during the 1930s was, of course, the depression.

THE ASSOCIATION AS A SOCIAL ORGANIZATION

Although the association is primarily a benevolent organization, it has provided its share of social activities for the New Orleans Yugoslavs and their friends. These social activities kept the early immigrants from feeling isolated and helped in the acculturation of the Yugoslav-born members.

During its early years when the membership consisted mainly of bachelors and of those whose families were in Dalmatia, the meetings, installation of officers, and all-male banquets were the principal social functions of the association. However, as the years went by, the social picture changed. The functions of the association became of such a nature that the families of the members and their American friends and neighbors could participate. The outdoor picnics, festivals, dances, and dinner dances became popular means of getting together and were given periodically. They served a dual purpose: an opportunity to gather socially and to raise money for the association's treasury.

Usually the picnics were given in a park where members, especially those who owned restaurants, did the catering. Food and drinks were always plentiful and games were provided for the children. In the early days—up to the passage of the Volstead Act in October, 1919 —a barrel or two of wine, usually imported from the Dalmatian vineyards, provided the beverage. Inevitably lamb was barbecued on an open rotary spit *razanj*. This type of outdoor cooking was imported from their native Dalmatia where no Dalmatian wedding feast or an outdoor social was ever complete without it.

There were several such picnics, the most important and successful one being that of July 27, 1934, celebrating the sixtieth anniversary of the founding of the association. The picnic was held on the grounds of the Holy Cross College. A young man, John P. Gentilich, who for many decades played a large role in the leadership of the association, served as the chairman of the affair. A nice sum of money was cleared by publishing a program with ads of businessmen-members and friends, and from sales of drinks and food at the picnic. All of the labor provided by the members was furnished free of charge and most of the food and drinks were donated.

The June 6, 1937, festival-dance celebrating the sixty-third anni-

United Slavonian Benevolent Association's 38th (1912) Anniversary Celebration Committee. Front row, left to right: Peter Bendich, John Radetich, John Kopajtich, John Balovich, Peter Kopanica, and John Bendich; second row: Rado Hihar, Luke Bajurin, Tony Dimak, Jack Kopanica, Matthew Antunica, and Nicholas Korac; back row; Marine Busko, Miho Kresich, Matthew Radetich, Peter Rozich, and Miho Perovich.

United Slavonian Benevolent Association's 60th Anniversary Celebration Committee, July, 1934, pictured at a picnic on the grounds of Holy Cross College, New Orleans. Front row, left to right: Leopold Taliancich, Miho Kresich, John P. Gentilich (chairman), Stipo Palihnich, John Carevich, Marko Butirich, and Nikola Butirich. Back row: H. Reidberg, Nicholas Jovanovich, Anthony Carevich (president), Jack Porobil, John M. Marcev, Anthony Seckso, Peter Kopanica, and Martin Butirich.

versary was held at Deutches Haus, New Orleans. It was the first successful affair of its kind. Several girls competed for the coveted title of
queen of the festival. The contest was decided by votes, each dollar
collected by the girls from their sponsor counting as one hundred
votes. This was a novel but effective idea of raising money for the association, and pricing each vote at one penny gave everyone a chance to
vote for the candidate of his choice, no matter how small the amount.
The depression was still being felt and dollars were scarce. Miss Marion Gerica reigned as the queen of the festival and Misses Marie Bilich and Theodora Vujnovich as Miss America and Miss Louisiana
respectively. The festival-dance was a social and financial success en-
riching the association's treasury by several thousand dollars, and it
set the pattern for subsequent socials of the association. Marine Gerica
was the general chairman of the affair and Mrs. Nicholas Levata the
chairlady of the ladies committee.

The Second World War precluded the celebration of another
such affair for nine years. On July 7, 1946, the seventy-second anniversary of the association was celebrated by a dance at the New Orleans Jerusalem Temple. Again the queen was chosen by the amount
of money she collected for the association from her "sponsors." The
runners-up were chosen maids. Miss Barbara Machella reigned as
queen with a full court of six beautiful maids and handsome dukes.
This, too, was a successful affair for it brought the treasury a substantial sum. Matthew J. Bilich served as the general chairman and Mrs.
Nicoline Matranga as the chairlady.

The seventy-third anniversary was celebrated on July 19, 1947.
Miss Rita Jurisich reigned as queen, accompanied by a full court.
The profit from the festival brought another substantial sum to the
treasury.

The Diamond Jubilee (seventy-fifth anniversary) was celebrated
on Sunday, June 5, 1949, in the Municipal Auditorium, New Orleans,
with John M. Marcev as chairman and Mrs. John Vezich as chairlady.
Miss Catherine Vezich reigned as queen with six maids and six dukes
in her court. To make the court complete the association chose Peter
Vujnovich to reign as king. This was a departure from earlier courts
which did not have kings, only escorts, for the queens. Again a large
sum was raised and given to the association to carry on its benevolent
work.

This seventy-fifth anniversary festival was repeated, with the same

Slavonian Association's 63rd Anniversary Court. Left to right: Zeljko Franks, Theodora Vujnovich, John Carevich, Marion Gerica (queen), Marie Bilich, Vlado Ivichevich, Molly Franicevich, and Marine Gerica.

Slavonian Association's 72nd Anniversary Court. Left to right: Eva Jurisich, Ernest Salatich, Marian Antunica, Nicholas Gerica, Rosemary Vezich, Joseph Taliancich, Barbara Machella (queen), Frank Kopanica, Madeline Pivach, Milos Vujnovich, Matthew Muhoberac, Catherine Bilich, Dr. Peter Salatich, Jr., and Norma Morovich. Sitting: J. P. Matranga (page) and Linda Morovich (attendant to the queen).

court, in Buras, Louisiana, on July 31, 1949, for the benefit of Plaquemines Parish Yugoslavs and their friends.

The last celebration of this type, with court and attendants, was
given on Sunday, June 15, 1952, in the Buras Auditorium. Miss Dominica Pausina reigned as queen and John Vela was king. John Muhoberac served as the chairman and Mrs. Marion Gerica Sabrio as the
chairlady. Something new was added for this celebration: Misses
Vanka Pausina and Carmelite Zibilich, dressed in Croatian national
costumes, entertained the assembly with Croatian folk dances. Needless to say this was the "hit" of the evening.

In 1954 the association initiated the annual celebration of its
founding with a lavish supper dance in one of the larger ballrooms in
a downtown hotel in New Orleans. These supper dances are well attended by Louisiana Yugoslavs and their friends. Usually, around six
hundred persons attend. Prizes are awarded to the lucky holders of
raffle tickets which have been selling months ahead of the scheduled
event.

From 1954 through 1959 Fred Barbier was the chairman of the
supper dances. John P. Gentilich served as the chairman of the 1960
affair. Since then Marine Gerica has become a regular chairman of
these parties. Needless to say, all of these chairmen have had the generous cooperation of other members, who somehow, year after year,
find time to help the association.

The ladies committee, without which a successful supper dance is
unimaginable, has been headed by Mrs. Katie Hihar Pausina and Mrs.
Eleonora Barbier Vogt.

As can be seen from the preceding paragraphs the association has
served as a nucleus for providing social get-togethers for the Yugoslavs
in Louisiana. Unfortunately, a ladies' auxiliary of the association was
never organized, and therefore all the socials have to be initiated by
men at one of the association's meetings. Consequently there are not
as many socials given as there would be if the ladies were organized.
There are no bingo games, cocktail parties, or other socials usually
given by the ladies in other similar organizations. However, the ladies
have always helped; they organize themselves into committees, function effectively and efficiently to assist in producing successful socials,
then disband until the next celebration.

Another ingredient necessary for an active social and cultural
life of an organization, a home, was never built. This is another facet

Marion Gerica Sabrio, 1937

Barbara Machella Ragas, 1946

Rita Jurisich Cotogno, 1947

Catherine Vezich Breaux, 1949

Dominica Pausina, 1952

Members of the United Slavonian Benevolent Association attending the January, 1971, meeting.

Photo courtesy Terry Friedman, the Times-Picayune

A friendly get-together at Johnny's Restaurant, October, 1965.

Photo courtesy the Plaquemines Gazette

in which the United Slavonian Benevolent Association differs from its sister organizations throughout America. Usually the main purpose of an ethnic organization is to provide a gathering place for its members where they can hold their meetings and socials or just drop in during their spare time. However, the "spare time" factor of other immigrants who worked in factories, construction gangs, and as longshoremen, was a luxury that Louisiana Yugoslavs never had. The members, particularly the officers, the leaders, the doers, who for the most part owned and operated their own business establishments, which commanded all their attention and constant presence, simply did not have any spare time for lonesomeness. Therefore they had no need for a home. Also, the membership is scattered throughout New Orleans, Plaquemines Parish, and Jefferson Parish. In Plaquemines and in Jefferson parishes they reside from Harahan to Venice and from Pointe a la Hache to Grand Isle.

The organization still attracts young members, the newcomers from Yugoslavia and those born here, and its future is assured for many generations to come. Its role of a strictly benevolent-medical association of yesteryear is changing to that of a more socially and culturally oriented organization. Whatever the future holds, it has played a major role during the transitional period in the acculturation of its members; it has provided a social and benevolent service which otherwise would not have been available to first-generation members.

LEADERSHIP: BIOGRAPHIES OF THE PRESIDENTS

Through the years the leadership of the organization has been provided by the presidents with strong assistance from the recording secretaries. Needless to say, the recording secretary, the financial secretary, and the treasurer have been doing the bulk of the work of running the business of the association. The other officers also do their share. The vice-presidents preside in the absence of the presidents, and the grand marshals keep order during the meetings and assist in conducting funerals of deceased members. The names of all officers who served the association are included in Table VI.

The presidents have always been close to the membership. Usually their occupation, education, roots, and background have been similar to those of the other members. The members have always felt that they were electing one of their own. The association was never run by an "intellectual class" as has been the case with many of the

Ladies Committee for the 1966 Slavonian Association Supper Dance. Standing, left to right: Mesdames Lena Matranga, Marie Slavich, Eleonora Vogt, Katie Pausina, Dominica Greco, and Leonie Jurisich; seated: Katie Grusich, Helen Franks, Katie Carevich, Theresa Ficovich, and Vera Vujnovich.

Photo courtesy the Plaquemines Gazette

Marine Gerica, representing the Slavonian Association, presents a check to Judge Leander H. Perez to help rebuild Plaquemines Parish after Hurricane Betsy in 1965.

Photo courtesy the Plaquemines Gazette

northern ethnic organizations. Consequently the separatism between the leaders and the general membership, the cause of premature demise of many a similar organization, has never developed.

Fortunately the portraits of all the presidents of the association are available and are published in this volume. The biographical notes on the presidents, which span the last hundred years, are very similar to the biographies of most of the Yugoslav immigrants. Therefore by describing the lives of the presidents we are, by projection, describing the lives of the Yugoslav immigrants and their descendants in Louisiana.

JOHN RADOVICH, 1874–1891

The first president of the association, John Radovich, was elected to the presidency at the organizational meeting of May 1, 1874, and was reelected every year thereafter for sixteen years. He served longer than any other president of the association. He died on December 26, 1890, while serving his seventeenth year as president and was buried in the association's tomb in St. Louis Cemetery, No. 3. Born in 1825 in Lustice, Boka Kotorska, what is now Yugoslavia, he came to Louisiana on one of the Boka Kotorska sailing vessels, which traded with New Orleans, and settled here. He owned and operated a fruit stand at the Treme Market, 178 Villere Street. During the American Civil War, he served in the Slavonian Rifles Company, European Brigade, Louisiana Militia.

An effective leader and an adroit administrator, he successfully led the young organization during its formative years when the basic groundwork for the association—which essentially is still in effect— was determined. During this time the membership increased threefold, from 54 in 1874 to over 150 in 1890. Building the association's tomb in New Orleans; compiling, codifying, adopting, and printing the charter; writing the constitution and the bylaws were the three outstanding accomplishments of the association under his tutelage.

RADOSLAV ABRAMOVICH, 1891–1897

Radoslav (Rade) Abramovich came to Louisiana from Boka Kotorska and until 1875 worked as a bartender in Luke Jovanovich's New Bazaar Café, and in that year he and Bogdan Abramovich became owners of this saloon and operated it for many years. He joined the association as a charter member on May 1, 1874 and on May 11,

TABLE VI

Officers of the United Slavonian Benevolent Association, 1874–1974

	PRESIDENT	VICE-PRESIDENT	RECORDING SECRETARY	FINANCIAL SECRETARY	TREASURER	GRAND MARSHAL
1874–75	John Radovich	Anthony Fucich	Krsto Vukasovich		Marko Popovich	Joko Ramadanovich
1875–76	Anthony Fucich	Nicholas Garbini	Krsto Vukasovich		Michael Draskovich	Joko Ramadanovich
	John Radovich		Luka Jovanovich			
1876–77	John Radovich	Nicholas Garbini	Luka Jovanovich	Luke Jovanovich	Joseph Kutzum	Joko Ramadanovich
1877–78	John Radovich	Nicholas Garbini	Krsto Vukasovich	Luke Jovanovich	Joseph Kutzum	Joko Ramadanovich
1878–79	John Radovich	Nicholas Garbini	Krsto Vukasovich	Luke Jovanovich	Frank Masich	Jero Lukinovich
			Vlaho Salatich			
1879–80	John Radovich	Anthony Bajurin	Vlaho Salatich	B. L. Fucich	Frank Masich	Jero Lukinovich
1880–81	John Radovich	Anthony Bajurin	Matt Radovich	Jero Lukinovich	Frank Masich	L. Jurgielewicz
1881–82	John Radovich	Anthony Bajurin	Matt Radovich	Jero Lukinovich	Frank Masich	L. Jurgielewicz
1882–83	John Radovich	Gaspar Slabowski	Matt Radovich	Bozo Sevelj	Frank Masich	L. Jurgielewicz
1883–84	John Radovich	Gaspar Slabowski	Matt Radovich	Bozo Sevelj	Frank Masich	Michael Sansovich
1884–85	John Radovich	Gaspar Slabowski	Matt Radovich	Rade K. Petrovich	Nicholas Garbini	Peter Popovich
1885–86	John Radovich	Gaspar Slabowski	Matt Radovich	Rade K. Petrovich	Nicholas Garbini	John Popovich
1886–87	John Radovich	Gaspar Slabowski	Matt Radovich	Rade K. Petrovich	Frank Masich	John Balovich
1887–88	John Radovich	Gaspar Slabowski	Ferdo C. Bautovich	Rade K. Petrovich	Frank Masich	John Popovich
1888–89	John Radovich	Gaspar Slabowski	Ferdo C. Bautovich	Rade K. Petrovich	Frank Masich	John Popovich
1889–90	John Radovich	Gaspar Slabowski	George D. Zibilich	Rade K. Petrovich	Frank Masich	John Popovich
1890–91	John Radovich	Radoslav Abramovich	George D. Zibilich	Rade K. Petrovich	Frank Masich	John Popovich
	Radoslav Abramovich		Ignazio Grabre			
1891–92	Radoslav Abramovich	Anthony Tomasovich	Ignazio Grabre	Rade K. Petrovich	Frank Masich	John Popovich
1892–93	Radoslav Abramovich	Anthony Tomasovich	Ignazio Grabre	Rade K. Petrovich	Frank Masich	John Popovich
1893–94	Radoslav Abramovich	Rade K. Petrovich	Vlaho Salatich	Joseph Jurisich	Anthony Masich	John Popovich
1894–95	Radoslav Abramovich	Ignazio Gabre	Vlaho Salatich	Joseph Jurisich	Anthony Masich	John Popovich
1895–96	Radoslav Abramovich	Samuel M. Fucich	Jacob Prislich	Joseph Jurisich	Anthony Masich	John Popovich
1896–97	Radoslav Abramovich	Samuel M. Fucich	Jacob Prislich	Joseph Jurisich	Anthony Masich	John Popovich:

Year						
1897–98	Ferdo C. Bautovich	Jacob Prislich	John Lupis-Vukich	Joseph Jurisich	Anthony Masich	Jack Simich
1898–99	Jacob Prislich	Joseph Jurisich	Anthony Jasprica	John Balovich	Anthony Masich	Michael Toso
1899–00	Jacob Prislich	Joseph Jurisich	Peter Borcich	Anthony Jasprica	Anthony Masich	Michael Toso
1900–01	Jacob Prislich	Ferdo C. Bautovich	Joseph Jurisich	John Balovich	Anthony Masich	N. Jasprica
1901–02	Samuel M. Fucich	Frank Starcich	Joseph Jurisich	Anthony Jasprica	Anthony Masich	N. Jasprica
1902–03	Samuel M. Fucich	Frank Starcich	Joseph Jurisich	John Balovich	Anthony Masich	N. Jasprica
1903–04	Joseph Jurisich	Ferdo C. Bautovich	George D. Zibilich	John Balovich	Anthony Masich	N. Jasprica
1904–05	Joseph Jurisich	Ferdo C. Bautovich	Baldo Senko	John Balovich	Anthony Masich	Anthony Jasprica
1905–06	Joseph Jurisich	Ferdo C. Bautovich	Baldo Senko	George D. Zibilich	Anthony Masich	N. Jasprica
1906–07	Joseph Jurisich	Ferdo C. Bautovich	Nicholas Kosich	John Gentilich	Anthony Masich	Baldo Senko
1907–08	Joseph Jurisich	Ferdo C. Bautovich	Matt Belin	John Gentilich	Anthony Masich	John Glavina
1908–09	Joseph Jurisich	Nicholas Kosich	John Seput	A. A. Nesanovich	Anthony Masich	John Glavina
1909–10	Samuel M. Fucich	Andrew Vidak	Joseph Jurisich	John Balovich	Anthony Masich	John Petrovich
1910–11	Andrew Vidak	George D. Zibilich	Joseph Jurisich	John Petrovich	Anthony Masich	Miho Zibilich
1911–12	Andrew Vidak	John Gentilich	Joseph Jurisich	John Petrovich	Anthony Masich	Miho Zibilich
1912–13	Andrew Vidak	John Gentilich	Joseph Jurisich	John Petrovich	Anthony Masich	Miho Zibilich
1913–14	Andrew Vidak	Ferdo C. Bautovich	Joseph Jurisich	John Porobilo	Anthony Masich	Matt Belin
1914–15	Andrew Vidak	Ferdo C. Bautovich	Joseph Jurisich	John Porobilo	Anthony Masich	Matt Belin
1915–16	Joseph Jurisich	John Glavina	George D. Zibilich	Anthony Vezich	Anthony Masich	Matt Belin
1916–17	George D. Zibilich	Ferdo C. Bautovich	Joseph Jurisich	Anthony Vezich	Andrew Vidak	Matt Belin
1917–18	Anthony A. Nesanovich	John Glavina	Joseph Jurisich	Anthony Vezich	Miho A. Zibilich	Frank Belin
1918–19	Anthony A. Nesanovich	Joseph Jurisich	Stephen Palihnich	Anthony Vezich	Miho A. Zibilich	Frank Belin
1919–20	George D. Zibilich	Ferdo C. Bautovich	John Glavina	Anthony Vezich	John Sukno	Frank Belin
1920–21	George D. Zibilich	Ferdo C. Bautovich	Stephen Palihnich	Matt Parun	Anthony Vezich	Anthony Carevich
1921–22	George D. Zibilich	Joseph Jurisich	Stephen Palihnich	Matt Parun	Anthony Vezich	Anthony Carevich
1922–23	John Jurovich	Anthony A. Nesanovich	Stephen Palihnich	Matt A. Zibilich	Anthony Carevich	Anthony A. Nesanovich
1923–24	George D. Zibilich	John Glavina	Stephen Palihnich	Benjamin Bilich	Miho A. Zibilich	Peter Kopanica
1924–25	Anthony M. Zibilich	Anthony A. Nesanovich	Stephen Palihnich	Benjamin Bilich	Anthony Carevich	Peter Kopanica
1925–26	Anthony M. Zibilich	Anthony A. Nesanovich	Stephen Palihnich	Benjamin Bilich	Anthony Carevich	Peter Kopanica
1926–27	Anthony M. Zibilich	Anthony A. Nesanovich	Stephen Palihnich	Benjamin Bilich	Anthony Carevich	Peter Kopanica
1927–28	Peter Kopanica	Anthony A. Nesanovich	Matt A. Zibilich	Benjamin Bilich	John Sukno	Peter Kopanica
1928–29	Peter Kopanica	Anthony A. Nesanovich	Matt A. Zibilich	Benjamin Bilich	John Sukno	John Muhoberac
1929–30	Stephen Palihnich	Anthony A. Nesanovich	Matt A. Zibilich	Benjamin Bilich	Anthony Vezich	John Muhoberac
1930–31	Stephen Palihnich	Peter Kopanica	Anthony M. Zibilich	Benjamin Bilich	Anthony Vezich	Miho A. Zibilich

TABLE VI (Continued)

	PRESIDENT	VICE-PRESIDENT	RECORDING SECRETARY	FINANCIAL SECRETARY	TREASURER	GRAND MARSHAL
1931–32	Anthony M. Zibilich	Peter Kopanica	Matt A. Zibilich	Benjamin Bilich	Anthony Vezich	Anthony A. Nesanovich
1932–33	John Gentilich	Peter Kopanica	Matt A. Zibilich	Benjamin Bilich	Anthony Vezich	Vincent Jasprica
1933–34	Anthony Carevich	Peter Kopanica	John Persich	Benjamin Bilich	Anthony Vezich	Anthony Antunica
1934–35	Anthony Carevich	Peter Kopanica	John Persich	Benjamin Bilich	Anthony Vezich	John M. Marcev
1935–36	John Gentilich	Jack A. Porobil	Anthony Zanki	Benjamin Bilich	Peter Taliancich	John A. Carevich
1936–37	Jack A. Porobil	John P. Gentilich	Anthony Zanki	Benjamin Bilich	Peter Taliancich	John A. Carevich
1937–38	Jack A. Porobil	John P. Gentilich	Anthony Zanki	Benjamin Bilich	John M. Marcev	John A. Carevich
1938–39	Jack A. Porobil	John P. Gentilich	Anthony Zanki	Benjamin Bilich	John M. Marcev	John A. Carevich
1939–40	John P. Gentilich	John Sukno	Anthony Zanki	Benjamin Bilich	John M. Marcev	John A. Carevich
1940–41	John P. Gentilich	John Sukno	Anthony Zanki	Benjamin Bilich	Peter Kopanica	John A. Carevich
1941–42	John P. Gentilich	John Sukno	Anthony Zanki	Benjamin Bilich	Peter Kopanica	John A. Carevich
1942–43	John Sukno	Dr. A. G. Juracovich	John Persich	Benjamin Bilich	John Lulich	John A. Carevich
1943–44	John Sukno	Dr. A. G. Juracovich	John Persich	Benjamin Bilich	John Lulich	John A. Carevich
1944–45	John Sukno	Dr. A. G. Juracovich	John Persich	Benjamin Bilich	John Lulich	Anthony Antunica
1945–46	John M. Marcev	Matt J. Bilich	John Persich	Benjamin Bilich	John Lulich	Anthony Antunica
1946–47	John M. Marcev	Matt J. Bilich	John Persich	Benjamin Bilich	John Lulich	Anthony Antunica
1947–48	John M. Marcev	Matt J. Bilich	Steve Bilich John Persich	Benjamin Bilich	John Lulich	Anthony Antunica
1948–49	Matt J. Bilich	Marine Gerica	John Persich	Benjamin Bilich	John P. Gentilich	Joseph Strgacich
1949–50	Matt J. Bilich	Marine Gerica	John Persich	Benjamin Bilich	John P. Gentilich	Joseph Strgacich
1950–51	Marine Gerica	Matt A. Zibilich	John Persich	Benjamin Bilich	John P. Gentilich	Joseph Strgacich
1951–52	Marine Gerica	John Muhoberac	John Persich	John M. Marcev	John P. Gentilich	Joseph Strgacich
1952–53	Marine Gerica	John Muhoberac	John Persich	John M. Marcev	John P. Gentilich	Simo Slavich
1953–54	John Muhoberac	Peter Vujnovich	John Persich	John M. Marcev	John P. Gentilich	Simo Slavich
1954–55	Dr. A. G. Juracovich	Peter Vujnovich	Milos M. Vujnovich	John M. Marcev	John P. Gentilich	Andrew Taliancich
1955–56	Dr. A. G. Juracovich	Peter Vujnovich	Milos M. Vujnovich	John M. Marcev	John P. Gentilich	Andrew Taliancich
1956–57	Peter Vujnovich	Benjamin Bilich	Milos M. Vujnovich	John M. Marcev	John P. Gentilich	Andrew Taliancich
1957–58	Peter Vujnovich	Benjamin Bilich	Milos M. Vujnovich	John M. Marcev	John P. Gentilich	Andrew Taliancich
1958–59	Benjamin Bilich	Fred Barbier	Milos M. Vujnovich	John M. Marcev	John P. Gentilich	Andrew Taliancich

1959–60	Fred Barbier	Frank Glavina	Milos M. Vujnovich	John M. Marcev	John P. Gentilich	Andrew Taliancich
1960–61	Fred Barbier	Frank Glavina	Milos M. Vujnovich	John M. Marcev	John P. Gentilich	Thomas Biskupovich
1961–62	Frank Glavina	Frank Kopanica	Milos M. Vujnovich	John M. Marcev	John P. Gentilich	Thomas Biskupovich
1962–63	Frank Glavina	Frank Kopanica	Milos M. Vujnovich	John M. Marcev	John P. Gentilich	Thomas Biskupovich
1963–	Frank Kopanica	Matt J. Ficovich	Milos M. Vujnovich	John M. Marcev	John P. Gentilich	Matt N. Anzulovich
1964*	Frank Kopanica	Matt J. Ficovich	Milos M. Vujnovich	John M. Marcev	John P. Gentilich	Matt N. Anzulovich
1965	Frank Kopanica	Matt J. Ficovich	Milos M. Vujnovich	John M. Marcev	John P. Gentilich	Matt N. Anzulovich
1966	Matt J. Ficovich	Robert Gegen	Milos M. Vujnovich	John M. Marcev	John P. Gentilich	Matt N. Anzulovich
1967	Matt J. Ficovich	Robert Gegen	Milos M. Vujnovich	John M. Marcev	John P. Gentilich	Matt N. Anzulovich
1968	Robert Gegen	Frank Kopanica	Milos M. Vujnovich	John M. Marcev	John P. Gentilich	Matt N. Anzulovich
1969	Robert Gegen	Frank Kopanica	Milos M. Vujnovich	John M. Marcev	John P. Gentilich	Matt N. Anzulovich
1970	Robert Gegen	Frank Kopanica	Milos M. Vujnovich	John M. Marcev	John P. Gentilich	Drago Cvitanovich
1971	Milos M. Vujnovich	Frank Kopanica	Peter Vujnovich	John M. Marcev	John P. Gentilich	Drago Cvitanovich
1972	Milos M. Vujnovich	Baldo V. Pausina	Peter Vujnovich	John M. Marcev	John P. Gentilich	Drago Cvitanovich
1973	Baldo V. Pausina	Drago Cvitanovich	Milos M. Vujnovich	John M. Marcev	John P. Gentilich	Zeljko Franks

* From 1874 through 1963 the elections of officers were held on the second Sunday in May of each year; therefore the term of office was from May of one year to May of the following year. Since January, 1964, the elections have been held on the second Sunday in January of each year, and the term of office is on the calendar-year basis.

1890, was elected its vice-president. As such he became the second president of the association when the first president, Radovich, died in office on December 26, 1890. Abramovich remained president for six years—until May, 1897—and guided the association through its most trying experience. It was during his administration that the hurricane of 1893 struck the South Louisiana coast and killed a large number of members. He immediately called an emergency meeting, unselfishly provided the vital leadership in this crisis, swiftly appointed the necessary committees, and tirelessly supervised the various rescue operations. He and Radovich were the only two presidents who came from the original charter members of 1874. Abramovich died on June 20, 1900, and was buried in the association's tomb alongside fellow members who preceded him in death.

FREDERICK C. BAUTOVICH, 1897–1898

Frederick (Ferdo) C. Bautovich was born in 1865 in the city of Dubrovnik. He came to New Orleans in 1881 and, by attending night school and studying diligently, learned the English language thoroughly. In March of 1884, he became a member of the United Slavonian Benevolent Association and only three years later, in May of 1887, was elected its recording secretary and on May 9, 1897, its third president. He served in that capacity until May 9, 1898. He also served as the vice-president of the association during 1900–1901, 1903–1908, 1913–1915, 1916–1917, and 1919–1921. While still in his early twenties he operated a restaurant and a coffee stand in the French Market area. In 1894 he married Pauline Pons, who bore him ten children, eight daughters and two sons. After the turn of the century he entered the real estate business and bought and sold many buildings in the Canal Street area. He also operated a curio store in one of his buildings in the 600 block of Canal Street. He was active in the real estate business until his death in 1938. Both of his two sons, Dr. Colenda F. Bautovich and Dr. Thomas P. Bautovich, became members of the association at an early age.

JACOB PRISLICH, 1898–1901

The fourth president of the association, Jacob Prislich, was born in Rijeka Dubrovacka, a town near Dubrovnik. He came to New Orleans in 1885 and joined the association in May of 1890. In 1897 he was elected to the vice-presidency of the association and kept this of-

Presidents of the United Slavonian Benevolent Association
1874–1974

John Radovich,
1874–1891

Radoslav Abramovich,
1891–1897

Frederick C. Bautovich,
1897–1898

Jacob Prislich,
1898–1901

fice for one year. He served as president from May 9, 1898, to May 12, 1901. To him belongs the honor of leading the still young association into the twentieth century. He worked in Michael Baccich's general store at 915 Decatur Street from 1896 to 1898, and in 1898 opened his own grocery store which he operated for many years.

SAMUEL M. FUCICH, 1901–1903, and 1909–1910

The fifth president of the association, Samuel M. Fucich, was born on the island of Losinj in northern Dalmatia. He was educated in the marine academies of Dalmatia where he was trained to serve as an officer in the merchant marine. He spoke nine languages. When he first arrived in the United States he settled in Donaldsonville, Louisiana, with his uncle and remained there for several years. He moved to New Orleans in mid-1870s and opened an oyster shop on Calliope Street between Magnolia and Clara streets. In 1892 he moved to 530–32 Dumaine Street where he dealt in shucked and in-shell oysters on a large scale. His shop extended through the block to Madison Street. As many as fifty oyster fishermen supplied him with oysters. To facilitate the delivery and insure an ample supply of oysters, he had the Nestor Canal at Nestor, Louisiana, dug so that the fishermen could bring them to the Mississippi River where the S.S. *Grover Cleveland* and the M.V. *Reliance* and other vessels could pick up oysters and bring them to the Picayune Wharf in New Orleans. He constructed camps on either side of the canal where the fishermen lived, and operated his business on a sort of sharecropper system where he would supply the oystermen with food, tools, and housing and they in turn would sell all their oysters to him. He was the first Yugoslav oyster dealer. Many were to follow his example and buy oysters from their countrymen, but none operated in this manner or on such a large scale. He employed many Yugoslavs in his shop in the city, including his three sons.

Fucich Bayou near Pointe a la Hache is named in his honor.

During the late 1890s when the tug-of-war contests were held regularly in New Orleans between various national immigrant groups, he was the captain of the South Slav team. Under his expert coaching they were the undefeated champions for many years.

Fucich joined the United Slavonian Benevolent Association in May, 1875, and served as its vice-president from 1895 to 1897, and its

Samuel M. Fucich,
1901–1903; 1909–1910

Joseph J. Jurisich,
1903–1909; 1915–1916

Andrew Vidak,
1910–1915

George D. Zibilich,
1916–1917; 1919–1922; 1923–1924

president from May 12, 1901, to May 10, 1903. He remained active in the association, and in May of 1909 was elected president for another year.

JOSEPH J. JURISICH, 1903–1909, and 1915–1916

Fucich was succeeded by Joseph John Jurisich, who was born on March 12, 1853, in Janjina on the Peljesac Peninsula. He came to New Orleans in 1873 and a few years later founded the Morning Call Coffee Stand located in the famous French Market. His descendants still own and operate the coffee stand.

Jurisich joined the association in March, 1891, and only two years later was elected its financial secretary, which office he kept until May, 1898, when he was elected vice-president. This position he relinquished in May, 1900, to accept the post of recording secretary. He was the association's recording secretary until May 10, 1903, when he was elected its sixth president; he remained in that position until May 9, 1909, when again he was elected recording secretary, and he served in that capacity until May 9, 1915. Once more he served as president, this time from May 9, 1915, to May 14, 1916. On the latter date he again accepted the post of recording secretary, in which he served for another two years.

A born leader, he was an officer of the association as a president, financial secretary, vice-president, or recording secretary, continuously, from 1893 to 1919. He served as chairman of the committee which coordinated the burials and the recovery activities of the Yugoslav oystermen who were the victims of the 1893 hurricane.

During World War I he was active in promoting the independence of his brethren in the old country and the creation of the Yugoslav state. To this end, he, with several other prominent Dalmatians, organized the Yugoslav League, through which they sent financial and material aid to the war victims. He was one of the leaders of the league and, together with other officers, signed the telegrams and documents sent to President Wilson and other Allied leaders. He died on February 3, 1924.

ANDREW VIDAK, 1910–1915

Andrew Vidak, the seventh president of the association, was born in 1873 in Molunat, Konavli, and came to Louisiana in 1892. He became a member in September of 1895 and on May 9, 1909, was elected vice-president, and a year later, on May 8, 1910, president of the association. He remained president until May 9, 1915, when he was succeeded by Joseph Jurisich. Vidak and Peter Spremich owned and operated the Vidak and Spremich Saloon and Boarding House at 760 Camp Street for many years. During World War I he was active as a member and an organizer of the Yugoslav League in New Orleans. From 1915 until his death on July 30, 1948, he served on the Board of Directors of the association as one of its most active members.

GEORGE D. ZIBILICH, 1916–1917, 1919–1922, and 1923–1924

George D. Zibilich, who was born in Duba on the Peljesac Peninsula on April 23, 1857, was the only president who served on three separate occasions.

Upon coming to Louisiana in 1874 he entered the oyster fishing business with his brother Jack. A year or so later he sold his part of the partnership and came to New Orleans where he opened a coffee stand with Frederick Bautovich at St. Ann and Decatur streets.

Sometime during early 1890s he quit the coffee stand and opened a grocery at Touro and Urquhart streets, but this store burned to the ground in 1895. In 1899 he again entered the coffee stand business, this time in old Treme Market at Orleans and Villere streets. Between 1900 and 1906 he interrupted his coffee stand business to enter the insurance field. He and a partner organized their own company, "The United States Relief Society," but due to ill health he had to sell his interest to his partner. From 1906 to 1916 he operated various businesses, first a restaurant, then a charcoal business, and a coffee stand which he sold in 1916 to enter the picture show business. This business prospered. He owned and operated several theaters throughout New Orleans. In 1929 he retired from the theater business and turned their management over to his two sons, Dominick and Joseph.

Zibilich joined the association in January of 1878, and from 1889 to 1891 served as its recording secretary, and from 1903 to 1906 as the association's financial secretary. In May, 1915, he was elected vice-president and the following year, on May 14, 1916, president of the association, serving in that post until May 13, 1917. On May 11, 1919 he was again elected president and served until May 14, 1922. Apparently he was popular with the members, for on May 13, 1923, after an absence of only one year, he was elected to the presidency for a third time. He remained active in the association, serving on various committees until the late 1930s when his failing eyesight compelled him to withdraw from active participation.

Zibilich's life in Louisiana, from 1874 to his death on January 1, 1950, spans a period of transition of the Yugoslavs from immigrants to full-fledged participants in the American way of life. He, himself, was a best example of this. He arrived as a penniless immigrant and through persistent struggles, through failures and successes, he became a prominent New Orleans businessman. He lived a full life, highly respected by his American friends and beloved by his family and fellow Yugoslavs.

Anthony A. Nesanovich, 1917–1919

The ninth president of the association, Anthony A. Nesanovich, was born in 1868 in Trpanj on the Peljesac Peninsula. He came to Louisiana in 1886 where he became an oyster grower, in which occupation he remained for fifteen years. For a few years he tried the restaurant business only to return to the oyster business this time as a dealer buying from his countrymen and selling to the New Orleans hotels and restaurants. For over four decades—until his retirement in late 1940s—he remained one of the principal New Orleans oyster dealers.

Nesanovich joined the United Slavonian Benevolent Association in February of 1890. For one year—from May 1908 to May, 1909—he served as the association's financial secretary and on May 13, 1917, was elected its president which post he held until May 11, 1919. He also served as the vice-president of the association during the 1922–1923 and 1924–1930 periods. He remained an active member, serving on the Board of Directors, until his death on April 7, 1951.

He presided over the association during the United States participation in World War I. It was during this time that many young men took a leave of absence and joined the United States armed forces and that the members saw their brethren in Dalmatia finally liberated from the Austrian yoke and united in a new South Slavic state: Yugoslavia. Nesanovich, with the rest of the members, rejoiced over this and helped the new nation materially through the New Orleans Yugoslav League.

John Jurovich, 1922–1923

John Jurovich was born in the village of Kuna on the Peljesac Peninsula in 1889. He joined the association on January 5, 1913, and

Anthony A. Nesanovich,
1917–1919

John Jurovich,
1922–1923

Anthony M. Zibilich,
1924–1927; 1931–1932

Peter J. Kopanica,
1927–1929

on May 14, 1922, was elected as the association's tenth president, serving until May 13, 1923. From 1923 until his death on June 26, 1963, he served as a director of the association. For many years Jurovich was the Louisiana Yugoslavs' "insurance man." He was an executive with the Pontchartrain District of the Metropolitan Life Insurance Company and in that capacity insured most Yugoslavs in the New Orleans area. He was also active in Masonic organizations and was a member of the Forum Lodge Number 395, Free and Accepted Masons for many years.

ANTHONY M. ZIBILICH, 1924–1927 and 1931–1932

Anthony M. Zibilich was the first second-generation president of the association. He was born in New Orleans on December 14, 1897, and received his primary and secondary education there. After completing high school he enrolled at Tulane University from which he received his bachelor's degree in civil engineering in 1918. Upon graduation he entered the services of the United States Navy Department in Washington, D.C., and after one year of service he was transferred to New Orleans. He remained in the service of the federal government, achieving the rank of captain in the United States Coast Guard.

Under the expert tutelage of his parents, Miho and Marija Zibilich, who came from Duba, he mastered the speaking, writing, and reading of the Croatian language thoroughly. This is convincingly evident from the scrupulously kept minutes and other records (in Croatian) during his tenure as recording secretary.

He married Elmira Bautovich, daughter of the third president of the association, Frederick Bautovich, and Pauline Pons Bautovich. They had four children: three sons and one daughter.

Zibilich joined the association as a minor member on January 8, 1911. He became active in the affairs of the association at an early age. As a chairman of the Committee on Revision of the Constitution and By-Laws, he thoroughly revised and properly codified the association's rules. He also rewrote the Croatian section (which until then was written in the provincial Croatian) in the modern literary Croatian language. The revised statutes were published in September, 1923.

On May 11, 1924, at the youthful age of twenty-six, he was elected as the eleventh president of the association, and served for three years —until May 8, 1927.

For the 1930–1931 year he held the office of the recording secretary and on May 10, 1931, was again elected to the presidency and served until May 8, 1932. When he died, at the age of fifty-two, on May 21, 1951, the association lost one of its most valuable members, and the Yugoslavs in Louisiana, especially the oystermen, one of its most unselfish, useful, and benevolent friends.

PETER J. KOPANICA, 1927–1929

The twelfth president of the association, Peter J. Kopanica, was born in Cesvinica near Ston in 1877 and came to Louisiana in 1893. For the first twenty-three years in Louisiana he cultivated and sold oysters in the Louisiana bayous. In 1916 he quit the oyster growing business, moved to New Orleans, and became an oyster dealer. For the next three and a half decades he was one of the principal oyster dealers in New Orleans. He had a fleet of trucks which transported the oysters from the boats to his many customers and to his own shop where they were opened, packed in gallon containers, and sold to New Orleans restaurants for frying. The "PK" brand became famous among the gourmets in the New Orleans area. He remained in this business until shortly before his death on August 29, 1953.

Papa Peter, as we affectionately called him, joined the association on March 5, 1899. On May 14, 1922, he was elected grand marshal, which post he relinguished on May 8, 1927, to become president of the association. He remained president until May 12, 1929, when he was succeeded by Stephen Palihnich. In May, 1930, he was elected vice-president and remained in that office until May, 1935. For the rest of his life he remained one of the staunchest supporters of the association, serving on the Board of Directors and on several committees and regularly and punctually attending the association's meetings.

Besides holding membership in the United Slavonian Benevolent Association he was an active member of Knights Templar, the Jerusalem Temple of the Shrine, and the Grand Chapter, Royal Arch Masons of Louisiana, and one of the charter members of the Slavonian Pleasure Club. A bachelor all his life, he was an immaculate dresser, always effusing continental charm, a southern gentleman by adoption.

STEPHEN I. PALIHNICH, 1929–1931

Stephen I. Palihnich joined the association on July 6, 1913, and seven years later, on May 9, 1920, was elected its recording secretary which office he held until May 8, 1927. During this time the constitution and the bylaws of the association were completely revised and printed in proper form. From May 12, 1929, to May 10, 1931, he served as the thirteenth president of the association.

Palihnich was born in Kuna on the Peljesac Peninsula in 1877 and came to New Orleans in 1892. Upon arrival he obtained employment at Joseph Jurisich's Morning Call Coffee Stand where he was eventually advanced to become manager of the establishment. He remained there until his retirement. He was very active in the civic affairs of his fellow Yugoslavs, serving as president of the Slavonian Pleasure Club for many years and as an officer of the Yugoslav League during World War I. He willingly contributed his spare time to the activities of the United Slavonian Benevolent Association, for which the grateful members awarded him a gold watch.

John Gentilich, 1932–1933, and 1935–1936

John Gentilich was born in Molat on the island of the same name in 1874 and came to Louisiana in 1895. He entered the restaurant business which he followed for the rest of his life. He owned and operated the Marble Hall Café on Lafayette Street for over thirty years. Due to his superior ability he was active in many other fields, but the restaurant business commanded his chief interest.

Up to 1895 the Yugoslavs of Louisiana came mostly from southern Dalmatia, but with Gentilich's coming to New Orleans, the homogeneity of the Louisiana Yugoslavs was changed somewhat (Molat is in northern Dalmatia). Shortly after Gentilich's arrival in New Orleans many other Yugoslavs—his relatives and friends—followed him here, and eventually a substantial number from Molat and the immediate area settled in New Orleans.

Gentilich joined the United Slavonian Benevolent Association on August 7, 1892, and soon became active in the affairs of the young organization. From May, 1906, to May, 1908, he served as financial secretary of the association and from May, 1911, to May, 1913, as its vice-president. However he did not follow the usual procedure of becoming president after serving in the vice-presidency, but waited until May, 1932, when he was elected the association's fourteenth president. He served until May 14, 1933. In May of 1935 he was again elected to the presidency and served until May 10, 1936.

From 1892 until his death on September 24, 1940, he was active in the association's affairs, serving on its Board of Directors and on

Stephen I. Palihnich,
1929–1931

John Gentilich,
1932–1933; 1935–1936

Anthony J. Carevich,
1933–1935

Jack A. Porobil,
1936–1939

various committees for over four decades. During the First World War he helped to organize the Yugoslav League and was instrumental in sending letters and telegrams to President Wilson and other Allied leaders explaining the just cause of the Dalmatian Croats in their struggle for self-determination. He was a member of the Slavonian Pleasure Club, and Level Lodge No. 373 Free and Accepted Masons, Indivisible Friends Commandery No. 1 Knights Templar, and Grand Consistory of Louisiana A.A.S.R.M. Orleans Guards of the Delta Chapter No. 1, Royal Arch Masons.

ANTHONY J. CAREVICH, 1933–1935

The fifteenth president, Anthony J. Carevich, joined the association on May 7, 1911, and eight years later was elected grand marshal, which post he kept until May, 1921. He served as treasurer of the association during the 1922–1923 year. On May 14, 1933, he was elected president and served until May 12, 1935. He was at the helm of the association during the difficult depression years when many members had difficulty paying their dues. However, due to Carevich's understanding nature and the generosity of the association, they remained members and many were helped financially. The sixtieth anniversary of the founding of the association was celebrated during his administration on July 27, 1934, with a festival and picnic on the grounds of the Holy Cross College.

Carevich was born in Korcula, southern Dalmatia, in 1880 and came to Louisiana in 1909. Upon arrival he fished oysters for a living. Two years later he moved to New Orleans and opened a grocery store at 818 Chartres Street, which he operated until shortly before his death on July 5, 1937.

JACK A. POROBIL, 1936–1939

Jack Anthony Porobil joined the association as a minor member on May 1, 1910. Although born and raised in Louisiana he speaks the Croatian language fluently. With this asset and his amiable and dynamic personality, he soon won the friendship and confidence of the old-timers and the leaders of the association, who entrusted him with responsible positions while he was still a young man. He took a sincere interest in the affairs of the association and served as a member of its Real Estate and of the Finance committees for many years. In May of 1935 he was elected vice-president and a year later, on May 10,

1936, president of the association. He served in that capacity for three years until May 14, 1939. When he became president, the association was having financial difficulties (as was the whole country due to the depression), but when he left the association's presidency, its treasury was on the upswing. The June 6, 1937, festival—the first of its kind—was a social and financial success, largely due to Porobil's skillful leadership.

The sixteenth president of the association was born in Leeville, Louisiana, on January 14, 1902, and educated in New Orleans schools. He entered the world of finance and in April, 1931, organized his own investment and lending institution: the Safety Finance Service, Inc., which he still heads. The finance company prospered, and its offices became an unofficial headquarters for the Yugoslavs in this area. Here they can get their documents translated and notarized, and get their papers prepared to travel to Yugoslavia or to bring a relative here.

Jack, as he is known to his many friends, is well respected in the New Orleans financial circles. He is a member of the Executive Committee of the First Homestead and Savings Association and has also been a member of the Board of Directors of that institution since 1935. He is looked upon by his fellow Yugoslavs as an "elder statesman," a Yugoslav Bernard Baruch, and is often asked for advice on financial, business, and travel matters. His two sons, Jack, Jr., executive vice-president of Safety Finance Service, Inc., and Gregory, an attorney, both members of the association, are following in their father's footsteps and are fast becoming adept at friendliness and dependability in dealing with Yugoslavs and native Louisianians.

JOHN P. GENTILICH, 1939–1942

The seventeenth president of the association, John P. Gentilich, became a member of the association on February 3, 1924, and on that same day was appointed by the late Nicholas Jovanovich—who served the association as a chairman of the Finance Committee most of his adult life—to serve on the Finance Committee as Jovanovich's assistant. Gentilich has been serving the association ever since, a half century of humanitarian service. On May 10, 1936, he was elected vice-president and three years later, on May 14, 1939, president of the association. He served the association in this capacity for three years, until May 10, 1942. After a six-year respite he was again elected to an office, this time to the responsible position of treasurer of the association. He has handled this position so well that he has been re-elected every year since 1948. Besides holding the above-mentioned offices, he held several other responsible positions in the organization: in July, 1934, he was the general chairman of the sixtieth anniversary celebration of the association, and in 1960 he served as the chairman of the supper dance. He also served as an assistant chairman, and co-chairman, and a member of many other activities and committees.

Gentilich was born on April 14, 1905, in the seaside town of Molat. He attended the elementary school there and three years of upper gymnasium in the nearby city of Zadar. Upon coming to New Orleans he attended night school and shortly thereafter entered the restaurant business with his father, Anthony, and an uncle, John Gentilich. In 1934 he became the owner of the Marble Hall Café near Gallier Hall (then City Hall), which he operated until 1969 when he took well-deserved retirement.

When Gentilich retired, he also closed for good a 114-year institution, which, as the New Orleans *Times-Picayune* stated editorially, "was a veritable Second City Hall to generations of statesmen and politicians . . . and a 'Second City Room' for workers of the *Times-Picayune, New Orleans States*, and the *States-Item.*" On its closing day he was honored by the presence of New Orleans Mayor Victor Schiro, U.S. Representative F. Edward Hebert, and many officials from the *Times-Picayune* and the *States-Item*, who with Gentilich, lamented the passing of such a venerable and friendly establishment. However, his retirement does not mean idleness, for Gentilich keeps busy with his social, civic, and benevolent activities, and therein lies the secret of his exuberant youth. He is married to Theresa Siegen-thaler with whom he has shared the trials and tribulations and successes of his interesting and active life. They had one son, John Jr., who died in 1968. A personal friend of mayors and governors, Gentilich is always ready to help his fellow Yugoslavs. A long-time member of the Board of Directors of the Safety Finance Company, he is presently serving as its vice-president. He also served ten years as a member of the Parkway and Parks Commission of New Orleans and actively participates in Masonic and civic organizations.

JOHN SUKNO, 1942–1945

Gentilich was succeeded by John Sukno, who was born in the village of Komaje, Konavli, in 1884 and came to New Orleans in

John P. Gentilich,
1939–1942

John Sukno,
1942–1945

John M. Marcev,
1945–1948

Matthew J. Bilich,
1948–1950

1900. He joined the association on October 4, 1903, and served as its treasurer from May, 1919, to May, 1920, and from May, 1927, to May, 1929. On May 14, 1939, he was elected vice-president and three years later, on May 10, 1942, president of the association. He remained in that post until May 13, 1945. Sukno guided the association during the trying years of World War II, when most of its young members were absent fighting the enemy, several sacrificing their lives.

In addition to membership in the United Slavonian Benevolent Association, he held membership in the following organizations: Slavonian Pleasure Club, Perfect Union Lodge No. 1, F. and A.M.; Grand Consistory of Louisiana, Jerusalem Temple, A.A.O.N.M.S., of New Orleans, and New Orleans No. 30 B.P.O.E., and the Ancient Order of Druids. He took an active part in the activities of the association throughout his tenure as a member and as a fully participating member of its Board of Directors, until his death on April 6, 1953.

JOHN M. MARCEV, 1945–1948

The nineteenth president of the association, John M. Marcev, became a member of the association on April 7, 1923, and on May 13, 1934, was elected its grand marshal. He held that position for one year. During the 1937–1939 period he served as the treasurer. On May 13, 1945, he was elected president and served for three years, until May 9, 1948. During his tenure as president two financially and socially successful festivals were held; July 7, 1946, and July 19, 1947, celebrating the seventy-second and seventy-third anniversaries respectively. On May 13, 1951, he was elected financial secretary of the association to which position the members—cognizant of his outstanding efficiency—have unanimously reelected him every year. He is still serving as the financial secretary.

Marcev was born on July 4, 1902, in Molat, Yugoslavia, and came to New Orleans in 1921. Soon after, he found employment in a restaurant and by self-study mastered the English language and the restaurant-managing business. In 1930 he and Joseph Baricev opened the Auditorium Restaurant on N. Rampart and St. Peter streets and three years later, in March, 1934, he opened his own restaurant—Johnny's—which he operated until his retirement in 1971. Due to the central location (1000 N. Rampart) of Marcev's restaurant and his gregarious personality, Johnny's became a meeting place of the Louisiana Yugoslavs.

Although his restaurant duties kept him busy he found time to actively participate in the affairs of the association and in carnival and Masonic organizations in which he holds membership. He continues to do so in his retirement.

On October 8, 1930, he married Frances Marie Ingegnores. They have two sons, John, Jr., and Joseph.

MATTHEW J. BILICH, 1948–1950

The twentieth president of the association, Matthew J. Bilich, was born in Duba on the Peljesac Peninsula on November 9, 1894, and came to New Orleans in 1906. When he came to Louisiana he became an oyster fisherman. Since his early years here were similar to those of many a Dalmatian lad, I think it appropriate to let him tell us about it, as he narrated his experiences in the *New Orleanian* magazine.

> At the age of twelve I began work with my father at a place located in Bayou Cook and continued work with him for four years until 1911 when I went into business for myself at my father's old place. I was considered a very capable young fisherman and an able seaman, working tirelessly many hours each day. I ordinarily worked fourteen hours a day, many a time eighteen and sometimes, under various circumstances, even a full twenty-four hours, so desirous was I of earning money. But inevitably my fortune was poor, trailing me as it has almost all of the other fishermen. When I thought my financial worries were ended along would come disaster resulting in the loss of most of my crop. That is what happened in 1915 when the storm of that year destroyed eighty per cent of my crop.

He remained in the oyster growing business for a number of years after 1915 and then moved to New Orleans to become an oyster dealer, establishing his own company: The M. J. Bilich Oyster Company which his family still runs. He remained active in the oyster dealership until two years before his death on April 24, 1970.

Bilich joined the association on March 5, 1911. After years of unselfish work for the association he was elected vice-president on May 13, 1945, and three years later, on May 9, 1948, president of the association. He served until May 15, 1950. He remained active in its affairs until the late 1960s when ill health forced him into semiretirement. He was married to Frances Hihar. They had three children: two daughters and a son.

As a former fisherman and a dealer of oysters he was sincerely interested in improving the conditions of the oysterman. To this end, in early 1930s, he helped organize the Association of Louisiana Oystermen, Inc., and served as its vice-president for many years. He was also a charter member of the Yugoslav American Club; a charter member of the Slavonian Pleasure Club; a charter member of the Louisiana Oyster Dealers and Growers Association; a member of Level Lodge 373, F. and A.M.; a 32nd degree Mason in the Grand Consistory of Louisiana; a noble in the Jerusalem Temple; a member of the Jerusalem Temple Mounted Escort Patrol, the Babylon Chapter No. 66 Royal Arch Masons, and Ivanhoe Commandery of the Knights Templar.

MARINE GERICA, 1950–1953

Marine Gerica joined the association on January 7, 1912. During the early 1930s he became active in its affairs and was, at this time, appointed to the Board of Directors. He was the general chairman of the June 6, 1937, festival-dance celebrating the sixty-third anniversary of the association. It is partly due to Gerica's hard work and indomitable persistence that this festival—during the twilight of the depression—was financially successful.

On May 9, 1948, he was elected vice-president and two years later, on May 14, 1950, president of the association. He served the association as its chief executive for three years until May 10, 1953. He is one of the association's most ardent workers and a champion fund collector. He has served the association efficiently and unselfishly as the chairman of Relief Committee and of the Tombs and Halls Committee for many years. He has also taken active part in the association's supper dances, serving from 1954 through 1960 as an assistant chairman, and from 1961 to the present as the chairman of the affair.

Gerica was born on March 5, 1894, in Ston and came to Louisiana in August, 1904. His first job in the New World was as an oysterman in the Louisiana bayous, where he worked for two years and then became a clerk in Mato Parun's grocery store at Olga. He remained there for four years. From 1910 to 1917, he worked in his uncle Marko Gerica's shipyard at Olga where he learned the shipbuilding trade. In 1917 he and a partner, Ante Bjelancich, bought the shipyard and when Bjelancich died in June, 1932, Gerica assumed full ownership. He ran the shipyard until 1942 repairing and building vessels for the Yugoslav oystermen. In 1942 he became manager for

Marine Gerica,
1950–1953

John Muhoberac,
1953–1954

Dr. Anthony G. Jurakovich,
1954–1956

Peter G. Vujnovich,
1956–1958

the New Orleans-Burrwood Packet Company. Later this firm merged with the El Rito Company, owned by Peter Taliancich and Marko Cibilich, into a new company: The Majestic-El Rito Freight Service. This company ran a freight and passenger service from New Orleans to Burrwood and return, stopping at points along the river. It transported passengers and all kinds of freight—machinery, oil, medical supplies, foodstuff, and building supplies from New Orleans and all kinds of produce, oranges, oysters, fish, shrimp, animal skins, and stock to New Orleans. During World War II it performed invaluable service to the United States Government and other governmental agencies in carrying vitally needed cargo to points near the mouth of the river. After logging hundreds of thousands of miles on the Mississippi in all kinds of weather, Gerica retired from the river in 1960 to a more sedate life.

He is married to Anne Machela. They have one daughter Marion (Mrs. Henry Sabrio) who reigned as queen of the 1937 USBA festival. Besides the above-mentioned activities in the association he was a long-time member and president for six years of the Grand Prairie Levee Board, a member of the Slavonian Pleasure Club, and a member of the Okeanos carnival organization over which he reigned as its king during the 1956 carnival season.

JOHN M. MUHOBERAC, 1953–1954

John M. Muhoberac, whose father Captain Matthew Muhoberac, came from Osojnik near Dubrovnik, Yugoslavia, in 1870s, was born in 1890 in Olga, Louisiana. By trade a carpenter and a boat builder, he entered the restaurant business later in life and owned and operated the Metry Café in Metairie for many years.

Muhoberac joined the association in April, 1920, and on May 13, 1951, was elected its vice-president, then president on May 10, 1953. He served until May 9, 1954. He was also a member of the Metairie Lions Club, Metairie Business Association, George Washington No. 65 F. and A.M., Grand Consistory of Louisiana A.A.S.R.M., and a noble of Jerusalem Temple. He was active in the association until shortly before his death, on December 22, 1962.

ANTHONY G. JURACOVICH, 1954–1956

The twenty-third president, Anthony G. Juracovich, joined the association on September 7, 1913. In the late 1920s he was appointed to the Board of Directors of which he is still a member. From May, 1942, to May, 1945, he served as the association's vice-president and from May 9, 1954, to May 13, 1956, as its president. During his administration the first supper dance celebrating the association's anniversary was held in June, 1954. Since then these supper dances have become the main social gatherings of the association.

Juracovich was born on October 24, 1886, in Zivogošće near Makarska and came to Louisiana, to join his father in Plaquemines Parish, in September, 1899. After attending public schools he entered Chenit Institute, from which he graduated in 1909. He followed that with the study of pharmacy and graduated in 1912 from the New Orleans College of Pharmacy. After practicing pharmacy for several years, he studied medicine at Tulane University Medical School, and when in his sophomore year war was declared, he entered the military service of the United States. He served in the Medical Corps in Isolation Hospital. After the war he joined the staff of the Eye, Ear, Nose, and Throat Hospital in New Orleans. Consequently he became interested in dental diseases and entered Loyola Dental School from which he graduated in 1924. After graduation he practiced dentistry in New Orleans until his retirement in 1958.

In 1924 he married Clara (Dolly) Bautovich. Their two children are Mrs. Rosary J. Walker and Dr. Joseph G. Juracovich.

PETER G. VUJNOVICH, 1956–1958

Peter G. Vujnovich was born in Sucuraj on the island of Hvar on May 8, 1922, and came to Louisiana in January, 1931. Upon completion of elementary grades in the Louisiana public schools he entered the oyster growing business with his father, Captain George Vujnovich, in the Grand Ecaille area. In 1952 he expanded his oyster business to include an oyster dealership in New Orleans. He is still engaged in both the cultivating and growing of oysters in the Louisiana bayous and in oyster dealership under the name of Capt. Pete's Oysters. He is married to Eva Jurisich; they have six children: Mary Jane, Anna Rose, Lana Jean, Peter, Jr., Anthony, and Frank. The three boys are minor members of the association. He is a long-time member of the Slavonian Pleasure Club, a member of the Yugoslav Club, whose president he was for many years, and a member of the Louisiana Oyster Dealers and Growers Association where he held the position of treasurer from 1967 to 1973 when he was elected president.

Vujnovich joined the association as a minor on April 5, 1936. He reigned as king of the seventy-fifth (Diamond Jubilee) celebration of the founding of the association. The festival was held in the Municipal Auditorium in New Orleans on June 5, 1949, and in Buras on July 31, 1949. He was elected to the vice-presidency on May 10, 1953, and three years later, on May 13, 1956, to the presidency of the association and served until May 11, 1958. On January 3, 1971, he was elected recording secretary and served in that capacity until January, 1973.

BENJAMIN BILICH, 1958–1959

Benjamin Bilich, affectionately known as Ben to his many friends, became a member of the association in October, 1912. On May 13, 1923, he was elected financial secretary and performed his duties with such dedicated efficiency that the members reelected him every year for twenty-eight years until May 14, 1951. His is the longest continuous tenure of any office in the history of the association. On May 13, 1956, he was elected vice-president and on May 11, 1958, president of the association. He served until May 10, 1959. Since that time he has remained a regular member of the Board of Directors and takes an active part in the affairs of the association.

Bilich was born in Duba on the Peljesac Peninsula on April 18, 1894, and came to New Orleans in September, 1910. Unlike his compatriots from Duba, who usually enter the oyster growing field upon coming to Louisiana, he opened a restaurant. At first he owned and operated a restaurant at 831 Decatur Street and later, Ben's Restaurant at 141 Decatur from which he retired in 1951. He is a charter member of the Slavonian Pleasure Club and a long-time member of the Board of Directors of the Safety Finance Company. He is married to Marija Gentilich. They have one daughter, Marie, who reigned as Miss America in the June 6, 1937, USBA Festival. Marie's husband, the late Dr. Jules C. Guidry, a dentist, although not of Yugoslav ancestry, was well known and readily accepted by the Yugoslavs in Louisiana whom he usually greeted in Croatian.

FRED J. BARBIER, 1959–1961

The twenty-sixth president, Fred J. Barbier, joined the association as a minor on March 6, 1927. During the late 1940s he became involved in the activities of the association and soon demonstrated

Benjamin Bilich,
1958–1959

Fred J. Barbier,
1959–1961

Frank J. Glavina,
1961–1963

Frank Kopanica,
1963–1966

exceptional leadership qualities. On May 11, 1958, he was elected vice-president and a year later, on May 10, 1959, president of the association. He remained president for two years. It was during his administration that the practice of presenting twenty-five-year and fifty-year membership certificates to the members was inaugurated. He also appointed the committee to revise the charter, constitution, and bylaws. These documents were completely revised, and adopted, and the association was rechartered well ahead of the charter expiration date of May, 1964.

Barbier was one of the initiators, and the driving force, of the annual supper dances to celebrate the association's anniversaries. He served as the chairman and the master of ceremonies of the initial supper dance in 1954. He also served as the master of ceremonies on many other occasions. He is the first, and so far the only, president of the association from the ranks of the third generation Yugoslavs.

It was primarily through his efforts that the old practice of conducting the business of the association in Croatian only and the requirement that presidents must speak Croatian language was abolished, thereby paving the way for the participation of the second and the third generation members and assuring the continuity of the association.

Born in New Orleans on October 12, 1920, he is married to Melva Weber, and they have one daughter, Carol. Barbier is engaged in the paper and janitorial distribution business in an executive position of secretary-treasurer of Advance Paper Company. He is also president of Advance Export Company. He has held office as president of the Yugoslav-American Club, president of the Slavonian Pleasure Club, past master of Fidelity Lodge No. 426 F. and A.M., and is currently vice-president of the Southern Paper Trade Association. During the Second World War he served in the United States Navy for four years, primarily in the European Theater of Operations, and was honorably discharged with a rating of chief yeoman.

FRANK JOHN GLAVINA, 1961–1963

Frank John Glavina, whose father, John Glavina, came from Trpanj at the turn of the century, and maternal grandfather, John Barbier, from Dusine near Vrgorac, Yugoslavia, during the late 1870s, joined the United Slavonian Benevolent Association as a minor member on October 3, 1926. During the late 1940s he became active in the association and was at that time appointed to the Board of Directors, which position he still holds. Following in the footsteps of his father, who held several offices in the association, Frank was elected vice-president in May of 1959 and two years later, on May 7, 1961, president of the association. He served until May 12, 1963. From the late 1940s to the present he has remained an active member of the association, serving on various committees, and is especially active on the Supper Dance Committee where he has served since the first supper dance of 1954.

Glavina was born in New Orleans on January 17, 1922. There he received his elementary and secondary education. From October, 1942, to February, 1946, he served in the United States Coast Guard and was assigned to a destroyer escort, the U.S.S. *Lansing*, which was engaged in convoy and other duties in the Atlantic and the Mediterranean.

He joined the New Orleans Police Department in December of 1946 where he received intensive training to become one of "New Orleans' finest." He is a graduate of the New Orleans Police Academy and the Louisiana State Police Training School. As a police officer he served his city with devotion and distinction, receiving several certificates of merit and numerous letters of commendation from appreciative citizens. In January, 1963—after seventeen years of devoted service—he retired from the Police Department with a rank of sergeant in the Detective Bureau. Presently he is employed as a warehouse superintendent by the Advance Paper Company.

He is a member of the Slavonian Pleasure Club; Veterans of Foreign Wars, John Dibert Post; Police Mutual Benevolent Association; Fraternal Order of Police; International Conference of Police Associations; Louisiana Peace Officers Association; and a past president of the Yugoslav American Club.

On December 22, 1946, Frank married Eleanor Thompson of New Orleans. They have three children: Melanie, who is married to Dr. Wayne Lyerly, a dentist; Marlene, married to Chester G. Cooke, a detective in the New Orleans Police Department; and a son, Martin John, who is attending Louisiana State University and who is a member of the Slavonian Association; and a grandson, Michael Cooke.

FRANK KOPANICA, 1963–1966

The twenty-eighth president of the association, Frank Kopanica, joined the association on October 1, 1939. Immediately after the Second World War he became active in the affairs of the association and to the present day remains one of its most productive workers. In 1946 he became a member of the Board of Directors and of several committees, notably the Finance Committee, to which he has contributed many hours of diligent work. On May 7, 1961, he was elected vice-president and on May 12, 1963, president of the association. He remained in that office until January 9, 1966. It was during his tenure in office that the association was rechartered and a new set of bylaws adopted. The working year of the association was changed from May of one year to May of the following year to the calendar year. Hence his term in office ended in January instead of in the traditional May. During the last year of his administration, in September, 1965, Hurricane Betsy struck the lower Louisiana coast and the association, under his leadership, canceled its October-scheduled supper dance and donated the entire proceeds of the raffle ticket sales (three thousand dollars) to the victims of the storm in Plaquemines Parish. A few years later—on January 14, 1968—he was again elected to an office in the association, this time to the vice-presidency. He served in that position until January, 1972.

Frank was born in Ćesvinica near Ston, Yugoslavia, on October 4, 1923, and came to Louisiana in August, 1939. Upon coming here he attended the New Orleans public schools for one year and Saint Stanislaus High School in Bay St. Louis, Mississippi, for three years. Subsequently he attended Soulé Business College in New Orleans. During the Second World War he served in the United States Navy for three years. He is a retired Louisiana state trooper and is presently employed as a revenue officer with the Louisiana Department of Revenue. He is a member and past president of the Slavonian Pleasure Club, and a member of the American Legion, Louisiana Peace Officers Association, Ocean Lodge No. 144, Grand Consistory of Louisiana, 32nd degree, and of Jerusalem Temple. Frank is married to Cecile Tabary. They have four daughters: Cecile, Nike, Tina Marie, and Kate.

MATTHEW J. FICOVICH, 1966–1968

Matthew J. Ficovich became a member of the association on February 7, 1926, and although residing at Empire, some sixty miles downriver from New Orleans, he took an active part in the association. He drives regularly from Empire (even if it means canceling a scheduled fishing trip) to attend the meetings and other functions of the association. On May 12, 1963, he was elected vice-president and on January 9, 1966, president of the association. He served until January 14, 1968. He was the first, and so far the only, president residing outside of the Greater New Orleans area. He is a member of the Board of Directors of the association, chairman of the Emergency Relief Committee for the Port Sulphur–Empire area, and the chairman of the Committee of Hall and Tombs for the Buras area. He is a regular member of the Supper Dance Committee and for the past few years has been serving as its Plaquemines Parish cochairman.

Ficovich was born in Ston, Yugoslavia, on January 12, 1909, and came to Louisiana in September, 1925. For the next eight years he fished oysters in the Louisiana bayous with his uncle, John Marinovich. From 1933 to 1946 he worked for the Freeport Sulphur Company and from 1946 to 1971, when he retired, he operated a marine fuel supply station at Empire, Louisiana. He is married to the former Theresa Jurisich; they have four daughters. He is a member of the Triumph Lodge No. 422, F. and A.M.; Grand Consistory of Louisiana, 32nd degree, A.A.S.R.M.; Jerusalem Temple of New Orleans; and of the Slavonian Pleasure Club. An avid fisherman, he spends much of his spare time in the great outdoors.

ROBERT A. GEGEN, 1968–1970

The thirtieth president of the association, Robert A. Gegen, joined the association on June 7, 1959. Immediately upon joining he became an active member of the organization, participating in various committees and serving willingly when called upon. In 1960 he was elected to the Board of Directors and has remained a member ever since. On January 9, 1966, he was elected vice-president and two years later, on January 14, 1968, president of the association. He served until January 3, 1971. During his tenure of office, Hurricane Camille struck the Louisiana coast and devastated Plaquemines Parish. The association, under his leadership, rose to the occasion and gave generous financial assistance to its widows and donated three thousand dollars to the Plaquemines Parish Camille Relief Fund.

Although he was not a native Louisianian, Gegen's leadership was readily accepted by all the members.

Gegen, whose parents Anthony Gegen and File Matulich came from Molat, was born in Hoquiam, Washington, on December 17, 1923. During the 1920s so many Yugoslav immigrants settled in Hoquiam, especially from Molat, that it was sometimes known as "second Molat." In this Yugoslav-American atmosphere young Gegen learned the Croatian language and also the customs of the old country which the Hoquiam Yugoslavs followed.

After graduating from Hoquiam High School he worked as a commercial fisherman in and around the Puget Sound. From May, 1943, to February, 1946, he served in the United States Navy and saw service in the Pacific where he took part in three campaigns. In July, 1946, he came to New Orleans—on a vacation with his uncle Mike Matulich—and so liked the Sunny South that he has remained here ever since. For a while he worked in John P. Gentilich's Marble Hall Café but decided not to make the restaurant business his lifetime work. Two years later, in 1948, he became an employee of the United States Government. For the first four years he worked in the Department of Agriculture and in March, 1952, became associated with the Department of Health, Education and Welfare, where, in the Social Security Administration, he presently performs the responsible duties of a claims representative. In this position he has come in contact with many Yugoslavs who sought his help and his experienced counsel regarding their retirement. To this he has responded generously and willingly. During the last twenty-one years with the Social Security he has assisted thousands to receive their rightfully due compensation in their twilight years. It is this work of helping his fellow man—as a government employee and as an ardent worker in the Slavonian Association—that gives Gegen his greatest satisfaction and a feeling of accomplishment.

Milos Michael Vujnovich, 1971–1973

Milos Michael Vujnovich was born in the seaside town of Sucuraj on the island of Hvar, Yugoslavia, on February 10, 1924, and came to Louisiana in November, 1938. He completed his elementary education in New Orleans, where he learned the English language. For a while he worked on the oyster reefs in Plaquemines Parish with his father, the late Captain George Vujnovich, and afterwards attended Delgado Trades School, where he studied cabinetmaking and the machine shop trades. In October, 1943, he joined the United States Army and served in the European Theater of Operation as a sergeant in the Signal Corps, Psychological Warfare Branch. He was awarded five battle stars.

Matthew J. Ficovich,
1966–1968

Robert J. Gegen,
1968–1971

Milos M. Vujnovich,
1971–1973

Baldo V. Pausina,
1973–

Honorably discharged from the army in December, 1945, he entered the University of Southwestern Louisiana in September, 1946, and graduated with a B.S. degree in education with a physics and mathematics major in June, 1949. Subsequently he received a Master of Education degree from Louisiana State University and a Master of Science degree from Loyola University. After his graduation from Southwestern he taught mathematics in the Westwego High School for two years. For the past eighteen years he has been associated with Delgado Junior College where he holds a rank of professor of physics and the chairmanship of the Science Department. In July, 1953, he married Vera Perret. They have three daughters, Wendy, Sandra, and Janice, and a son, George.

Vujnovich joined the United Slavonian Benevolent Association on February 4, 1940. On May 9, 1954, he was elected recording secretary, an office he held until January 3, 1971, when he was elected president of the association. He served for two years. During his tenure as president a financially and socially successful supper dance was given, and the revised constitution and bylaws of the association were compiled, printed, and distributed to the members. On January 7, 1973, he relinquished the office of president of the association to once again accept the post of recording secretary.

Ever since his college days he has been interested in the Yugoslav immigration to America in general and to Louisiana in particular. Although his major fields of interest are education and physics, he still finds time to pursue his secondary interest. As an immigrant by origin and an American by adoption and education he has always been intrigued by the melting-pot process by which this primarily—up to the 1850s—Anglo-Saxon nation absorbed millions of immigrants of varied backgrounds and cultures and still retained its original democratic structure which the Founding Fathers gave it at its inception.

In 1955 his article "Yugoslavs in Louisiana" was published in an emigrants' almanac *Matica* at Zagreb, Yugoslavia. During the last few years he has delivered several lectures on the Louisiana Yugoslavs to organizations interested in the Slavic immigration to the Gulf South. For the past five years or so—during his spare time—he has been busy researching, compiling material through correspondence and interviews, and writing on the Yugoslav immigration to Louisiana, the result of which is this book.

During the late 1940s he helped to reorganize and revitalize the

Yugoslav American Club and served as its secretary for several years. He is also a member of the Slavonian Pleasure Club, American Physics Association, Knights of Columbus, Delta Sigma Phi Fraternity, and a charter member of the LSUNO chapter of an education society, the Phi Delta Kappa, and an executive secretary of the Louisiana Oyster Dealers and Growers Association.

W. C. V., guest biographer.

BALDO V. PAUSINA, 1973–

The thirty-second president of the United Slavonian Benevolent Association, Captain Baldo V. Pausina, joined the association on November 3, 1918. After serving as a member of the Board of Directors and as a member of various committees for several years, he was elected vice-president in January, 1972, and on January 7, 1973, president of the association.

Pausina was born on February 22, 1904, in Vrucica on the Peljesac Peninsula. He came to Louisiana with his mother and a sister in 1908. His father, Vincent, preceded them to Louisiana by a few years and once he had established his oyster fishing business, he sent for his family (a typical procedure of Yugoslav immigrants practiced to this day). The elder Pausina died in 1917 and two years later, at the age of fifteen, young Baldo quit school to go to work to help support the family.

In 1934 he married Katherine Hihar. They have two children, a daughter Dominica and a son Ralph. Mrs. Pausina, or Mrs. Katie as she is known to her many friends, has been active in the social functions of the association since the early 1940s and has served as chairlady for many of its supper dances and celebrations. She is also active in the social affairs of the Louisiana Oyster Dealers and Growers Association and has served as president of the Ladies Auxiliary of that organization since its founding in February, 1971. Daughter Dominica reigned as queen of the 1952 festival. Son Ralph has taken over the family oyster business and runs it successfully.

An oysterman all his adult life, Pausina has acquired—through practical experience and by keeping abreast of the latest developments through literature and personal contacts—such extensive knowledge about the Louisiana oysters that he is considered an authority on the subject. He has been interviewed many times by the local and the regional press. In 1970 he delivered a paper entitled "Louisiana Oyster Culture" at a meeting of the World Mariculture Society in Baton Rouge, Louisiana, which was published in the 1970 proceedings of the society and thereby became a part of the Louisiana oyster literature.

During the early 1930s he helped to organize the Association of Louisiana Oystermen and served as its secretary-treasurer until it was dissolved several years later. Although he is busy with his own oyster growing and cultivating business, he always finds time to help promote the oyster industry. In 1950 he became a member of the Oyster Institute of North America (since renamed the Shellfish Institute of North America) and from 1951 to 1969 was a member of its Board of Directors, representing the Louisiana oystermen. In 1952 he was one of the prime organizers of the Louisiana Oyster Dealers and Growers Association and was elected its first president, serving in that office for several years. In 1953 he was a cochairman for the Shellfish Institute's National Convention which was held in New Orleans. For bringing the convention to New Orleans and to the Gulf South for the first time in the history of the organization, he received a citation from the New Orleans Chamber of Commerce and from the city of New Orleans.

He is still active in the cultivation and production of oysters, serving as the vice-president of the Pausina Oyster Corporation.

He is a charter member of the Yugoslav American Club, a member of the Board of Directors of the Foti Finance Company, a member of the Slavonian Pleasure Club, and of the Greater New Orleans Chamber of Commerce.

BENEFICIAL RESULTS OF JOINING AN ETHNIC ORGANIZATION

The tendency of the European newcomers to form and join their ethnic organizations has been criticized as the means of perpetuating the old country habits; of preventing the immigrants from adopting the American way of life; of keeping them from learning the English language and permitting them to retreat to islands of isolation thereby creating a deterrent in the melting-pot process. I wholeheartedly disagree with these charges. I am thoroughly convinced that these social and benevolent organizations help the immigrants become better citizens and speed up the process of Americanization.

American society is an organization-oriented society composed of many organizations in all strata of life, from the federal to the precinct level. From the very beginning, American life has been affected and influenced by organizations, from Samuel Adams' Committee on Correspondence to the present-day presidential commissions. There are political, social, educational, labor, fraternal, and service organizations which are interwoven with the everyday life of Americans, be they company executives or hourly wage earners. There are Elks, Eagles, Garden Clubs, Masons, Knights of Columbus, Shriners, Odd Fellows, Kiwanis International, Lions International, Rotary International, Variety Clubs International, Loyal Order of Moose, YMCA, and YWCA and many more. The *World Almanacs* list pages and pages of them. If the Americans want to have a voice in local politics or to be elected to a political office, they join a precinct or ward political organization; to get adequate compensation for their labors they join a labor union; to get maximum benefits for their profession, a professional organization be it AMA or NEA; to be socially accepted, a country club; to help run and influence the local schools, a PTA; to show off that they did their share for America, a veteran organization; to protect, and to get maximum price for, their products, a business association, and so on. Therefore, it is only natural that newly arrived and bewildered immigrants, without the knowledge of the English language and most of the time without a usable skill and without any acquaintances outside their countrymen, seek out and join an organization composed of persons similar to themselves.

These organizations do not slow down their Americanization process but rather accelerate and improve it. First of all, here they find acceptance and companionship and thereby acquire some confidence which is so essential for the well-being of immigrants, especially eastern Europeans. The benevolent organizations give them some security in case of need and sickness; and in case of their death they know that their widows and orphans will be cared for, and they themselves will be given a decent Christian burial. For many of them the attendance at the meetings and participation in the discussions is their first experience in American democracy. Most of the ethnic organizations are chartered by the states where they are located, and thereby their constitutions and bylaws have to obey state laws and are democratic in nature. The constitutions and bylaws are written in both languages so that newcomers can read about their rights and privileges in an organization. Another advantage of bilingual documents and correspondence is that it provides an opportunity for learning the written word in English. The laws and rules of these organizations are written in both languages alongside each other so that the comparison of meanings, if not of individual words, suggests itself and thereby provides their first lesson in the English language. Also, if they want to actively participate in the affairs of an organization, the knowledge of English is a prerequisite and it compels them to learn the language and sends them to *Robert's Rules of Order*.

Socially it helps them to adjust in the New World. If an association has a home/lodge they go there on Sunday afternoons and evenings; sometimes for a game of cards, sometimes for a drink, but occasionally to read a newspaper, a periodical, or even a book. At picnics, dances, and other socials they meet the members of the opposite sex of their nationality as well as native Americans. Many a romance between a European (Yugoslav) immigrant and an American took root at such gatherings, thereby assuring complete acculturation during the first generation.

The officers of these organizations are usually well-established members of a community and are able to help the newcomers with employment, limited financial assistance, a place to live, minor legal assistance, and direct them to proper agencies when they need help, and to serve as interpreters. Also it is from these organizations that newcomers get the experience and skills which give them confidence to join and actively participate in native American organizations such as masonic, religious, or trade organizations from which, as uninformed immigrants, they shy away.

As enumerated above, the ethnic organizations still help the present-day immigrants in their endeavor to become regular Americans. However, their functions as the transitional agencies were much more beneficial and necessary during the past generations before the enactment of present-day protective social legislation.

Appendixes

APPENDIX I

Some of the Business Establishments Presently Owned or Once Owned by the Yugoslavs in Louisiana, Showing the Name of the Owner and Some, Where Significant, the Year Founded. Source: Soard's and R. L. Polk's New Orleans City Directories and Author's Personal Census. All Addresses in New Orleans Unless Otherwise Stated.*

ABRAMOVICH AND PETROVICH GROCERY AND SHIP CHANDLERS, 235 and 237 Decatur Street, Radoslav G. Abramovich and Raphael C. Petrovich, 1887.

ABRAMOVICH, RADOSLAV G., RESTAURANT, Carondelet near corner of Poydras Street, 1893.

ABRAMOVICH SALOON, 233 Decatur Street, Michael Abramovich, 1875.

ADRIATIC BEER PARLOR, 509 Dumaine Street, John Vuiovich.

AJMARICH, D., GROCERY, St. Thomas Street, 1840.

AJMARICH, FRANK, COFFEE HOUSE, 88 Dauphine Street, 1840.

ALACH AND LUCICH OYSTERS, 3200 St. Claude Avenue, Stephen Lucich and Andrew Alach.

AMANOVICH, GEORGE, SALOON, 910 Bienville Street.

AUDITORIUM RESTAURANT, N. Rampart and St. Peter streets, Joseph Baricev and John M. Marcev.

BACCICH, MICHAEL A., GROCERY, 915 Decatur Street, 1894.

BACCICH AND SON, REAL ESTATE, M. A. Baccich and George Baccich.

BAJANOVICH FRUIT STAND, 17 Apollo Street, Andrew Bajanovich, 1855.

BAJURIN RESTAURANT, 57 North Street, John A. Bajurin, 1872.

---

* The oyster growers are not listed here for they are discussed fully in Chapter 4.

KOPANICA OYSTER BAR, 133 Exchange Place, Frank Kopanica.

KOPANICA'S OYSTER HOUSE, oyster dealer, 837 N. Rampart Street, Peter Kopanica.

KRESICH, MATTHEW P., SALOON, 200 Gravier Street.

KRESICH AND VUJEVICH EMPIRE CAFE, Empire, La., Miho Kresich and John Vujevich.

KUMARICH RESTAURANT, 603 Chartres Street, Dinko Kumarich.

LAKESIDE SEAFOOD RESTAURANT AND OYSTER BAR BY DRAGO, 3232 N. Arnoult Road, Metairie, Drago Cvitanovich.

LETINICH, BARTOL, RESTAURANT, 1437 St. Bernard Avenue.

LEVATA'S RESTAURANT, 1548 N. Claiborne Avenue, Anthony Levata, Joseph Tomasovich.

LOUISIANA STATE COFFEE HOUSE, 187 Chartres Street, Peter Masich, 1857.

LUKINOVICH FRUIT STAND, 179 Camp Street, Jerome Lukinovich, 1872.

LUKINOVICH, JEROME, OYSTER SALOON, 179 Camp Street, 1873.

LUKINOVICH, JEROME, RESTAURANT, 190½ Camp Street, 1887.

LUKINOVICH, MARTIN, RESTAURANT, 748 Camp Street, 1892.

LUKINOVICH RESTAURANT, 176 Camp Street, Marco Lukinovich, 1875.

LULICH, JOHN, oyster dealer, 210 Solomon Street.

MAJESTIC-ELRITO FREIGHT SERVICE, INC., Press Street Wharf, Peter Taliancich, Marine Gerica, Marko Cibilich.

MANDICH CAFÉ, 1201 N. Rampart Street, Chris Mandich.

MANDICH, JOHN, RESTAURANT, 3801 Magazine Street.

MANDICH RESTAURANT AND BAR, 3200 St. Claude Avenue, John Mandich.

MANDICH, SAMUEL, RESTAURANT, 138 S. Claiborne Avenue.

MARACICH, GEORGE, SALOON, 1012 Tchoupitoulas Street, 1893.

MARBLE HALL CAFÉ BRANCH, S. Rampart and St. Ann streets, John Peter Marcev, 1919.

MARBLE HALL CAFÉ RESTAURANT, 720 Lafayette Street, John Gentilich, 1902; John P. Gentilich, 1934.

MARCEV, JOHN, RESTAURANT, 401 Baronne Street.

MARCEV, PETER, RESTAURANT, 8501 Oak Street.

MARICH, N., GROCERY, 292 Burgundy Street, 1848.

MASCOVICH FRUIT STAND, Dauphine corner St. Louis Street, George Mascovich, 1853.

MASICH CIGARS AND TOBACCO IMPORTERS, 56 Gravier Street, Frank Masich, 1861.

MASICH AND CO., FRUIT DEALERS AND IMPORTERS, wholesale, 83 and 84 Old Levee Street, Frank Masich, G. Masich, and C. Jovanovich, 1857.

MASICH AND COSULICH, SHIP BROKERS, 159 Common Street, Frank Masich and A. Cosulich, 1881.

MASICH GROCERY, 921 Decatur Street, Anthony M. Masich.

MATCOVICH FRUIT STAND, 589 Magazine Street, Luke Matcovich, 1871.

MATULICH, CHRIS, RESTAURANT, 901 Louisiana Avenue.

MATULICH RESTAURANT AND BAR, 938 St. Roch Avenue, M. Matulich.

MAVAR, MIRO, RESTAURANT, 1839 Canal Street.

MAVAR RESTAURANT, 2101 Bienville Street, Sam Mavar.

METRY CAFE AND BAR, 502 Metairie Road, Metairie, John Muhoberac.

MORNING CALL COFFEE STAND, French Market corner St. Philip Street, Joseph Jurisich, Jurisich family.

MID-CITY RESTAURANT, 4139 Canal Street, Anthony Zanki and Pascal Taliancich, Anthony Zanki.

MIHOJEVICH, LAZAR, RESTAURANT, 1731 Dryades Street, 1894.

MILADIN, MICHAEL, SALOON, 761 Tchoupitoulas Street, 1894.

MILJAK, MITCHELL, SOFT DRINK STORE, 901 Bourbon Street.

MILINOVICH, DOMINICK, SALOON, 410 Julia Street, 1893.

MILINOVICH FRUIT DEALER, 32–36 Treme Market, D. Milinovich, 1873.

MILINOVICH, LAZAR J., SALOON, 1100 Howard Avenue.

MILINOVICH AND RADOVICH OYSTER SALOON AND BAR, Chartres corner Frenchmen Street, Marco Radovich and Adam Milinovich, 1873.

NAZORICH, LUKE, SALOON, 184 Bienville Street, 1872.

NESANOVICH, ANTHONY A., OYSTER DEALER, 1348 St. Bernard Avenue.

NESANOVICH, ANTHONY, RESTAURANT, 1504 St. Bernard Avenue.

NEW BAZAAR CAFÉ AND HALL, 233 Old Levee Street (later Decatur), Luke Jovanovich, 1872–74; Bogdan Abramovich, 1874–78; Radoslav Abramovich, 1879.

NORICH, JAMES M., FRUIT STAND, wholesale, 94 Canal Street, 1874.

OAK STREET RESTAURANT, 8242 Oak Street, Anthony Cvitanovich.

OCHIGLEVICH SAIL MAKING, 23 Front Levee Street near United States Mint, John Ochiglevich, 1858.

OCHIGLEVICH OYSTERS, Levee near St. Ferdinard Street, Peter Ochiglevich, 1859.

OLGA SHIPYARD, Olga, La., Marko Gerica, Marine Gerica.

ORLICH, LUKE, BILLIARDS, 103 St. Charles Avenue, 1855.

PABLOVICH, L., FRUIT STAND, 134 St. Louis Street, 1848.

PAVELICH COFFEE HOUSE, "On Patterson Street between Chestnut and Goslin, Algiers," Henry Pavelich, 1848.

PERICICH, MATTHEW, SALOON, 802 N. Rampart Street.

PEROVICH, ALEXANDER, SALOON, 933 Decatur Street.

PEROVICH, ANTHONY, RESTAURANT, 2429 Ursuline Avenue.

PERSICH DRUG STORE, Port Sulphur, La., John Persich.

PETER'S RESTAURANT, 8328 Oak Street, Peter Marcev.

PETROVICH, D., FRUIT STAND, Ursuline corner Old Levee, 1858.

PETROVICH, GEORGE, FRUITS, 111 Chartres Street, 1859.

PETROVICH, J., FRUITS, Dauphine corner St. Louis Street, 1850.

PETROVICH, JOHN, SHOES, corner Magazine and St. Mary streets, 1849.

PETROVICH, LUKE, SALOON, 169½ S. Rampart Street, 1885.

PETROVICH AND MASICH GROCERY, 921 Decatur Street, Raphael C. Petrovich and Anthony M. Masich, 1894.

PETROVICH, MARKO, GROCERY, corner St. Philip and Roman streets, 1849.

PETROVICH'S SUPER MARKET, Empire, La., Troje Petrovich.

PIACUN RESTAURANT, 3037 Tulane Avenue, Matthew A. Piacun.

PIACUN, THOMAS, RESTAURANT, 1536 St. Bernard Avenue.

PIVACH INSURANCE AGENCY, INC., Port Sulphur, Belle Chase, La., George Pivach.

POPICH HOTEL, Buras, La., Nick Popich.

POPICH AND JURISICH, OYSTER DEALERS, 542 N. Rampart Street, John Popich and Joseph M. Jurisich.

POPOVICH, MARKO, COFFEE HOUSE AND GROCERY, 3 Ursuline Avenue, 1868.

PRISLICH GROCERY, 1007 Decatur Street, Jacob Prislich, 1898.

PROTICH, NICK, RESTAURANT, 2633 Daneel Street.

PYANICH, MICHAEL, SALOON, 3923 Magazine Street.

RACHICH JEWELRY, 186 Royal Street, Nicholas Rachich, 1858.

RADETICH, NIKOLA, RESTAURANT, 222 Camp Street, 1876.

RADOVICH FRUITS, wholesale, 23 Front Levee Street, Vincent Radovich, 1858.

RADOVICH FRUIT STAND, 302–308 Treme Market, 178 Villere Street, John Radovich, 1858

RADOVICH OYSTERS, 131 Bienville Street, Marko Radovich, 1875.

RADULOVICH BOARDINGHOUSE, 21 St. Philip Street, John Radulovich, 1873.

RADULOVICH FRUITS, 26 Front Levee Street, Vincent Radulovich, 1858.

RADULOVICH OYSTER SALOON, 21 St. Philip Street, John Radulovich, 1873.

RAGUSIN, MARKO, SALOON, 1301 Julia Street, 1908.

RAICEVICH FRUIT STAND, 15 Front Levee Street, Tripo Raicevich, 1848.

RAMADANOVICH RESTAURANT, 77 Royal Street, John Ramadanovich, 1872.

RASICA SALOON, 14 Dumaine Street, Peter Rasica, 1870.

SAFETY FINANCE SERVICE, INC., Audubon Bldg., Jack Porobil, president.

SALATICH AND BACCICH GROCERY AND GENERAL STORE, 231 Decatur Street, Michael Baccich and Vlaho Salatich, 1882.

SALATICH, VLAHO P., GROCERY, 231 Decatur Street, 1879.

SAMOVICH, PETER, VEGETABLES, French Market, 1893.

SANSOVICH, MICHAEL, OYSTER DEALER, 236 Chartres Street, 1890.

SANSOVICH, M., & CO., OYSTERS, 530 Toulouse Street, Michel Sansovich and Vincent Scurich, 1908.

SANSOVICH, PETER, RESTAURANT, 500 Robert E. Lee Boulevard

SARICH RESTAURANT, 438 Carondelet Street, John Sarich.

SAVICH, JOSEPH, SALOON, 193 S. Rampart Street, 1892.

SCENEVICH COFFEE STAND, 38 Mandeville Street, G. Scenevich, 1857.

SIGALOVICH CIGARS, cigar making, 839 New Levee Street, E. Sigalovich, 1859.

SKROKOV, LOUIS, RESTAURANT, 1701 N. Broad Street.

SIMICH, MICHAEL, RESTAURANT, 810 Camp Street, 1893.

SIROVICH, CHARLES E., FRUITS, WHOLESALE, 55 Gravier Street, 1873.

SMIRCICH, JOSEPH, RESTAURANT, 712 S. Rampart Street.

SPANJA RESTAURANT, 717 N. Claiborne Avenue, Roko Spanja.

SPREMICH, PETER, RESTAURANT, 546 S. Rampart Street.

STANICH, THEODORE, FRUIT MERCHANT, 13 Madison Street, 1840.

STARCICH, FRANK, RESTAURANT, 91 Baronne Street, 1887.

STEPISICH FRUIT DEALER, 149½ Camp Street, Dominick Stepisich, 1870.

SUBAT, ANDREW, SALOON, 910 Decatur Street, 1909.

SUKNO, JOHN, RESTAURANT, 900 Magazine Street.

SUKNO, LUKE, SALOON, 261 N. Poydras Street, 1893.

SUNICH FRUIT STAND, St. Bernard between Derbigny and Claiborne streets, Anthony Sunich, 1873.

TADIN, JOHN, RESTAURANT, 1800 N. Rampart Street.

TALIANCICH, LEOPOLD, RESTAURANT, 1543 N. Claiborne Avenue.

TOM'S PLACE, Empire, La., Thomas Morovich, Thomas Morovich, Jr.

TONY'S BAR, Buras, La., Anthony Smokovich.

TONY'S RESTAURANT, 2419 Orleans Avenue, Anthony Spanich.

TURSICH, ANTHONY, SALOON, 1031 Annunciation St., 1910.

UGLESICH RESTAURANT AND BAR, 1238 Baronne Street, Sam Uglesich.

VIDAK, ANDREW, RESTAURANT, 801 Camp Street.

VIDAK AND SPREMICH SALOON AND BOARDING, 760 Camp Street, Andrew Vidak and Peter Spremich, 1894.

VIDICH, P., COFFEE HOUSE, Poydras and Circus streets, 1848.

VIENNA GARDEN RESTAURANT, 1101 N. Rampart Street, Matt Franicevich.

VISKO'S RESTAURANT, 516 Gretna Blvd., Gretna, Vincent Vuskovich.

VISKOVICH, THOMAS, RESTAURANT, 865 Magazine Street.

VLAHO, MATTHEW, RESTAURANT, 548 S. Rampart Street.

VODANOVICH, BOZO, OYSTER DEALER, 2713 St. Ann Street.

VODANOVICH, GEORGE, HOTEL AND RESTAURANT, 1839 Canal Street.

VODANOVICH, VINCENT, RESTAURANT, 500 Jackson Avenue.

VUJNOVICH OYSTER HOUSE, 1731 N. Rampart Street, Peter Vujnovich.

VUKOVICH FRUIT STAND, Claiborne Market, Matthew Vukovich, 1858.

VULEVICH, JOHN, RESTAURANT, 1725 S. Peters Street.

YURATICH SEAFOOD MART, Buras, La.

ZAR, LUKE, RESTAURANT, 940 St. Ann Street.

ZIBILICH, GEORGE D., RESTAURANT, 281 Camp Street, 1889.

ZIBILICH, PAUL, CO., INC., OYSTER DEALERS, 940 N. Peters Street.

ZIBILICH RESTAURANT, 3750 S. Claiborne Ave., Anthony and Matt Zibilich, Matt Zibilich, Prvenka and Stanley Pausina.

ZIBILICH AND ZANKI RESTAURANT, 1008 Common Street, Matt Zibilich and Anthony Zanki.

ZUVICH, VALERIAN, BOAT BUILDER, foot of Walnut Street, *ca.* 1910.

APPENDIX II

Showing the member's name, month and year he became a member, and city of birth (Yugoslavia unless otherwise indicated).

Abramovich, Bogdan, May, 1874, Boka Kotorska
Abramovich, Rade, May, 1874, Boka Kotorska
Abramovich, Steven, May, 1874, Boka Kotorska
Africh, Anthony, November, 1932, Prvic Luka
Africh, Joseph, March, 1925, Prvic Luka
Alach, Andrew, January, 1924, Drasnice
Alikasovich, Theodore, March, 1938, Tetovo
Amanovich, Nicholas, February, 1913, Velicane near Hercegnovi
Andrich, Jerome, July, 1916, Jurice
Anticich, John, May, 1912, Igrane
Anticich, John M., October, 1917, Gradac
Anticich, Thomas, March, 1912, Igrane
Antoncich, Thomas, May, 1874, Dubrovnik
Antulovich, Vincent, May, 1874, Dubrovnik
Antunica, Anthony M., May, 1903, Hodilje
Antunica, Anthony V., November, 1902, Hodilje
Antunica, Matthew, March, 1900, Hodilje
Antunica, Nicholas, January, 1922, New Orleans, La.
Antunovich, Anthony, July, 1911, Zivogosce
Antunovich, Jack, June, 1934, New Orleans, La.
Antunovich, John, July, 1922, Zivogosce

Antunovich, Steve, April, 1937, New Orleans, La.
Anzulovich, Anthony M., June, 1911, Kneza
Anzulovich, Mato, April, 1973, Kneza
Anzulovïch, Matthew N., March, 1922, Kneza
Apoloneo, John, May, 1874, Dubrovnik

Bajurin, Anthony, May, 1874, Ston
Bajurin, Luke, July, 1912, Hodilje
Bakalich, Anthony M., August, 1918, Igrane
Bakalich, Matthew, November, 1917, Igrane
Bakalich, Matthew B., May, 1911, Igrane
Balovich, Nicholas, April, 1916, Duba near Ston
Ban, Anthony, May, 1874, Konavli
Bandera, Frank, December, 1909, Beli
Barach, Andrew, November, 1912, Trpanj
Baranich, Peter, March, 1938, Molat
Barbalich, Peter S., August, 1936, New Orleans, La.
Barbier, August John, June, 1905, New Orleans, La.
Barbier, August John, Jr., August, 1937, New Orleans, La.
Barbier, Fred J., March, 1927, New Orleans, La.
Barbier, George, March, 1910, New Orleans, La.
Barbier, John, January, 1884, Dusine near Vrgorac
Barbier, Joseph John, July, 1897, New Orleans, La.
Barbier, Matthew, November, 1889, New Orleans, La.
Barbier, Matthew, Jr., February, 1925, New Orleans, La.
Barbir, Andrew, July, 1911, Vrgorac
Barbir, Lawrence, May, 1884, Vrgorac
Barbir, Lawrence, Jr., February, 1947, New Orleans, La.
Baricev, Joseph, Jr., June, 1937, New Orleans, La.
Baricev, Joseph P., September, 1932, Molat
Baricev, Joseph Slavko, March, 1939, Molat
Baricev, Peter, November, 1921, Molat
Baricev, Robert, June, 1937, New Orleans, La.
Baricevich, John, June, 1940, Jesenice
Barisich, Anthony K., October, 1911, Sucuraj
Barisich, George, February, 1967, New Orleans, La.
Barisich, John K., March, 1949, Sucuraj
Barisich, Joseph, February, 1967, New Orleans, La.
Batinich, Dragutin, June, 1944, Molat
Batinich, Sam, May, 1926, Molat
Bautovich, Colenda F., September, 1924, New Orleans, La.
Bautovich, Frederick C., March, 1884, Dubrovnik
Bautovich, Thomas P., September, 1930, New Orleans, La.
Bekavac, John, January, 1918, Brela near Makarska
Belin, Frank, December, 1904, Trpanj

Belin, Matthew, December, 1896, Trpanj
Belin, Matthew F., November, 1962, New Orleans, La.
Bendich, George M., December, 1890, Plaquemines Parish, La.
Bendich, John, June, 1916, New Orleans, La.
Bendich, Lawrence, March, 1897, New Orleans, La.
Bendich, Nicholas, January, 1920, New Orleans, La.
Bendich, Peter, March, 1904, New Orleans, La.
Benovich, Kristo, May, 1889, Grbanj, Boka Kotorska
Berbera, John, May, 1874, Bol near Dubrovnik
Berberovich, Ilija, May, 1874, Boka Kotorska
Bilich, Anthony John, July, 1928, Duba near Trpanj
Bilich, Anthony Joseph, April, 1956, Duba near Trpanj
Bilich, Benjamin, October, 1912, Duba near Trpanj
Bilich, Jack, March, 1919, Trogir
Bilich, John, Jr., May, 1928, Duba near Trpanj
Bilich, John R., February, 1938, New Orleans, La.
Bilich, Luke J., May, 1928, Duba near Trpanj
Bilich, Matthew, Jr., July, 1959, Duba near Trpanj
Bilich, Matthew John, March, 1911, Duba near Trpanj
Bilich, Matthew M., June, 1911, Duba near Trpanj
Bilich, Steve, March, 1941, Kobas
Biskupovich, Thomas, March, 1940, New Orleans, La.
Biskupovich, Thomas J., Jr., July, 1959, New Orleans, La.
Bjelancich, Anthony, November, 1899, Kuna
Bjelancich, Baldo, March, 1916, Kuna
Bjelich, Alexander, November, 1925, Kotor
Bogdanovich, Nicholas, August, 1919, Stari Zadar
Bozanja, Vincent, April, 1921, Rozat near Dubrovnik
Brajkovich, George, November, 1928, New Orleans, La.
Bubich, Anthony, September, 1918, Plamin
Bubrig, Nicholas, May, 1919, Boothville, La.
Bubrig, Steve, November, 1926, New Orleans, La.
Budinich, Matthew, August, 1903, Budva
Bujacich, Cirijak J., August, 1923, Olga, La.
Bujacich, Donko, February, 1919, Premuda
Bujacich, Joseph, September, 1940, Olga, La.
Bukaran, Joseph, March, 1930, Nerezine on Losinj
Bulich, Simo, October, 1912, Sukosane near Zadar
Burich, Simo, March, 1919, Zirana
Busurelo, Robert, June, 1946, Blata on Mljet
Butirich, Baldo, April, 1925, Trpanj
Butirich, John, September, 1912, Trpanj
Butirich, John M., May, 1918, Trpanj
Butirich, Martin, September, 1912, Trpanj
Butirich, Steve Marko, May, 1922, Trpanj
Buzolich, Steve, March, 1938, Bobovisce, Brac

Cace, Anthony, November, 1917, Prvic Luka
Cace, John, February, 1918, Prvic Luka
Carevich, Anthony, May, 1911, Korcula
Carevich, John A., April, 1922, New Orleans, La.
Carevich, Rudolf, June, 1920, Korcula
Carevich, Samuel, December, 1923, Korcula
Carevich, Samuel John, Jr., February, 1966, New Orleans, La.
Cibilich, Anthony, May, 1968, Duba near Trpanj
Cibilich, Bozo Toma, July, 1929, Duba near Trpanj
Cibilich, John B., August, 1913, Duba near Trpanj
Cibilich, John Mata, July, 1924, Duba near Trpanj
Cibilich, Marko A., August, 1911, Duba near Trpanj
Cibilich, Matthew M., October, 1928, Duba near Trpanj
Cibilich, Peter B., August, 1913, Duba near Trpanj
Ciko, George Jules, April, 1938, New Orleans, La.
Ciko, George, February, 1906, Stolivo
Coludrovich, Adrian, August, 1955, New Orleans, La.
Coludrovich, Rennie Lee, December, 1961, New Orleans, La.
Coludrovich Virgil, August, 1955, New Orleans, La.
Crnjak, John, July, 1892, Trnovo
Crnjak, John J., April, 1920, Empire, La.
Curich, Nicholas, May, 1919, Zrnovo
Curovich, Frank, February, 1928, Krapan, Sibenik
Cvitanovich, Anthony, July, 1935, Iz Veliki
Cvitanovich, Anthony, September, 1912, Igrane
Cvitanovich, David, July, 1932, Igrane
Cvitanovich, David Peter, October, 1969, Port Sulphur, La.
Cvitanovich, Dominick, April, 1919, Igrane
Cvitanovich, Dragutin, December, 1962, Igrane
Cvitanovich, Frank, October, 1939, New Orleans, La.
Cvitanovich, John T., October, 1939, New Orleans, La.
Cvitanovich, Luke, January, 1966, Igrane
Cvitanovich, Nicholas, December, 1912, Igrane
Cvitanovich, Peter, June, 1918, Igrane
Cvjetkovich, Andrew, May, 1874, Dubrovnik

Dean, Stanley J., June, 1920, Podgora
Delo, Marine, August, 1912, Hodilje
Delo, Steve, May, 1937, New Orleans, La.
Devcich, Matthew, November, 1912, Podgora
Digovich, Vlaho, July, 1927, Pijavicino
Dimak, Anthony F., September, 1950, New Orleans, La.
Dimak, Anthony S., July, 1898, Brijesta, Peljesac
Dimak, John, May, 1928, New Orleans, La.
Dimak, Nicholas, June, 1917, Brijesta, Peljesac
Dimak, Steve, November, 1923, New Orleans, La.

Dimak, Steve N., December, 1939, New Orleans, La.
Dolanich, Peter M., September, 1924, Grbalj, Boka Kotorska
Dragicevich, Silve, December, 1914, Donja Vrucica
Draskovich, Michael, May, 1874, Konavli
Drcelja, Matthew, May, 1874, Dubrovnik
Druskovich, Vincent, March, 1940, Racisce, Korcula
Dujmich, Andrew, February, 1893, Sveta Lucija Kostrena
Dujmov, Dominick, November, 1921, Molat
Dujmov, Milan J., March, 1952, Molat

Ercegovich, Joseph, July, 1891, Josiza, Boka Kotorska

Farac, John, September, 1917, Blata, Korcula
Farac, Matthew, July, 1968, Honorary Member, Empire, La.
Ficovich, Matthew, November, 1921, Cesvinica
Ficovich, Matthew J., February, 1926, Ston
Fiscur, John, July, 1935, Ostrica, La.
Foretich, Salvie, August, 1928, New Orleans, La.
Franceski, Simo, July, 1934, Plaquemines Parish, La.
Franicevic, Nikola, September, 1959, Sucuraj
Franicevich, Anthony, December, 1923, Sucuraj
Franicevich, Bosko, February, 1922, Sucuraj
Franicevich, Frank, March, 1918, Sucuraj
Franicevich, Joseph, August, 1919, Zivogosce
Franicevich, Ljubo, June, 1925, Sucuraj
Franicevich, Marijan, May, 1923, Zivogosce
Franicevich, Matthew, March, 1920, Sucuraj
Franicevich, Matthew, June, 1940, Ostrica, La.
Frankovich, Matthew, May, 1890, Trpanj
Franks, Joseph V., April, 1933, Sucuraj
Franks, Joseph, II, September, 1959, New Orleans, La.
Franks, Zeljko, April, 1936, Sucuraj
Franks, Zvonimir, November, 1939, Sucuraj
Franovich, Spiro, March, 1929, Rezevic, Boka Kotorska
Fucich, Anthony, May, 1874, Losinj
Fucich, Bozo L., May, 1874, Losinj
Fucich, Fortune J., December, 1919, New Orleans, La.
Fucich, Simeon M., May, 1875, Losinj
Fucich, Simeon M., Jr., February, 1918, Donaldsonville, La.
Fucich, Simeon, M., III December, 1919, New Orleans, La.
Fucich, Vladimir, December, 1919, New Orleans, La.

Garbini, Nicholas, May, 1874, Hodilje
Garma, Anthony, August, 1924, Krapanj
Gegen, Robert A., June, 1959, Hoquiam, Washington
Gentilich, John, August, 1892, Molat

Gentilich, John P., February, 1924, Molat
Gentilich, Nicholas S., June, 1922, Molat
Gentilich, Nicholas S., Jr., May, 1940, New Orleans, La.
Gerica, John M., April, 1922, New Orleans, La.
Gerica, Marine, January, 1912, Ston
Gerica, Nicholas, February, 1916, Plaquemines Parish, La.
Gerica, Peter M., July, 1960, New Orleans, La.
Giona, John, May, 1874, Dubrovnik
Gjenero, Marko, June, 1967, Krucica, Slano
Gjuratovich, Andrew, December, 1911, Vitalena, Konavli
Glavina, Frank, October, 1926, New Orleans, La.
Glavina, John F., March, 1904, Trpanj
Glavina, Martin, August, 1906, Trpanj
Glavina, Martin J., January, 1962, New Orleans, La.
Glavocich, Simo, April, 1892, Olib
Gojkovich, Nicholas, March, 1891, Ercegnovi
Grabre, Ignacio, November, 1877, Voloska
Grusich, Marko, February, 1926, New Orleans, La.
Grusich, Thomas, July, 1897, Melbourne, Australia
Grusich, Wilfred, September, 1926, New Orleans, La.
Gusina, George, May, 1874, Dubrovnik

Hajtilovich, Baldo, February, 1926, Luka, Ston
Hihar, Maro, February, 1973, Mali Ston
Hihar, Rado, September, 1923, New Orleans, La.
Hrboka, John, August, 1925, Zman
Hrboka, Zakarija, May, 1927, Zman

Ilijich, Vincent, March, 1877, Brac
Ivicevich, Steve, June, 1922, Trpanj
Ivicevich, Vladimir, February, 1939, Trpanj
Ivosich, John, August, 1941, Molat
Ivovich, Tripo, April, 1886, Lastva, Boka Kotorska

Jasich, Frank, May, 1896, Supetar on Brac
Jasich, Matthew, October, 1918, Buras, La.
Jasich, Paul, February, 1889, Supetar on Brac
Jasprica, Vincent, October, 1923, New Orleans, La.
Jovanovich, Luke, May, 1874, Hercegovina
Jovanovich, Luke Victor, June, 1914, New Orleans, La.
Jovanovich, Nicholas S., December, 1878, New Orleans, La.
Jovanovich, Nicholas S., Jr., November, 1948, New Orleans, La.
Jurakovich, Anthony G., September, 1913, Zivogosce
Jurakovich, Joseph G., October, 1955, New Orleans, La.
Jurich, Nicholas, June, 1913, Osojnik
Jurich, Spiro, August, 1922, Krapanj

Jurisich, Alvin, May, 1938, New Orleans, La.
Jurisich, Frank, February, 1918, Brist near Makarska
Jurisich, John E., August, 1954, New Orleans, La.
Jurisich, John J., November, 1918, Duba near Trpanj
Jurisich, Joseph, Sr., April, 1904, Duba near Trpanj
Jurisich, Joseph, Jr., July, 1918, New Orleans, La.
Jurisich, Joseph, Jr., September, 1946, New Orleans, La.
Jurisich, Joseph Edward, December, 1909, New Orleans, La.
Jurisich, Joseph John, March, 1891, Janjina on Peljesac
Jurisich, Joseph Michael, March, 1931, New Orleans, La.
Jurisich, Lawrence C., April, 1924, New Orleans, La.
Jurisich, Luke A., Jr., May, 1952, New Orleans, La.
Jurisich, Luke A., Sr., March, 1912, New Orleans, La.
Jurisich, Luke V., April, 1930, Duba near Trpanj
Jurisich, Malcolm, September, 1971, Port Sulphur, La.
Jurisich, Melko, July, 1925, New Orleans, La.
Jurisich, Mitchell F., May, 1941, Empire, La.
Jurisich, Peter P., October, 1918, New Orleans, La.
Jurisich, Vlaho J., November, 1908, Duba near Trpanj
Jurjevich, Joseph, March, 1917, Salina, La.
Juka, Marko, March, 1927, Supetar on Brac
Jurovich, Edward F., December, 1934, New Orleans, La.
Jurovich, Frank A., June, 1928, New Orleans, La.
Jurovich, John, January, 1913, Kuna on Peljesac
Jurovich, John, Jr., July, 1927, New Orelans, La.

Kandich, Damjan, January, 1913, Visnice, Konavli
Kandich, Nicholas, November, 1913, Durinici, Konavli
Kaus, Konrad, December, 1917, Istria
Keko, Anthony, August, 1937, New Orleans La.
Keko, Gregory, January, 1913, Trpanj
Koljevina, Nicholas, March, 1926, St. George
Koludrovich, Zvonimir, September, 1934, Orebic
Kopajtich, Marko, March, 1879, Senjska Rijeka
Kopanica, Frank, October, 1939, Cesvinica, Ston
Kopanica, Peter, March, 1899, Cesvinica, Ston
Korac, Anthony, May, 1918, Duba near Ston
Korac, John, March, 1919, Duba near Ston
Korac, Nicholas, February, 1919, Mali Ston
Kos, Anthony, December, 1920, Labin, Istria
Kos, John, January, 1926, Grand, Istria
Koskina, Joseph, May, 1874, Split
Kovacevich, Dominick, April, 1878, Stari Grad on Hvar
Krajina, Branislav, December, 1963, Sarajevo
Kresich, Miho, August, 1905, Ston
Kristicevich, Stephen, February, 1918, Podobuce on Peljesac

Krsanac, Joko, May, 1874, Lustice, Hercegnovi
Krstelj, John, May, 1918, Viganj on Peljesac
Kuluz, Anthony M., January, 1918, Sucuraj
Kumarich, Dominick, October, 1917, Sucuraj
Kutzum, Matthew, May, 1874, Dubrovnik

Lalich, Marijan, June, 1925, Tucep
Lalich, Mijo, March, 1914, Tucep
Letinich, Bartol, January, 1927, Iz Veliki
Letinich, John T., March, 1941, Havana, Cuba
Levata, Anthony, March, 1914, Cilipi, Konavli
Levata, Anthony, Jr., April, 1927, New Orleans, La.
Levata, Anthony N., May, 1919, New York, N.Y.
Levata, Nicholas, January, 1915, Cilipi, Konavli
Lovich, David A., July, 1969, Igrane
Lovretich, Anthony J., May, 1918, New Orleans, La.
Lucich, Stephen, April, 1940, Tisna
Lukinovich, Jero, May, 1876, Brac
Lulich, Anthony, May, 1920, Igrane
Lulich, Anthony, August, 1941, New Orleans, La.
Lulich, John, Jr., June, 1936, New Orleans, La.
Lulich, John, Sr., May, 1918, Igrane
Lulich, John S., June, 1921, Igrane
Lulich, Michael A., March, 1968, New Orleans, La.
Lulich, Mitchell, August, 1941, New Orleans, La.
Lulich, Pasko, July, 1924, Igrane
Lupis, John, May, 1891, Viganj on Peljesac

Machela, John, January, 1935, Olga, La.
Machela, Matthew, January, 1949, Buras, La.
Mandich, Chris, March, 1924, Molat
Mandich, John, June, 1922, Molat
Mandich, John Joseph, May, 1945, New Orleans, La.
Maracich, George, June, 1876, Kukuljanovo
Marcev, Clifton, October, 1946, New Orleans, La.
Marcev, Hilliard P., October, 1946, New Orleans, La.
Marcev, John, February, 1918, Molat
Marcev, John M., April, 1923, Molat
Marcev, John M., Jr., October, 1938, New Orleans, La.
Marcev, John P., Jr., July, 1924, New Orleans, La.
Marcev, Joseph A., June, 1944, New Orleans La.
Marcev, Pascal, November, 1921, Molat
Marcev, Peter, February, 1924, Molat
Marinkovich, Anthony, June, 1942, Sukovac
Marinovich, Anthony, May, 1918, Zivogosce
Marinovich, Anthony J., February, 1927, Buras, La.

Marinovich, Milton, January, 1929, Buras, La.
Marinovich, Nicholas, June, 1922, Hodilje
Marinovich, Peter, January, 1922, Buras, La.
Markezich, Joseph C., August, 1966, New Orleans, La.
Markotich, Dominick Anthony, May, 1909, Trpanj
Masich, Anthony M., February, 1890, Sreser on Peljesac
Masich, Frank, May, 1874, Sreser on Peljesac
Masich, John J., September, 1928, Sreser on Peljesac
Masich, Ralph F., December, 1923, New Orleans, La.
Matesich, Eugene, June, 1926, Molat
Matulich, Chris, October, 1925, Molat
Matulich, Ljubo, April, 1940, Molat
Matulich, Marko, January, 1938, Molat
Matulich, Nicholas, December, 1925, Molat
Matulich, Nicholas, December, 1939, New Orleans, La.
Matulich, Simo, April, 1914, Molat
Matulich, Stanley, May, 1936, Molat
Mavar, Sam, August, 1920, Molat
Mavar, Vladimir, June, 1937, Molat
Mazuran, John, August, 1909, Viganj on Peljesac
Mestrovich, Anthony, April, 1919, Kuna on Peljesac
Mestrovich, George, May, 1918, Kuna on Peljesac
Mialjevich, Joseph, March, 1891, Dusine near Vrgorac
Mihaljevich, Thomas, August, 1913, Igrane
Mihocevich, Nicholas, September, 1918, Duba near Trpanj
Mijoch, Bosko, May, 1874, Konavli
Miladin, William, August, 1921, New Orleans, La.
Milicich, Slavko, November, 1941, Podgora
Miljak, Miho, September, 1912, Trpanj
Miljak, Marion, October, 1941, New Orleans, La.
Miscenich, John, August, 1917, Istria
Mladineo, Nicholas, May, 1874, Hvar
Morovich, Anthony, November, 1910, Igrane
Morovich, Anthony P., August, 1949, New Orleans, La.
Morovich, John, August, 1918, Igrane
Morovich, Luke, July, 1922, Igrane
Morovich, Matthew, October, 1915, Igrane
Morovich, Thomas G., Jr., November, 1957, Empire, La.
Mrlais, Anthony L., October, 1918, Borje on Peljesac
Mucalo, Matthew, September, 1912, Trpanj
Muhoberac, Frank, July, 1927, New Orleans, La.
Muhoberac, John M., April, 1920, Olga, La.
Muhoberac, Joseph, October, 1940, New Orleans, La.
Muhoberac, Joseph S., Jr., February, 1950, New Orleans, La.
Muhoberac, Lawrence, July, 1927, New Orleans, La.
Muhoberac, Matthew M., April, 1918, Olga, La.

Muhoberac, Matthew M., September, 1932, New Orleans, La.
Muhoberac, Peter J., July, 1927, New Orleans, La.
Muhoberac, Peter M., April, 1918, Olga, La.
Muhoberac, Thomas, February, 1919, Olga, La.
Muhoberac, Vlaho M., April, 1918, Olga, La.
Murina, John, December, 1913, Duba near Trpanj
Murina, John, September, 1923, New Orleans, La.
Murina, Joseph, July, 1897, Duba near Trpanj
Murina, Kristo, May, 1910, Duba near Trpanj
Murina, Kuzma, April, 1961, Duba near Trpanj
Murina, Simo, March, 1892, Duba near Trpanj
Mustahinich, Bosko, May, 1874, Konavli

Negodich, Anthony, May, 1886, Sveti Ivan on Brac
Nemarich, Peter, July, 1926, Petrocana
Nesanovich, Anthony A., February, 1890, Trpanj
Nesanovich, Anthony Joseph, May, 1913, New Orleans, La.
Nesanovich, Jack, July, 1907, Trpanj
Nesanovich, Joseph M., April, 1918, New Orleans, La.
Nesanovich, Matthew A., August, 1903, Trpanj
Nesanovich, Matthew J., April, 1918, New Orleans, La.
Nikolac, Anthony, May, 1908, Grlina near Neretva
Nozica, Stephen, January, 1898, Janjina on Peljesac

Palihnich, Stephen, July, 1913, Kuna on Peljesac
Parun, Bernard, September, 1913, Igrane
Parun, Bernard, Jr., March, 1957, New Orleans, La.
Parun, George, June, 1893, Igrane
Parun, Matthew, April, 1892, Igrane
Parun, Peter, April, 1928, Igrane
Pausina, Baldo V., November, 1918, Vrucica
Pausina, Frank, April, 1939, New Orleans, La.
Pausina, Luke, Jr., January, 1936, New Orleans, La.
Pausina, Milenko, November, 1930, New Orleans, La.
Pausina, Ralph F., May, 1969, New Orleans, La.
Pausina, Ralph V., August, 1945, New Orleans, La.
Pausina, Stanley V., September, 1927, Empire, La.
Pausina, Stanley V., Jr., February, 1951, New Orleans, La.
Pausina, Vincent, September, 1924, New Orleans, La.
Pausina, Vincent, May, 1909, Vrucica
Pavlich, Blaz, February, 1928, Gerovo
Pavlovich, August G., December, 1938, New Orleans, La.
Pavlovich, John P., August, 1922, Krusevica, Boka Kotorska
Pavlovich, Milos, August, 1921, Krusevica, Boka Kotorska
Pavlovich, Ostoja, January, 1917, Krusevica, Boka Kotorska
Pavlovich, Spiro, October, 1892, Krusevica, Boka Kotorska

Pavlovich, Spiro, December, 1947, Buras, La.
Pavlovich, Spiro M., January, 1924, Buras, La.
Pekich, Anthony S., April, 1921, Janjina
Pendo, Ilija, May, 1874, Ston
Perovich, Alexander L., February, 1911, Orahovac, Boka Kotorska
Perovich, Theodor, April, 1921, New Orleans, La.
Persich, J. Donald, April, 1948, New Orleans, La.
Persich, John N., March, 1912, New Orleans, La.
Persich, Joseph, January, 1923, New Orleans, La.
Persich, Nicholas, August, 1895, Korcula
Persich, Nicholas N., June, 1913, New Orleans, La.
Petesich, John, September, 1940, Privlaka near Nin
Petricevich, Dominick, October, 1923, Sucuraj
Petrovich, Andrew L., March, 1918, Duba near Trpanj
Petrovich, Anthony, April, 1945, Duba near Trpanj
Petrovich, Anthony A., May, 1936, Duba near Trpanj
Petrovich, Anthony M., February, 1944, Empire, La.
Petrovich, Bozo L., August, 1918, Duba near Trpanj
Petrovich, Kuzma A., September, 1953, Duba near Trpanj
Petrovich, Luke, May, 1874, Duba near Trpanj
Petrovich, Luke A., March, 1944, New Orleans, La.
Petrovich, Luke L., February, 1876, Duba near Trpanj
Petrovich, Luke V., April, 1951, New Orleans, La.
Petrovich, Rade, May, 1885, Duba near Trpanj
Petrovich, Roko, December, 1927, Duba near Trpanj
Petrovich, Troje R., July, 1927, Duba near Trpanj
Petrovich, Troje R., Jr., August, 1952, Empire, La.
Petrovich, Vlaho, May, 1874, Duba near Trpanj
Petrovich, Vlaho A., June, 1927, Duba near Trpanj
Piacun, Joseph, July, 1969, Sucuraj
Piacun, Matthew, November, 1917, Sucuraj
Piacun, Thomas, February, 1918, Sucuraj
Picinich, Matthew, September, 1892, Susak
Picinich, Samuel, May, 1874, Susak
Picoli, Philip, May, 1874, Dubrovnik
Pivach, Anthony, July, 1924, Podgora
Pivach, George, May, 1919, Podgora
Pivach, George L., Jr., November, 1939, Triumph, La.
Pobrica, Andrew L., June, 1940, Igrane
Pobrica, John, June, 1940, Igrane
Pobrica, Lovro, February, 1931, Igrane
Poluta, Anthony, July, 1918, New Orleans, La.
Poluta, John, October, 1918, New Orleans, La.
Poluta, Matthew, March, 1922, New Orleans, La.
Poluta, Peter, June, 1910, Empire, La.
Popich, Anthony J., May, 1931, New Orleans, La.

Popich, Dinko, November, 1959, Brijesta
Popich, Dragutin, April, 1955, Brijesta
Popich, John, September, 1912, Brijesta
Popich, John N., January, 1966, Brijesta
Popich, John N. P., May, 1924, Buras, La.
Popich, Joseph A., December, 1941, Brijesta
Popich, Joseph A., April, 1949, Buras, La.
Popich, Nedjeljko, March, 1972, Brijesta
Popich, Nicholas P., February, 1944, Buras, La.
Popich, Nicholas T., June, 1922, New Orleans, La.
Popich, Richard Anthony, November, 1959, Buras, La.
Popich, Thomas Peter, June, 1947, Buras, La.
Popovich, Marko, May, 1874, Lucisce, Boka Kotorska
Porobil, Gregory M., January, 1953, New Orleans, La.
Porobil, Jack A., May, 1910, Leeville, La.
Porobil, Jack A., Jr., January, 1953, New Orleans, La.
Porobilo, John, July, 1897, Trpanj
Porobilo, Ljubo, February, 1918, Trpanj
Prcevich, Vlaho, January, 1927, Brijesta on Peljesac
Prgomet, Anthony, April, 1918, Drenica
Prislich, Jacob, May, 1890, Rijeka Dubrovacka
Protich, Anthony, March, 1939, New Orleans, La.
Protich, Frank, December, 1919, New Orleans, La.
Protich, Leo, January, 1931, New Orleans, La.
Protich, Nicholas, June, 1925, New Orleans, La.
Puh, Stephen, May, 1874, Konavli

Radetich, Matthew, March, 1924, New Orleans, La.
Radetich, Matthew M., May, 1919, New Orleans, La.
Radetich, Nicholas, October, 1912, New Orleans, La.
Radovanovich, Marine, February, 1927, Kneza on Korcula
Radovich, George, March, 1892, Lustica, Boka Kotorska
Radovich, John, May, 1874, Lustica, Boka Kotorska
Radovich, Lazar, May, 1874, Lustica, Boka Kotorska
Radovich, Philip, May, 1945, Kaprije near Sibenik
Radovich, Vincent, May, 1874, Lustica, Boka Kotorska
Ramadanovich, Joko, May, 1874, Boka Kotorska
Rasica, Peter, May, 1874, Konavli
Ribica, Nicholas, May, 1889, Lastva, Boka Kotorska
Rikoski, Ilija, May, 1874, Dubrovnik
Rodolf, George A., July, 1911, Bayou Cook, La.
Rosandich, Zivko, March, 1971, Sucuraj
Rozich, John P., November, 1910, Cesvinica near Ston
Rozich, Peter P., March, 1912, New Orleans, La.
Rudez, John, September, 1917, Gradac
Rundich, Chris R., April, 1932, Dracevo, Gubinje

Rusich, Edward J., August, 1954, Buras, La.
Rusovich, Basil J., May, 1919, Krtoli, Boka Kotorska
Russin, John, May, 1874, Luka on Sipan
Ruvo, Matthew Marko, July, 1912, Orebic
Ruzich, Matthew, December, 1914, Kostrina

Sablich, Slavko, August, 1930, Krasica near Bakar
Salatich, Anthony, June, 1916, Empire, La.
Salatich, Archille, March, 1918, New Orleans, La.
Salatich, Ernest L., July, 1946, New Orleans, La.
Salatich, Eugene T., January, 1968, New Orleans, La.
Salatich, Malter A., February, 1945, New Orleans, La.
Salatich, Nicholas, June, 1889, Gruz
Salatich, Peter B., October, 1896, New Orleans, La.
Salatich, Peter B., Jr., October, 1946, New Orleans, La.
Salatich, Vlaho, May, 1884, Dubrovnik
Salinovich, Anthony, January, 1891, Dusine near Vrgorac
Sangaletti, Ambro, May, 1874, Lastovo
Sansovich, Michael, January, 1878, Stari Grad, Hvar
Sarich, John, July, 1897, Gruljane, Hercegovina
Satara, Nicholas, August, 1927, Danca
Seckso, Anthony, July, 1920, Sibenik
Seckso, Paul N., July, 1930, New Orleans, La.
Seferovich, Andrew Sargent, June, 1931, New Orleans, La.
Seferovich, Cedomir, January, 1884, Morinj, Boka Kotorska
Seferovich, Cedomir Archille, June, 1931, New Orleans, La.
Seferovich, George Henry, June, 1931, New Orleans, La.
Separovich, Marko, April, 1918, Blato on Korcula
Seput, Anthony A., July, 1923, Donja Vrucica
Seput, Frank, February, 1914, Donja Vrucica
Seput, Gaspar, November, 1939, Vrucica
Seput, John, May, 1951, New Orleans, La.
Seput, John A., May, 1890, Vrucica
Seput, John J., August, 1916, New Orleans, La.
Skalamija, Peter, May, 1874, Konavli
Skobelj, Luke, May, 1874, Rijeka Dubrovacka
Skorlich, Joseph, August, 1912, Iz Veliki
Skrokov, Luke, August, 1927, Nevidane near Zadar
Skrokov, Robert Louis, August, 1954, New Orleans, La.
Skurich, John, April, 1921, Port Eads, La.
Slabowski, Gaspar, May, 1874, Dubrovnik
Slavich, Anthony F., April, 1918, Duba near Trpanj
Slavich, Anthony S., August, 1936, Duba near Trpanj
Slavich, Danny R., July, 1968, New Orleans, La.
Slavich, Frank A., January, 1941, Duba near Trpanj
Slavich, Frank S., August, 1936, Duba near Trpanj

Slavich, Frank S., Jr., July, 1968, New Orleans, La.
Slavich, Gregory, September, 1912, Sucuraj
Slavich, Jack I., January, 1919, Kucisce on Peljesac
Slavich, John George, May, 1910, Duba near Trpanj
Slavich, Joseph George, August, 1926, Duba near Trpanj
Slavich, Mario, September, 1948, Sucuraj
Slavich, Randy Lee, July, 1968, New Orleans, La.
Slavich, Sam Dennis, June, 1958, New Orleans, La.
Slavich Simo A., July, 1909, Duba near Trpanj
Smojo, Mijo, January, 1921, Bjelo Polje, Hercegovina
Smokovich, Anthony, August, 1939, Pula
Soljacich, Baro, May, 1874, Dubrovnik
Sortan, Joko, May, 1874, Dubrovnik
Spanich, Anthony M., July, 1935, Molat
Spanich, Rudolph, April, 1941, Molat
Spanja, Kristo, November, 1941, Krapanj
Spanja, Matthew, September, 1936, Buras, La.
Spanja, Roko, January, 1919, Krapanj
Spanja, Simo, September, 1919, Krapanj
Spremich, Bozo, November, 1912, Vitalena, Konavli
Spremich, Nicholas, September, 1918, Mikulici, Konavli
Spremich, Peter, September, 1886, Mikulici, Konavli
Spremich, Peter P., May, 1911, New Orleans, La.
Spremich, Rudolph, April, 1926, New Orleans, La.
Spremich, Vlaho, May, 1911, New Orleans, La.
Starcevich, Frank, February, 1884, Bakar
Starcich, Frank, May, 1898, Bakar
Stefanovich, Simo, August, 1918, Kostajnica
Stella, Karlo, December, 1917, Korcula
Stella, Mitchell, May, 1944, Empire, La.
Stiglich, Mato, May, 1874, Hrvatsko Primorje
Stipeljkovich, Peter, July, 1889, Vrucica
Strbinich, John, May, 1874, Dubrovnik
Strgacich, Joseph, April, 1922, Iz Veliki
Stuk, Donko, June, 1893, Vrucica
Stuk, John, May, 1910, Vrucica
Stuk, Matthew, November, 1915, Donja Vrucica
Stuparich, Vincent, May, 1908, Iz Mali
Subat, Andrew, September, 1904, Susak
Sucich, Dominick, August, 1913, Premuda
Sukno, John, October, 1903, Komaje, Konavli
Sukno, Luke, March, 1879, Komaje, Konavli
Sukno, Luke, Jr., October, 1910, Komaje, Konavli
Suljaga, Peter, August, 1922, Trpanj
Sumich, John, March, 1918, Podgora
Sumich, Matthew N., November, 1939, Buras, La.

Sumich, Vlado, May, 1959, Podgora
Surdich, Stephen, May, 1874, Boka Kotorska

Tadin, John, April, 1917, Povlje on Brac
Tadin, Nicholas, June, 1927, New Orleans, La.
Taliancich, Bozo, April, 1936, New Orleans, La.
Taliancich, Emil, December, 1922, New Orleans, La.
Taliancich, John P., March, 1922, New Orleans, La.
Taliancich, Joseph P., July, 1927, New Orleans, La.
Taliancich, Lawrence P., July, 1927, New Orleans, La.
Taliancich, Leopold, August, 1913, Igrane
Taliancich, Paul D., May, 1950, New Orleans, La.
Taliancich, Peter, February, 1912, Igrane
Taliancich, Peter P., July, 1927, New Orleans, La.
Taliancich, Peter R., May, 1950, New Orleans, La.
Taliancich, Sam, September, 1921, New Orleans, La.
Taliancich, Stephen S., May, 1950, New Orleans, La.
Talijancich, Andrew I., March, 1911, Igrane
Talijancich, Anthony, November, 1914, Igrane
Talijancich, Dominick, July, 1918, Igrane
Talijancich, Matthew, March, 1924, Igrane
Talijancich, Pascal F., July, 1932, Igrane
Tesvich, Anthony, May, 1922, Donja Vrucica
Tesvich, Anthony, Jr., June, 1952, New Orleans, La.
Tesvich, Kuzma F., March, 1916, Donja Vrucica
Tesvich, Kuzma John, November, 1929, Vrucica
Tesvich, John S., April, 1915, Donja Vrucica
Tesvich, Luke S., May, 1927, Donja Vrucica
Tesvich, Luke S., Jr., September, 1941, New Orleans, La.
Tesvich, Peter, July, 1944, New Orleans, La.
Tesvich, Stephen, June, 1952, New Orleans, La.
Tomasich, Arthur, February, 1932, Bay St. Louis, Miss.
Tomasovich, Anthony A., February, 1890, Duba near **Trpanj**
Tomasovich, Anthony A., Jr., May, 1920, New Orleans, La.
Tomasovich, Anthony B., May, 1909, Duba near Trpanj
Tomasovich, Anthony I., October, 1908, Duba near Trpanj
Tomasovich, John, October, 1930, Duba near Trpanj
Tomasovich, Joseph, October, 1928, Duba near Trpanj
Tomasovich, Joseph, Jr., December, 1969, New Orleans, La.
Tomasovich, Joseph John, July, 1888, Duba near Trpanj
Tomasovich, Matthew V., March, 1910, Duba near **Trpanj**
Tomasovich, Simo, October, 1910, Duba near Trpanj
Tonkovich, Anthony A., July, 1911, New Orleans, La.
Toso, Marko, June, 1923, New Orleans, La.
Tovarac, Frank, May, 1874, Ston
Trazivuk, Daniel G., December, 1936, Suez, Egypt

Trinaistich, Matthew, March, 1876, Volosko, Isria
Tripkovich, Theodore, May, 1874, Boka Kotorska
Turcich, John S., June, 1926, Sreser on Peljesac

Uglesich, Zdenko, July, 1959, Bozava on Dugi Otok
Urlich, Marijan S., January, 1931, Drasnice

Vasiljevich, John, August, 1920, Jasice, Hercegnovi
Vasiljevich, Spiro, June, 1942, Jasice, Hercegnovi
Vela, Emile, August, 1939, Podgora
Vela, John, June, 1917, Podgora
Vela, Joseph, December, 1912, Podgora
Vela, Marijan S., February, 1918, Podgora
Vela, Matthew, March, 1918, Podgora
Vela, Peter, February, 1913, Podgora
Vela, Peter, April, 1963, Podgora
Vela, Steve, December, 1917, Podgora
Veljacich, Nicholas, May, 1874, Peljesac
Vesich, Anthony J., May, 1906, New Orleans, La.
Vesich, Anthony J., Jr., May, 1930, New Orleans, La.
Vesich, Anthony J., III, February, 1967, New Orleans, La.
Vezich, Anthony, March, 1897, Trpanj
Vezich, John A., May, 1915, New Orleans, La.
Vezich, Joseph, January, 1910, New Orleans, La.
Vezich, Nicholas A., January, 1912, New Orleans, La.
Vezich, Thomas, January, 1910, New Orleans, La.
Vlaho, Harvey Matthew, June, 1930, New Orleans, La.
Vlaho, Marko, February, 1918, Cerno, Hercegovina
Vlaho, Matthew, October, 1917, Cerno, Hercegovina
Vidak, Andrew, September, 1895, Molunat, Konavli
Vidak, Vlaho, February, 1913, Molunat, Konavli
Vidos, Anthony, November, 1917, Kuna
Viskovich, Thomas, September, 1923, Podaca, Makarska
Vodanovich, Bozo, December, 1911, Podgora
Vodanovich, Chris, August, 1946, New Orleans, La.
Vodanovich, George, March, 1912, Podgora
Vodanovich, George, Jr., August, 1932, New Orleans, La.
Vodanovich, John, August, 1946, New Orleans, La.
Vodanovich, Steve A., December, 1936, New Orleans, La.
Vodanovich, Vincent, November, 1917, Podgora
Vodopija, Jerry, January, 1944, New Orleans, La.
Vodopija, John M., May, 1930, Murter
Vodopija, John M., Jr., January, 1944, New Orleans, La.
Vodopija, Matthew, January, 1944, New Orleans, La.
Vojkovich, John, August, 1931, Sucuraj
Vrsaljko, Anthony, February, 1959, Podgora

Vucinovich, Anthony, May, 1889, Lepetane, Boka Kotorska
Vuinovich, Risto, December, 1922, Nisici, Rudina
Vujevich, Anthony, November, 1921, Prapatnica, Vrgorac
Vujevich, John J., June, 1918, Prapatnica, Vrgorac
Vujnovich, Frank M., April, 1971, New Orleans, La.
Vujnovich, George A., February, 1918, Sucuraj
Vujnovich, George Michael, April, 1963, New Orleans, La.
Vujnovich, Marko, June, 1917, Sucuraj
Vujnovich, Milos M., February, 1940, Sucuraj
Vujnovich, Peter G., April, 1936, Sucuraj
Vujnovich, Peter G., Jr., April, 1971, New Orleans, La.
Vujnovich, Tony J., April, 1971, New Orleans, La.
Vujovich, John, July, 1916, Montenegro
Vukasovich, Krsto, May, 1874, Ubli, Boka Kotorska
Vukasovich, Rabo, May, 1890, Ubli, Boka Kotorska
Vukov, Matthew, July, 1911, Zlarin
Vulich, John, February, 1918, Duba near Ston
Vuljan, Joseph, June, 1939, Sucuraj
Vuljan, Nick, March, 1938, Sucuraj
Vuljan, Philip, September, 1938, Sucuraj
Vuskovich, Matthew, May, 1921, New Orleans, La.
Vuskovich, Spiro, May, 1874, Boka Kotorska
Vuskovich, Vincent M., January, 1964, Harvey, La.

Yacich, Chris, May, 1923, New Orleans, La.
Yacich, Frank, May, 1923, New Orleans, La.
Yuncevich, Marko, June, 1911, New Orleans, La.
Yuncevich, Savo, March, 1894, Zlijebi, Boka Kotorska
Yuratich, Merle, March, 1963, New Orleans, La.

Zaninovich, John, September, 1907, Trpanj
Zaninovich, Nicholas, March, 1918, Trpanj
Zanki, Anthony N., January, 1924, Makarska
Zanki, Anton N., January, 1939, New Orleans, La.
Zar, Luke, May, 1905, Crkvenica
Zarich, Henry, April, 1932, New Orleans, La.
Zegura, John, March, 1909, Duba near Trpanj
Zegura, John S., December, 1910, Donja Vrucica
Zegura, Stephen S., July, 1912, Donja Vrucica
Zelencich, Matthew, November, 1910, Kale, Dalmatia
Zibilich, Anthony A., December, 1916, Duba near Trpanj
Zibilich, Anthony L., February, 1890, Duba near Trpanj
Zibilich, Anthony M., January, 1911, New Orleans, La.
Zibilich, August A., March, 1927, Duba near Trpanj
Zibilich, August M., March, 1938, Duba near Trpanj
Zibilich, Bozo A., January, 1924, Duba near Trpanj

Zibilich, Bozo J., August, 1905, Duba near Trpanj
Zibilich, Bozo, Jr., June, 1936, New Orleans, La.
Zibilich, Bozo Matthew, July, 1930, Duba near Trpanj
Zibilich, Dominick C., June, 1920, New Orleans, La.
Zibilich, George D., January, 1878, Duba near Trpanj
Zibilich, George John, December, 1934, New Orleans, La.
Zibilich, Jack B., June, 1936, New Orleans, La.
Zibilich, John A., January, 1940, Duba near Trpanj
Zibilich, John Bozo, April, 1896, Duba near Trpanj
Zibilich, John Michael, December, 1934, New Orleans, La.
Zibilich, Joseph, June, 1945, Duba near Trpanj
Zibilich, Joseph George, April, 1920, New Orleans, La.
Zibilich, Kuzma M., May, 1910, Duba near Trpanj
Zibilich, Matt A., November, 1921, Duba near Trpanj
Zibilich, Matthew K., March, 1937, New Orleans, La.
Zibilich, Matthew M., August, 1929, Duba near Trpanj
Zibilich, Miho A., June, 1908, Duba near Trpanj
Zibilich, Milenko M., November, 1929, Duba near Trpanj
Zibilich, Peter B., May, 1893, Duba near Trpanj
Zibilich, Robert J., June, 1956, New Orleans, La.
Zibilich, Troje, April, 1929, Duba near Trpanj
Zibilich, William Martin, January, 1935, New Orleans, La.
Zile, Matthew, June, 1917, Cesvinica near Ston
Zupanovich, Peter, November, 1910, Vitalena, Konavli
Zuravich, Frank, August, 1922, Krapanj
Zuvich, Alfred, August, 1924, Buras, La.
Zuvich, Nicholas, May, 1924, New Orleans, La.
Zuvich, Stephen, March, 1892, Supetar on Brac

Bibliography

Adamic, Louis. *A Nation of Nations.* New York, 1944.

————. *My Native Land.* New York, 1943.

————. *The Native's Return.* New York, 1934.

Balch, Emily Greene. *Our Slavic Fellow Citizens.* New York, 1910.

Bilich, Matthew J. "Louisiana Oysterman," *The New Orleanian* (February 15, 1931).

Booth, Andrew D. *Records of Louisiana Confederate Soldiers and Louisiana Commands in Three Volumes.* New Orleans, 1920.

Bratulic, Vjekoslav, ed. *Jadranski Zbornik* (Adriatic Anthology). Rijeka, Yugoslavia, 1969.

Carter, Hodding, ed. *The Past as a Prelude: New Orleans, 1718–1968.* New Orleans, 1968.

Clissold, Stephen, ed. *A Short History of Yugoslavia.* London, 1966.

Enciklopedija Jugoslavije (Yugoslav Encyclopedia). Zagreb, Yugoslavia, 1955.

Falls, Rose C. *Cheniere Caminata* (The Wind of Death). New Orleans, 1893. A narrative of the 1893 hurricane.

Foretic, Vinko. "Cinjenice i Pretpostavke, Veze Starih Dubrovcana s Nono-otkrivenim Zemljama i Njihovo Iseljavanje" (Facts and Hypotheses, Connections of the People of Dubrovnik with the Newly Discovered Land and Their Emigration). *Iseljenicki Kalendar Matica* (Emigrants' Almanac). Zagreb (1960). 143–52.

Govorchin, Gerald G. *Americans from Yugoslavia.* Gainesville, Fla., 1961.

Holjevac, Veceslav. *Hrvati Izvan Domovine* (Croatians Outside Their Homeland). Zagreb, 1968.

Istre, G. "Speech of People in Plaquemines Parish of Slavic Descent." M.A. thesis. Louisiana State University, 1966.

Kerner, Robert J., ed. *Yugoslavia.* Berkeley, Calif., 1949.

Lahman, Otokar. "Nasi Iseljenici Oko Usca Mississippija" (Our Emigrants at the Mouth of the Mississippi). *Geografski Glasnik* (Geographic Herald). Zagreb. XI–XII (1949–50). 135–46.

Louisiana Almanac and Fact Book, 1949–50. ed. Stuart O. Landry. New Orleans, 1950.

Luetic, Josip. *1000 Godina Dubrovackog Brodarstva* (1000 years of Dubrovnik's Shipping). Zagreb, 1969.

Lupis, Ivan. "Najveca Katastrofa u Povijeti Naseg Iseljenistva." A contemporary report of the 1893 hurricane. (Unpublished paper.)

New Orleans City Directories, 1835–1973.

New Orleans Newspapers: *Daily Crescent, Daily Picayune, Item, States-Item, Times-Democrat,* and *Times-Picayune.*

Pausina, Baldo V. "Louisiana Oyster Culture." New Orleans, 1970 (Address presented at the Louisiana State University Marine Biologists' Meeting, February 10, 1970.)

Plaquemines Parish Gazette. 1950 through 1973.

Prpic, George J. *The Croatian Immigrants in America.* New York, 1971.

Seferovich, George H. "Marketing Louisiana Fresh Oysters." M.A. thesis. Louisiana State University, 1938.

Sisic, Ferdo. *Pregled Povijesti Hrvatskog Naroda* (A Survey of the History of the Croatian People). Zagreb, 1916.

Tadich, John V. "The Jugoslav Colony of San Francisco on My Arrival in 1871," in *Slavonic Pioneers in California,* ed. V. Meler. San Francisco, 1932.

Trazivuk, George. *Review of the Jugoslav Activities in New Orleans (1914–1920).* New Orleans, 1920.

United Slavonian Benevolent Association Charter, Constitution and By-laws, 1874, 1910, 1923, and 1972. New Orleans.

_____, *Membership Records,* 1874–1973.

_____, *Minutes,* 1921–1973.

United States Census (Louisiana Volume), 1850, 1860, 1870, 1920, 1930, 1940, 1950, 1960, and 1970.

Vojnovic, Lujo. *Kratka Istorija Dubrovacke Republike* (A Short History of the Republic of Dubrovnik). New York, 1962.

Vujnovich, Milos M. "Jugoslaveni u Luiziani" (Yugoslavs in Louisiana). *Maticin Iseljenicki Kalendar* (Emigrants' Almanac). Zagreb (1955). 61–66.

Yugoslav Club, Charter, Constitution and By-Laws. New Orleans, 1938.

Index

www.ingramcontent.com/pod-product-compliance
Lightning Source LLC
Chambersburg PA
CBHW020345270326
41926CB00007B/317